GRATEFUL DEAD GEAR

GRATEFUL DEAD GEAR

THE BAND'S INSTRUMENTS, SOUND SYSTEMS, AND RECORDING SESSIONS
FROM 1965 TO 1995

BLAIR JACKSON

Backbeat Books

GRATEFUL DEAD GEAR
Blair Jackson

Published by Backbeat Books
600 Harrison Street, San Francisco, CA 94107
www.backbeatbooks.com
email: books@musicplayer.com

An imprint of the Music Player Network
Publishers of *Guitar Player, Bass Player, Keyboard, EQ*, and other magazines

United Entertainment Media, Inc.
A CMP Information company

CMP
United Business Media

Distributed to the book trade in the US and Canada by
Publishers Group West, 1700 Fourth Street, Berkeley, CA 94710

Distributed to the music trade in the US and Canada by
Hal Leonard Publishing, P.O. Box 13819, Milwaukee, WI 53213

Text Design and Composition: Chris Gillespie, Happenstance Type-O-Rama
Cover Design: Richard Leeds—BigWigDesign.com
Front Cover Photos: Jay Blakesberg
Cover Background Art: Mary Ann Mayer
Back Cover Photo: Rosie McGee
Author's Photo: Dennis Callahan

Library of Congress Cataloging-in-Publication Data

Jackson, Blair.

  Grateful Dead gear : the band's instruments, sound systems, and recording sessions from 1965 to 1995 / Blair Jackson.

    p. cm.

  Includes bibliographical references (p. 275) and index.

  ISBN-13: 978-0-87930-893-3 (alk. paper)

  ISBN-10: 0-87930-893-1 (alk. paper)

  1. Grateful Dead (Musical group) 2. Grateful Dead (Musical group)–Equipment and supplies. 3. Rock groups–United States. 4. Sound–Recording and reproducing. I. Title.

  ML421.G72J27 2006

  782.42166092'2–dc22

                    2006027930

Printed in China

06 07 08 09 10   5 4 3 2 1

ACKNOWLEDGMENTS

I WILL be the first to admit that in the hardcore world of Grateful Dead tech, I am just a humble visitor passing through. There are so many people who know more than I, who have put in the time researching and writing about the topics covered in this book, they should probably share a byline with me. To start, I'd like to single out the great *Guitar Player* magazine writer/ photographer Jon Sievert, whose wonderfully detailed interviews with members of the Dead (and crew members) through the years were essential building blocks in my research. My good friend and colleague David Gans, likewise, has done magnificent work about the Dead through the years and was, as always, extremely generous with his interview transcripts and research materials.

Early on in the writing of the book, through the "Garcia" conference on dead.net, I hooked up with Tom Wright, who proved to be a fantastic resource for information about Garcia's and Weir's guitars and amps. He was uncommonly patient with a steady stream of questions, and I sincerely thank him for that. Ditto to Dan Schwartz, who helped me grasp the world of Phil Lesh's basses. Dan Healy probably got more phone calls from me than he wanted—he's always good for a clear explanation and a good story. Owsley Stanley—he'd rather you call him Bear; everyone does—was also a most helpful e-mail correspondent from his lair in Australia.

Thanks, too, to the many kind people who consented to be interviewed for this book (in no particular order): Bob Weir, Phil Lesh, Mickey Hart, Bill Kreutzmann, Bob Matthews, Betty Cantor-Jackson, David Nelson, Ron Wickersham, Howard Danchik, Bill Candelario, Peter Miller, John Curl, Dennis Leonard, Bob Bralove, Jim Gamble, Ken Smith, Geoff Gould, John Meyer, Steve Gagne, Dick Bogert, Janet Furman Bowman, Jeff Hasselberger, Harry Popick, Mark Dronge, Laird Grant, Bob Shumaker, Phill Sawyer, James Trussart, Rick Turner, Tim Scully, Adam Palow, Tom Constanten, Gary Brawer, and Steve Parish.

I'd also like to acknowledge the following folks for their valuable Help on the Way: Dennis McNally, Eileen Law, Justin Kreutzmann, Derek Jaskulski, Maureen Droney, Susan Wickersham, Billy Rothchild, David Goggin, Graham Nash, Steve Buzzard, Heather Johnson, David Lemieux,

Willie John Cashman, Harry Angus, Phil Garfinkel, Edwin Hurwitz, Donna McKay, Howard Cohen, and all the photographers whose work is represented in the book.

Special thanks to Richard Johnston of Backbeat Books for urging me to write this book and for his support throughout, and to my fine copy editor, Karl Coryat. On the art end, kudos to Maureen Forys and Chris Gillespie.

Finally, much love to my fabulous family—wife Regan and kids Kyle and Hayley—who ignored the unbelievable mess in my office for months, cut me slack for the nights and weekends I wasn't available to them, and put up with the disturbing sight of me obsessively examining gear photos for hours on end, never once calling in mental health professionals.

TABLE OF CONTENTS

INTRODUCTION

"THE BAND'S ALL PACKED AND GONE...."

The Grateful Dead was a fantastic ongoing experiment that swept up millions of people in its psychedelic wake over the course of 30 glorious years. Some people brushed up against this most peculiar beast and quickly turned away—too weird, too out of tune, too *something*. Others jumped on and off the Day-Glo Bus at different times depending on the circumstances of their lives and changes in their musical tastes. But a sizable number of folks—we'll never know precisely how many—*got it* Big Time and had that smiling skull crowned with a wreath of roses burned indelibly on their retinas. For these people, the Dead's music and the whole Grateful Dead experience became a vital part of their everyday lives. There were as many levels of appreciation as there were Deadheads, from casual fans who saw them every couple of years and maybe spun their records or tapes at home once in a while, to the truly obsessed, who followed them on tour, kept song lists, and collected everything they could that was associated with the band. It was a wonderful club with *no* requirements. But chances are, if you're checking out this book with interest, you know all that.

Many books have been written about the Grateful Dead through the years, but never one quite like this. This is the tech book: musical instruments, live sound systems, and recording sessions. Esoteric? I suppose. Arcane? Sure, but in a *good* way. And you know what? *Grateful Dead Gear* doesn't even capture the full breadth of those admittedly large subject areas. You want esoteric? During my first week of research, while cruising through an online discussion of Phil Lesh's basses in a Yahoo "Gearheads" conference, I came across a spirited debate about the material covering the Hagstrom pickups on Phil's Gibson SG bass in the late '60s. Different participants in the conference presented photographic evidence to support their positions, all in search of some sort of consensus: Yes, now we know *this* about that bass, that time period, that sound. This is what historians do; the microcosmic detail is almost limitless, and in the age of the Internet, everyone can be a participant.

Quite frankly, the Hagstrom discussion scared me a little. In a tech book about the Dead, how deep would I be expected to go? Could I possibly trace the evolution of the band's equipment and recording sessions with the kind of detail that would illuminate anything valuable for the sort of person who would enjoy a book like this in the first place? And what of my own limitations? I'm not a musician, I've never designed an integrated circuit, never mixed a concert. But I've been fascinated by the Dead from the first time I saw them—March 20, 1970 at the Capitol Theater in Port Chester, New York—and I've devoted much of my adult life to listening to them, studying them, and writing about them. I suppose this project fell to me because besides being a Dead historian I have also been an editor and writer for *Mix* magazine, the nation's leading audio journal, for the past 20-plus years. So, I've spent some time in studios, interviewed plenty of engineers, producers, and musicians about technical (and musical) matters, and I feel relatively comfortable in that world. After three decades of covering every conceivable angle of the Dead's world in books, articles, and liner notes (for nine years I even put out a Dead 'zine called *The Golden Road*), tackling *Grateful Dead Gear* sounded like a refreshing way to study this "band beyond description" from a new perspective. And it was. But, oh, what a gargantuan topic! I thought I knew a bit going in; it turns out I knew precious little.

This tome was inspired in part by a very cool book that Backbeat put out a few years ago, called *Beatles Gear*, by Andy Babiuk. That book spun stories about the instruments and amplifiers the Fab Four used from their childhood days until the end of the Beatles in 1970. It contained charming stories about the day this or that Beatle walked into a certain music store and laid down a few quid for some guitar or bass, and it traced the history of nearly every instrument a Beatle touched, from keyboards to drums. That seemed like a nice jumping-off point for a book about the Dead, except the time period would be 30 years (the Beatles' peak was just nine years), and we would also include information about the evolution of the Grateful Dead's vaunted live sound system—from the days when there really *was* no sound reinforcement industry to the complex setups of the '90s—and their recording sessions, since that, too, is an area that grew so much technically during the Dead's lifespan. What makes the Dead's tech side so fascinating is that they were not only part of the grand tradition of modern popular music—with their Gibsons and Fenders and McIntosh amps, etc.—but also trailblazers unafraid to take chances by using new custom instruments and hand-built equipment or devising innovative ways of delivering their music to arenas and stadiums. You've heard about the Wall of Sound; now read about the theory behind it and the Herculean task of putting it all together! Or the stories behind the incredible range of guitars and basses that helped create such magical music for three decades. It's quite a saga, and it's populated by dozens of interesting, sometimes strange, but always supremely dedicated people. This is a book about people getting machines to serve great art (and high times).

A few caveats are in order. Though this book traces the Dead's technological development chronologically, it is not a conventional history of the band, and it presumes a certain level of knowledge of the group's story and music. (For those readers looking for solid accounts of Dead history, I'd recommend Dennis McNally's *A Long Strange Trip*, or my own *Garcia: An American Life*.) This is also not the Grateful Dead *music* book, with elaborate discussions about the intricacies of the Dead's songwriting and improvisational genius—I hope someone in the know is slaving away on that project as we speak. Because of space considerations, I elected to limit my focus to the Grateful Dead proper and not discuss the many solo offshoots. And I chose to ignore the whole audience taping phenomenon which, though very interesting, has been extensively covered in the fine multi-volume opus *The Deadhead's Taping Compendium* by Michael Getz and John Dwork. Finally, I regretfully steered clear of the magnificent artistry of Grateful Dead lighting shaman Candace Brightman—that's another book waiting to be written.

I'd also like to note up front that though great effort was made to hunt down all the Dead's instruments and to track the unending permutations of their sound gear (which changed a little almost every night for 30 years, I'm convinced), there are unavoidable gaps—and, because of space limitations, certain hard choices about what *not* to include had to be made along the way. In an undertaking such as this, the writer is, to a degree, limited by the memories of those involved in the story (Phil Lesh once termed his years in the Dead as "a smoky haze") and the photographic record (which, fortunately, is quite extensive). In an ideal world, I would have had another few years to scour pictures and search through spec sheets and old warehouse files ... and another thousand pages to work with! But this book is at least a start: a coherent narrative that for the first time anywhere brings together various threads and streams of information, while also serving as a starting point for others' future research.

Enjoy the ride—even though it's in the equipment truck, instead of Jerry's limo!

— BLAIR JACKSON
  OAKLAND, CALIFORNIA
  MAY 1, 2006

ROOTS

IT'S A STORY Jerry Garcia never got tired of telling: On his 15th birthday—August 1, 1957—his mother, knowing that he loved music, finally gave him a musical instrument: an accordion! Yes, Jerry Garcia might have turned into the next Myron Floren (or, one would hope, Clifton Chenier), but "I railed and raved, and she finally turned it in, and I got a pawnshop electric guitar and an amplifier," he said many years ago in an interview. "I was beside myself with joy." Whew, that was a close one!

Chapter One
1957-1964

Garcia came from a musical family. His father, a Spanish immigrant named Jose (he went by Joe once he moved to San Francisco after World War I), was a professional musician and bandleader during the 1920s and '30s. He played saxophone and clarinet, and even though he had long since quit the music business by the time Jerry was born—instead he ran a seaman's bar and hotel near the S.F. waterfront—he still had instruments around the house, and Jerry fondly recalled the warm sound of his father's playing. Joe played mostly jazzy dance music and the pop standards of the day (he even named Jerry after the great American pop songwriter Jerome Kern), whereas Jerry's mother, Ruth, liked opera and classical music.

Joe drowned on a fishing trip just after Jerry turned five, but Ruth decided to stay in the bar business, so much of Jerry's early life was spent hanging out in that environment—listening to the colorful stories of old seadogs who would pass through, and hearing all sorts of different kinds of music on the bar's juke-box. Even more influential, though, was Jerry's older brother Clifford (a.k.a. Tiff), who introduced him to R&B and the pioneers of rock 'n' roll through a couple of hip local radio stations. Like a lot of adolescents in the mid '50s, he'd gotten a blast of primal rock energy from Bill Haley & the Comets through the film *Rock Around the Clock*, and flipped over Chuck Berry and Little Richard. But he also heard the top blues and R&B artists of the day, including Lightnin' Hopkins, Jimmy McCracklin, Howlin' Wolf, and others. And like so many kids his age, he was intoxicated by the sound of the electric guitar.

So, back to that birthday and his first guitar: It was a Danelectro Silvertone which was, as *Vintage Guitar* magazine put it, "a staple of the entry-level guitar market in the '50s and '60s." Company founder Nathan Daniel got his start building amplifiers for Epiphone from the mid '30s to the mid '40s, but in 1947, he started his own amp company, initially selling his products through Montgomery Ward. The following year he added Ward's' biggest competitor, Sears & Roebuck, to his client list, and that began a long and fruitful relationship with the retail and mail-order giant. In 1954, Danelectro began making inexpensive solidbody electric guitars in an effort to compete with popular models made by Gibson and Fender (which we'll discuss in future chapters). "Silvertone" was the brand name of the guitars marketed through Sears; other retailers sold the same guitars under the Danelectro name. Jerry never spoke in detail about the first guitar, and I've never run across a photograph of it, so we don't know precisely which model he had, though given that it was obtained in a pawnshop, we might presume it was perhaps a pre-1957 version.

As a "budget" guitar, the Silvertone was made from much cheaper materials than its better-regarded counterparts. The sides, neck, and bridge block were made of poplar stapled together and covered in masonite, and the top and back were painted, while the unfinished sides were covered in light-colored vinyl. The guitars came with either one or two pickups, which were stuffed inside surplus chrome-plated lipstick tubes under the melamine pickguard. Early models had aluminum frets. Though there are those who embraced various Danelectro models through the years for brief periods (including both Eric Clapton and Pete Townshend in the '60s, and David Lindley much later), they were never considered great guitars, any more than Sears' notorious brown and black plaid couches were considered great furniture. It's true, though, that some surviving Danelectros are treasured for their quirky sound. There is one other historical fact about the company worth noting: In 1956 Danelectro introduced a 6-string electric bass...which failed to catch on.

Garcia learned the rudiments of guitar from friends, from his brother, and from playing along with records and studying pictures of guitarists' hands. For a short time during his senior year in high school he was in a real band, but he dropped out of school later that year to join the army, and his interest in the electric guitar apparently waned when he made that move. Garcia once said that about the only good thing to come from his nine-month stint in the army (most of it spent in San Francisco, much to his disappointment) is he met someone who taught him the basics of fingerpicking acoustic guitar.

THE FOLK SCARE

When Garcia was discharged in the fall of 1960, he gravitated to a suburban area south of San Francisco known as the Peninsula, where he had lived with his mother and stepfather during his junior high school years, and where his best friend, Laird Grant, still lived. Palo Alto was the home of Stanford University and boasted a rich bohemian scene populated by all sorts of writers, artists, musicians, and dancers. Garcia immediately fell in with the folk music crowd (this being at the height of what he jokingly called "the folk scare"—when the likes of the Kingston Trio, the Rooftop Singers, and various other groups actually had hit records), and devoted much of his time to learning different guitar styles and playing in a succession of short-lived folk groups. He moved away from "commercial" folk relatively quickly and instead embraced old-time folk, country blues, and bluegrass, absorbing as much as he could from other pickers and from records.

During these first couple of years of the '60s, Garcia also met a number of musician friends who would figure prominently in his saga over the next three decades. These included David Nelson and Sandy Rothman, who played in groups with Garcia in the early '60s, and then again in the late '80s (the Jerry Garcia Acoustic Band); Robert Hunter, who became Garcia's songwriting partner in the late '60s and co-wrote all his greatest songs; John Dawson, whose interest in country music later led him to form the New Riders of

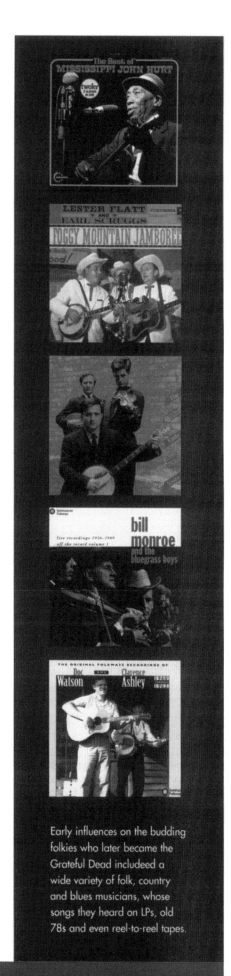

Early influences on the budding folkies who later became the Grateful Dead included a wide variety of folk, country and blues musicians, whose songs they heard on LPs, old 78s and even reel-to-reel tapes.

the Purple Sage with Garcia and Nelson; and Phil Lesh, a budding composer of modern classical and electronic music, who was now part of the same circle of hard-partying bohemians.

Garcia definitely owned some sort of acoustic guitar during his first months in Palo Alto/Menlo Park—he was rarely seen without it—but it's not clear what kind it might have been. Perennially broke and unemployed (he and Hunter even lived side-by-side in abandoned cars at one point), Garcia probably picked up instruments on the cheap from similarly impoverished friends, or as Nelson puts it, "Just as likely he would have traded something for it. Cash was not something any of us really had. I think the first guitar I saw him with was a big ol' Guild acoustic [perhaps an F-50, which was somewhat similar to the Gibson J-200]." The first solid story we have of Garcia *buying* a guitar comes from Nelson, and the axe wasn't exactly in mint condition:

Garcia, with his Martin guitar, waits to go onstage at a gig at Stanford University, 1963. That's David Nelson on the left behind him; Robert Hunter on the right.

PHOTO: JER MELROSE

"Back in '62, Jerry found this gorgeous 1940 Martin D-18," he told *Acoustic Guitar* magazine in 2002. "It had been used by some country outfit and had two little holes drilled right through the top where one of those old '50s electric pickups had been installed. The finish was worn and most of the top was bare wood. It was just incredible-sounding." Garcia with a Martin—not bad at all!

The C.F. Martin guitar company has been in operation since 1833, when German-born instrument maker Christian Frederick Martin emigrated to the United States and opened up a shop on New York City's Lower West Side. Through good times and bad, the company has always been a family business, with a Martin continuously at the helm from the outset. And though guitars have always been their principal focus, there was a period at the turn of the 20th century when mandolins took center stage, and in the 1920s, the ukulele boom helped spur company growth. Helping them out of the lean depression years was the introduction of the larger (and louder) "Dreadnought" guitars, which were also notable because they had 14 frets, rather than 12, clear of the body. (The Dreadnought name came from a type of World War I-era British battleship, and actually, the first guitars called Dreadnoughts were made by Martin around that time, but did not bear the Martin name—rather, they were marketed by the Oliver Ditson Company, and were considerably different from the Martin guitars carrying that name beginning in 1931.) Martin guitars were characterized by their distinctive X-bracing under the top, which augmented both the treble and bass tones of the guitar. The mahogany D-18 was an outgrowth of the original D-1; the 14-fret model, which became a standard of sorts in the industry, was introduced in 1934. The rise in popularity of the D-18 (and the D-28) was fueled primarily by country guitarists, who appreciated their power and richness. And in the folk world, if you could afford a Martin, that was considered a good score. There is also a photo of Garcia from slightly later posed with a Guild acoustic guitar; more on that company in the next chapter.

During this period, too, Garcia fell in love with the banjo and obsessively devoted himself to learning that instrument the same way he had the guitar. He picked up techniques and nuances from Earl Scruggs, Ralph Stanley, Don Reno, Bill Keith, and others, and learned many of the cornerstones of the classic bluegrass repertoire. In 1963 Garcia met and married his first wife, a Stanford student named Sara Katz, and had a baby named Heather. Sara was a musician, too, and they often played as a duo, as well as with other folkies on the scene.

"After we got married," Sara told me in 1996, "we traded in his old banjo, my dear little rosewood Martin, added to the money we'd received for wedding presents and from some wedding gifts we'd returned, and got him the fancy banjo of his dreams—a Weymann from the '30s with the name 'John' inlaid on the peghead. Everybody called the banjo 'John.' That banjo had a very distinctive tone: sharp and metallic. We invested in this instrument because it was to be the source of our livelihood, and Jer played that sucker night and day, and got to be very good. He was a very dedicated musician, an aspiring virtuoso. If he couldn't get in four hours of practice a day, he'd be in a foul mood."

David Nelson's memory in that *Acoustic Guitar* interview was a little different from Sara's: "Eventually he wanted a really good banjo, so when Lundburg [Jon Lundburg, who ran the best instrument shop in Berkeley in that era] found him a nice Weymann, I traded Jerry my D-18, a Paramount 5-string banjo, and a hundred bucks, which was just enough for him to get that Weymann. In return I got one of the best D-18s in the world—and that's what I ended up using on 'Cumberland Blues' [on the 1970 album *Workingman's Dead*]."

Whatever the particulars of the procurement, the Weymann was a wonderful instrument, as Nelson says, "one of the only banjos made in the '20s or '30s that was of comparable quality to a Gibson Mastertone, which was hands-down the best one. I remember Jerry playing that Weymann [at Lundburg's] and saying, 'Oh, I *love* it! I gotta have it!' He was just drooling."

Jerry picking a Paramount banjo owned by David Nelson, 1963.

PHOTO: JER MELROSE

By the time Garcia landed his prized banjo, H.A. Weymann & Son had long since stopped making instruments. Today, we think of banjos almost exclusively in the context of country and bluegrass music, but during the instrument's "golden age," between the end of the Civil War (1865) and the Great Depression (1929–35), the banjo was an integral part of popular music and jazz, in addition to both white and black "folk" music. The Weymann company was established in Philadelphia in 1864, and originally was a full-service distributor of musical instruments. They didn't start making banjos until 1900, and their business peaked between 1910 and 1929, when the founder's son left the instrument retail business to become an RCA phonograph dealer. (However, banjos bearing the Weymann name continued to be made for a while after that.) There were certainly more popular brands than Weymann, including Paramount, Bacon & Day, Vega, Gibson, and Epiphone, but Weymann's instruments were still highly regarded and noted for their fine craftsmanship. Their top models were also quite expensive: $400 in 1927 was *a lot* of money (and $140 for the cheapest was, too).

The most distinctive feature of the Weymann banjo was the "Megaphonic" tone rim, which was a slightly cone-shaped tapered rim made from ten layers of laminated wood (often set in lovely geometric patterns) that supposedly allowed the banjo to project more. It also had adjustable action by the simple turn of a nut located in the center of a brace in the dowelstick. Depending on the model, too, some Weymanns had beautifully intricate mother of pearl inlay work on the frets. Though Garcia's original Weymann was a relatively plain mid-line model, years later he purchased a top-of-the-line Weymann banjo: In a photo of Jerry in the booklet for the Old & In The Way CD *Breakdown* (recorded in 1973), clearly visible on the neck of his Weymann is a delicate inlaid vine crawling majestically up the length of the neck. Other Weymanns had double vines and other patterns on the neck, and the back of the banjo was frequently adorned with an elaborate wood inlay design or pattern.

To help make ends meet during this period, when he had a wife and baby daughter, Garcia worked part-time as a guitar and banjo teacher at a Palo Alto store called Dana Morgan's Music Shop. The money wasn't great, but the loose hours were perfect for someone who didn't want to work a 9-to-5 job, and it also brought Jerry into contact with both other pickers and the retail world of musical instruments. And, of course, he could occasionally trade work time for instruments, which he did.

THE JUG BAND

Sometime near the end of 1964, Garcia met an aspiring young musician from Atherton (a ritzy 'burb adjacent to Palo Alto) named Bob Weir. A high-spirited and good-natured misfit who had bounced around various public and private schools, never living up to his academic potential (being dyslexic certainly didn't help) and never quite fitting in, he was bitten by the music bug as a young teen. "When I became conscious of popular music," he told *Guitar Player*'s Jon Sievert in 1981, "Joan Baez was a big hit. It was really impressive to me that you could make all this music with just your guitar and voice, or maybe a couple of friends and their instruments. I started fingerpicking and did a little bit of flatpicking." His early influences included Baez and the Rev. Gary Davis, the great bluesman whom he heard both on record and through the exquisite fingerpicking of a then-unknown player who haunted the Peninsula's folk nightspots—Jorma Kaukonen, who would later gain fame as the lead guitarist of the Jefferson Airplane.

"My first guitar was a $17 Japanese model," Weir told Sievert. "Then I got a $36 Harmony classical [Harmony was another maker of inexpensive guitars aimed at "students"; the company was owned by Sears for many years], and it was okay. [Shortly after that he got a $79 Harmony Sovereign steel-string guitar.] When I was 15, I ran away from home to be a cowboy for a summer [in Wyoming] and make enough money to buy a Martin D-28 from a pawnshop. A little later I found a really nice 1944 Martin 000-21 in a pawnshop for less than

Suggested listening: A live recording of Mother McCree's Uptown Jug Champions, recorded in July 1964 and released in 1999, is the best surviving artifact of the jug band.

$100, as I recall." The '44 Martins had a spruce top, Brazilian rosewood sides and back, and a mahogany neck. That was also the last year Martins used a scalloped X-bracing, which added to the instrument's bass response.

As Bob Weir tells the story, it was New Year's Eve 1963–64 that he and two of his friends, Bob Matthews (who was studying banjo with Garcia) and Rich McCauley, were wandering the streets of Palo Alto looking for fun, when they heard banjo music wafting out of Dana Morgan's Music Shop. Inside, Garcia was picking away as he waited for a student to show up, seemingly unaware that it was New Year's Eve. Though they had met a couple of months earlier, this is the night Garcia and Weir really hit it off, and by the end of the evening Matthews had suggested they all start a jug band together. This wasn't as outrageous as it might sound today—jug bands were all the rage during that era in the folk community, with the Jim Kweskin Jug Band, the Even Dozen Jug Band (featuring future Garcia collaborator David Grisman), and various other outfits selling a surprising number of records coast to coast. The jug bands drew from the far-ranging blues, folk, and novelty repertoires of the original black string bands of the '20s and '30s and added their own elements. It was eclectic good-time music all the way. It didn't even require any particular instrumental proficiency: If you had a kazoo, you could be in a jug band!

Garcia, for one, was ready for something looser than the sort of rigorous, specialized banjo music he'd been playing in a succession of string bands on the Peninsula the previous year-plus. And so, a group called Mother McCree's Uptown Jug Champions was born. The core group consisted of Garcia (playing guitar *and* banjo), Weir, and Garcia's blues-playing buddy Ron McKernan, a soulful white kid from a depressed section of east Palo Alto who talked like a black man, drank cheap screw-top wine, and already had earned the nickname Pigpen, after an unkempt character from the comic strip "Peanuts." But that trio was supplemented by an ever-changing group of other friends, including Tom Stone, Dave Parker, Bob Matthews (the latter two would later work for the Dead in non-musical capacities), and many others. Basically, if you were a friend of someone in the band and could (maybe) play an instrument, hum on a kazoo, or sing a bit, you had a shot at playing with Mother McCree's at some point: Matthews estimated more than 20 different people played with the group between January and May 1964.

In retrospect, it was a very innocent time, a charming interlude before the music world changed forever and the folk boom faded.

ELECTRICITY

ALTHOUGH the jug band was tremendous fun and actually fairly successful on some levels, drawing decent-size crowds to the limited number of venues they played, no one had any illusions about making it to the Big Time with that group. (Plus, with its large, revolving membership nobody ever took home much money.) Pigpen may have been the first to agitate about the possibility of forming an electric band; after all, his heroes—Jimmy Reed, Muddy Waters, Howlin' Wolf, and others—all had electric blues bands. And then along came the Rolling Stones—young, rowdy, and white—playing their own infectious version of Chicago blues and primal rock 'n' roll, particularly on their first couple of albums, which were dominated by cover tunes. Mother McCree's played some of those same blues and early rock songs, but they didn't have quite the *snap* that electric instruments and drums afforded.

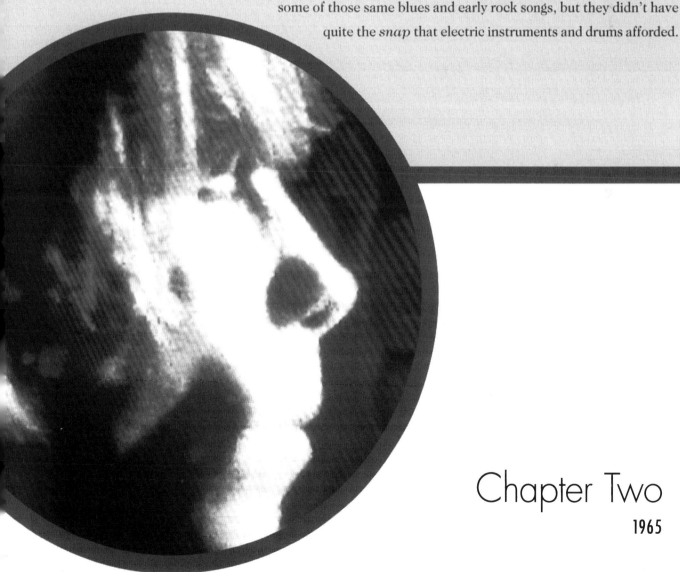

Chapter Two
1965

Weir and Garcia at the Inn Room with their Warlocks, 1965.

In the Beatles-versus-Stones debates that inevitably erupted among music fans in those days, the Mother McCree's musicians definitely leaned toward the Stones—they seemed looser and funkier. "For me, the most resonant thing was hearing the Rolling Stones play music that I'd grown up with, the Chess [Records] stuff," Garcia said in the March 1991 issue of *Musician* magazine. "That was surprising because it was music that had already happened in my life, and then hearing it again it was like, 'Right, that would be fun to play.' In the Grateful Dead's earliest version as a bar band, the option was to play Beatles stuff or Rolling Stones, and we always opted for whatever the Rolling Stones were doing—because we had a better understanding of where the music was coming from."

But who could deny that the Beatles were also onto something very, very cool? If that had not been clear to the McCree's crowd during the Beatles' first couple of *Ed Sullivan Show* appearances early in 1964, it was downright obvious by the time *A Hard Day's Night* hit American movie theaters in August of that year. Both Weir and Garcia cited that film as a pivotal factor in their eventual decision to move away from an acoustic format that was feeling more archaic by the day under the onslaught of freshly minted rock and pop groups crossing "the pond" from England and forming all over America, and finally plugging in. *A Hard Day's Night* was truly the film that launched a thousand bands. It made being in a rock 'n' roll group look like irresistible, non-stop fun: The music! The fame! The chicks! A finger-poke in the eye of Authority! Forget the coffee house circuit—next stop: *The Ed Sullivan Show*!

Well, even if their aspirations weren't quite that grandiose, Garcia, Weir, and Pigpen at least felt that playing electric music might be a *gas*. And actually, Garcia and Pigpen had already gotten a taste of it at the same time they were playing in Mother McCree's: Occasionally, Jerry picked up a bass (amazingly enough) and Pigpen sang with a local group called the Zodiacs, which played frat parties and other dances on the Peninsula, churning out the radio hits of the day along with hipper R&B selections. The group was fronted by a guitarist named Troy Weidenheimer, who could play Freddie King licks like the master himself, and who ended up being somewhat influential on Garcia's own approach to playing once he made the switch to electric music. It was also not unusual for Garcia and Weir to take electric instruments off the walls and out of the store window at Dana Morgan's and play them after hours. There was one rule: No new instruments; only used ones.

When talk of an electric band began in earnest in the spring of 1965, Dana Morgan Jr., son of the music store owner, signed on to play bass—and that, of course, gave the band a source for the guitars and amps Garcia and Weir would need, and a keyboard for Pigpen. For a drummer, they enlisted Bill Kreutzmann, who at 18 already had a reputation as one of the best skinsmen in the area. He'd played in a popular R&B band called the Legends, so in a sense he was the most experienced musician of the lot. They chose the funny/creepy name the Warlocks, which was neither stupider nor more clever than any of the monikers that were being attached to the dozens of other bands that were suddenly popping up like weeds in the wake of the British Invasion.

TURNED ON

The formation of the Warlocks also coincided with the arrival of a new drug in their social world: LSD. Garcia and the others had been smoking pot for some time, and speed in various forms had also made inroads into the Peninsula musical milieu. But LSD was different. The powerful hallucinogen—which was, incredibly enough, legal until it was banned in October 1966—seemed to open up an entirely new universe of possibilities to Garcia and the others: As he told me in a 1988 interview, "Psychedelics are still the most important thing that ever happened to me. Psychedelics is a lot of why I'm here and doing what I'm doing.... Nothing has opened me up like psychedelics. I mean, I was a different person [before I took them]."

And switching from acoustic instruments to electric guitar also fit in with the *turned-on* consciousness that psychedelics provided a window to. "For me, just going and playing the electric guitar represented freedom from the tremendous control trip that you have to have to be a banjo player," Garcia noted in an interview with the British magazine *Swing 51*. "I'd put so much energy and brainwork into controlling the banjo that, after psychedelics, what I wanted to do more than anything else was not be in control nearly so much. And playing the electric guitar freed me! So for me it was a combination of the times, a lucky moment, and it was much easier putting together a rock 'n' roll band or an electric band, than having a bluegrass band."

The truth of the matter is we don't precisely know what the first axe Garcia played in the Warlocks was. Because here's what happened: After rehearsing endlessly at the music store, in May '65 the group secured its first gigs at a Menlo Park pizza parlor called Magoo's. They were eclectic from the get-go (as Mother McCree's had been), playing a combination of blues, electrified folk and jug-band tunes, some Chuck Berry, Rolling Stones, and even some Dylan, now that he, too, had gone (partially) electric on his seminal *Bringing It All Back Home* album. At the third show at Magoo's, Phil Lesh and a couple of friends came boppin' in, high on acid, and grooved to the sounds of the young band—dancing freely even though dancing was supposedly *verboten* there. During a set break, Jerry confided to Phil that he was not happy with Dana Morgan Jr.'s bass playing and practically insisted that Phil take a stab at the instrument, despite the fact that the only stringed instrument he'd ever played regularly was the classical violin as a youth. After all, Phil was hip and brilliant—how hard could it be to play rudimentary bass in a rock 'n' roll band? Dana Jr. was also having trouble juggling his obligations to the store and being in a band at the same time, so it was no surprise that he quickly bowed out of the Warlocks.

Unfortunately, with his son out of the band, Dana Sr. quickly tired of the racket the Warlocks made during their rehearsals, so he banished them first to the carport outside the store, then from the premises altogether, and then he summarily sold their instruments. Yikes! With the band's lifeline to free equipment gone, Garcia was forced to ask his mother, with whom he'd had very little contact during that period, to help him buy a guitar and amp, and to her eternal credit, she agreed. So that's when Garcia went into a local store called Guitars Unlimited, where he also occasionally did some teaching, and purchased the instrument that is usually considered his "first" guitar with the Warlocks (and, later, the Grateful Dead): a cherry red Guild Starfire III. Might he have played some other guitar or guitars at those first couple of gigs before Phil joined? Yes, but without corroborating photographs or memories from those on the scene, we'll probably never know for sure.

Even in guitar-oriented interviews through the years, Garcia rarely spoke about that Guild guitar, so we don't know much about his motivations for buying it. There were no major guitar magazines or real rock 'zines in 1965—just the sort of teen-idol press that had followed Elvis and Ricky Nelson and Bobbys Darin, Rydell, and Vee through the late '50s and early '60s, and was now hopelessly devoted to the Beatles and Stones and the Dave Clark Five and the Animals and all the other acts with the appropriate hairstyles and matching outfits. Occasionally you'd find a picture of someone playing a guitar in one of those magazines, but mostly they were interested in shaggy hair and pearly-white teeth, and they weren't really concerned with music. As Garcia once said, "It was hard to even find out who played guitar in some of those early bands—

Scotty Moore [Elvis's guitarist] and James Burton [Nelson's guitarist] and Cliff Gallup [Gene Vincent's guitarist] and all those guys weren't getting mentioned anywhere. You had to dig for that stuff." So chances are Garcia wouldn't have known about Burton's Fender Telecaster, or Gallup's Gretsch Duo-Jet, or Buddy Holly's Stratocaster, or T-Bone Walker's "Charlie Christian" Gibson. Television was a better way to actually see instruments in action (albeit in black and white), so he had the opportunity to admire George Harrison's Gretsch Tennessean, John Lennon's 6- and 12-string Rickenbackers, Brian Jones's teardrop-shaped Vox, and Keith Richards's sunburst Les Paul in action.

GUILD, GRETSCH AND GIBSON

By 1965, New York City-based Guild Guitars had been in existence for just 13 years, but the company had established a sterling reputation for making quality instruments, starting with acoustic guitars and quickly moving into electric instruments in the mid '50s with the X-500 Stuart series (and the less expensive X-50), which were hollow-body jazz guitars aimed to compete with various higher-priced Gibson, Gretsch, and Epiphone models. Guild was founded by a Polish immigrant guitarist and music store owner named Alfred Dronge and former Epiphone executive George Mann, who also brought a couple of Epiphone luthiers over with him. Mann left the company after just a year, but Dronge (and later, his son) guided the company to considerable success in a relatively short time. Guild never seriously challenged Gibson or Fender, but Guild definitely had its niche, gaining a wide following among jazz players as well as in the folk community (though there, too, the company was no match for Martin or Gibson). Guild even gained a foothold with blues singers such as Muddy Waters and Howlin' Wolf, both of whom played 1963 Guild Thunderbirds for a while.

In 1960 Guild introduced the thin, light (just over six pounds), single-cutaway, hollow-body Starfire III, based on Guild's own T-100. It had a laminated Honduran mahogany body and neck and a Brazilian rosewood fingerboard. The early models had DeArmond Dynasonic single-coil pickups (also favored by Gretsch), but by the mid '60s Guild had switched to its own HB-1 humbucking pickups, which were slightly smaller than Gibson's. The bridge, Guild/Bigsby tailpiece (with the familiar Guild "harp" shape), and Bigsby tremolo were aluminum, and the pickguard was black Lucite. Like most Guild hollowbodies, the Starfire III was noted for its warmth, though it was picked up mostly in rock circles: At the time Garcia was mastering his Starfire, both the Kinks' Dave Davies and Zal Yanovksy of the Lovin' Spoonful were also using that axe. Garcia did have this to say about the Guild in a 1978 interview: "It had a thin body and two humbucking pickups and a kind of bright sound. I just liked the feel of it for some reason. It was before I was really developing what could be described as taste, and at that time I just liked the thin-body sound."

The Warlocks onstage at the Inn Room in Belmont, Calif. Phil has a Gibson EB-0, Weir a Gretsch Tennessean, Garcia a Guild Starfire, Pigpen a Farfisa organ and Billy's playing Ludwig drums.

Bob Weir's first guitar in the Warlocks was a Gretsch Chet Atkins Tennessean. In 1965, the Fred Gretsch Manufacturing Company (as it was formally called) was riding an incredible wave of success thanks to one very prominent picker: George Harrison, who played a maroon/brown Chet Atkins Country Gentleman on the Beatles' historic first *Ed Sullivan Show* appearance in February 1964, and a Tennessean on a later show. (Every piece of gear the Beatles touched—or, more accurately, were photographed with—turned to gold for manufacturers: Rickenbacker, Gibson, Ludwig, Hofner, Vox…so many companies thrived because of the Beatles association. See Andy Babiuk's excellent book *Beatles Gear* for lots more.)

Actually, though, Gretsch was a well-established company decades before Harrison came along. It was founded in Brooklyn in 1883 by a 27-year-old immigrant from Manheim, Germany named Friedrich Gretsch, who built and sold banjos, drums, and tambourines out of a small storefront. Upon Friedrich's untimely death in 1895, his son Fred took over the business, and over the course of the next two decades he expanded it tremendously, through both importing a wide range of musical instruments from Europe (it was Fred Gretsch who trademarked the Zildjian brand of cymbals in America in the mid '20s) and manufacturing more of its own instruments in a huge new building in Brooklyn. Even though drums (under the Gretsch-American name) and banjos (Broad-kaster brand) continued to be a lucrative part of the business through the 1930s, Fred saw the potential in guitars and moved the company in that direction: By 1939 Gretsch had introduced its Synchromatic line of guitars, which included Electromatic electric guitars. A year later Gretsch entered the booming Hawaiian lap-steel guitar market with a model made by Valco. In 1953—several years after Fred Gretsch Jr. took over the company from his father—Gretsch introduced its first solidbody electric guitars, the Roundup and Duojet.

However, most guitar historians agree that the Golden Age of Gretsch begins in 1955 with hollowbodies—the White Falcon and the PX6120—the first of many Gretsch axes to carry Chet Atkins's name. The various Chet Atkins models released in the late '50s (the Country Gentlemen in '57, the Tennessean in '58) became very popular with rockabilly and country-western performers, and one user—the great Duane Eddy—made the longest-charting instrumental album of all time (*Have Twangy Guitar, Will Travel*) in 1959 using a 6120.

Weir's guitar was a single-cutaway Tennessean, which was on the less expensive end of the Atkins signature guitar line. It was made of maple with a rosewood fingerboard, and it carried a walnut finish on the top and a mahogany finish on the back and sides. It had two single-coil HiLoTron pickups (a step below Gretsch's SuperTron pickups, in better models) and an aluminum Gretsch/Bigsby tailpiece and Bigsby whammy bar.

"It was a nice guitar," Weir opined in 2005. "I'd love to have one of those again. I'm pretty sure I found that in a pawnshop in San Francisco." How did he happen to choose it? "Sheer whimsy and how it played, how the neck felt. I had no idea at that point what I was looking for in terms of pickup response, tonal response, or anything like that. I was a complete novice at electric guitar. So I saw the Gretsch and I liked the way it felt. George Harrison played a Gretsch, and I thought that was pretty cool.

"When I started playing the electric guitar," he continued, "I was taking pretty directly from what I was doing on acoustic guitar, except I was playing a lot more up the neck, a lot more closed positions. But I was playing a chordal style because Jerry was playing lines. I would try to invert my positions as best I could, but I didn't know that many positions at that point. It was catch as catch can."

Once Phil Lesh joined the band, he had to move quickly to buy a bass, and thanks to the generosity of his then-girlfriend, Ruth Pakhala, he picked out a Gibson EB-O from Guitars Unlimited. "I always had a love-hate relationship with that bass," Phil wrote in his fine 2005 memoir *Searching for the Sound* (though he mistakenly called the bass an EB-1). "The neck was like a telephone pole, the strings weren't individually adjustable for height, and the one pickup seemed to be in the wrong place. On the other hand, it was a short-scale instrument, easy to play, and when I later replaced the Gibson pickup with a pair of Guild humbuckers, the little guy developed a rich, pear-shaped tone that worked really well in recording."

Gibson, of course, was one of the great names in American musical instruments then and now. The company took its name from Orville Gibson, who started making mandolins as a hobby in Kalamazoo, Michigan in 1894. He applied for and received a U.S. patent for his mandolin design, which differed considerably from the popular Italian models of the day, and by 1902 had entered into a partnership with several businessmen to form the Gibson Mandolin-Guitar Manufacturing Company. Gibson had only a minimal role in the company after its formation—though he did collect royalties on mandolins featuring his design—and he died in 1918. The company continued to grow as it began making banjos and then refined its designs for various flat-top and arch-top guitars. Although the Gibson company didn't invent the electric guitar—various individual innovators were messing with telephone pickups on acoustic guitars in the late '20s and early '30s, and Rickenbacker was making electric lap steels by 1932—Gibson went a long way toward popularizing it: In 1935, a team of engineers developed a new hexagonal pickup which Gibson put first in a lap-steel guitar and then, beginning in 1936, in an archtop guitar dubbed the ES-150 ("ES" for Electric Spanish). When that axe was adopted by jazz guitarist Charlie Christian (who'd been influenced to plug in by guitarist Eddie Durham of the Jimmy Lunceford Big Band), both the electric guitar and the Gibson company took off—particularly after Christian joined Benny Goodman's band in 1939.

Shortly after World War II, Gibson introduced its famous P-90 pickup, and a number of other models of electric guitars followed in the wake of the ES-150, including the ES-5, which had three pickups, and the first single-cutaway model, the ES-176. The next revolutions at Gibson came with the introduction of the Les Paul solidbody electric in 1952 and the semi-hollowbody ES-335 in 1958—more on those later.

Gibson first dabbled with electric basses as early as the mid '20s, when company engineer Lloyd Loar devised a crude experimental model. A decade later, when introducing the ES-150 guitar, Gibson attempted to make a bass along similar lines, but it never went into production. Finally, around the time the Les Paul was coming out, Gibson introduced its EB-1 solidbody (mahogany) bass, which was designed to look exactly like a giant violin—somewhat mimicking the orchestral double bass. (This came almost two years after Leo Fender came out with his electric Precision Bass, and a year after Kay's entry into the market.) Later, Gibson would produce basses that were influenced by the design of some of its popular electric guitars, including the single-pickup EB-O.

When it was introduced in 1959, the EB-0 was based on the design of the Les Paul Junior, but by 1961 it had adopted the "two-horned" look of the popular Gibson SG—that's the model that Phil owned. The EB-0, which proved to be one of Gibson's best sellers for many years, had a mahogany body and (until 1972) a mahogany neck with rosewood fingerboard. It had a single chrome-plated Gibson humbucking pickup wired to the tone and volume controls.

Drummer Bill Kreutzmann's kit when the Warlocks got going was a simple Ludwig setup, the third Ludwig kit he'd owned in his years of playing drums. "I knew literally nothing about drums," he told me in 2006, "so I just went with the most simple and basic kit, with a [15″] snare, a 22″ kick drum, a [16×16] floor tom, and one [9×13] rack tom. I had two Zildjian cymbals and a hi-hat. But I wasn't one of those guys who went to drum stores and checked out different snares and all that. I just wanted a kit that sounded good and felt right, and that wasn't hard to find."

Ludwig is yet another company that benefited from a close association with the Beatles, in this case Ringo Starr, whose Ludwig kit with the group's logo on the bass drum head was prominent in the 1964 *Ed Sullivan Show* appearances—"the first time I ever saw my name on TV," company president William Ludwig Jr. told *Beatles Gear* author Andy Babiuk. "It was also the first time I'd seen the Beatles and the first time I was aware of Ringo using Ludwig drums. Our company was besieged with calls the next day." It wasn't long before Ludwig had a back order of 85,000 sets—nine months' worth!

Like Friedrich Gretsch, brothers William and Theo Ludwig were German immigrants, but as children they settled in Chicago, where they established the Ludwig & Ludwig Drum Company in 1910. William is credited with the invention of the modern bass-drum pedal, so essential to playing rhythmic music. Their first pedals were made of wood, but their brother-in-law, who ran the machine shop at International Harvester, figured out a way to manufacture the pedal out of metal, and that helped launch the brothers' operation. The company had many ups and downs, particularly during the depression, when Ludwig's assets were acquired by the formidable C.G. Conn company of Elkhart, Indiana, as a way to survive, but with William still running the show. By 1936, though, William had left Conn to start his own concern again, the W.F.L. Drum Company, whose first product was the enormously successful Speed King foot pedal. Then, in 1955, William was able to buy back the Ludwig name, machinery, and designs from Conn, and that's when the modern Ludwig Drum Company begins, with William at the helm and son Bill (William Jr.) and daughter Betty joining dad. Things were progressing very well for the company during the early '60s—rock 'n' roll drummers seemed especially fond of Ludwig kits' bright sound—and then came that fateful day in 1963 when Ringo walked into a London store called Drum City and fell in love with an oyster-black pearl-finish Ludwig set, the kit that made drummers go ga-ga on *The Ed Sullivan Show*.

From a 1970 Gibson catalog, a description of the EB-0, Phil's first bass.

Though we think of the early Grateful Dead keyboard sound as being the distinctive wheedle of a Vox Continental organ, in the earliest known photos of the Warlocks, taken by Paul Ryan at the Inn Room club, Pigpen is definitely playing a Farfisa organ of some kind. The band's original equipment handler, Garcia's boyhood friend Laird Grant, also remembered that Pig's first organ was a Farfisa, though he couldn't remember which model. In all likelihood it was a Combo Compact, introduced by the Italian company the previous year. As a Farfisa ad at that time trumpeted: "The swinging rhythm and driving beat of today's music make the new electronic Combo Compact a 'natural' for young groups who play this modern sound!"

The boom in small, portable organs in the mid and late '60s was an outgrowth of a relatively recent change in instrument technology: specifically, the use of transistors, which Farfisa had originally put in its electronic accordions. The Combo Compact boasted 40 full-size keys, a 12-note manual bass on the far left of the keyboard, a swell-pedal volume control activated by the knee (dubbed the Tone Booster), a wide selection of switches (called tablet stops, or tabs) to make changes in vibrato and reverb, and tone stops that allowed the organ to (crudely) mimic the timbres of various orchestral instruments. Today, we think of the Farfisa and its ilk as sounding retro and cheesy, but in the '60s these organs provided a solid alternative to pianos and the heavy and expensive Hammond B-3, both of which were all but untransportable for young bands with limited means playing gigs in tiny clubs. By contrast, the Combo Compact weighed just 70 pounds in its handy single-handle carrying case, and it could easily be plugged into any kind of amplifier. Richard Wright of Pink Floyd played a Combo Compact during the group's early days, and that's a Farfisa on the Strawberry Alarm Clock's infamous slice of faux psychedelia, "Incense and Peppermints." Much more widely used by American rock bands was the somewhat similar Vox Continental, which we'll discuss shortly.

THE EARLY AMPS

Using the aforementioned Paul Ryan Warlocks photos as a guide, it is apparent that for amplification, the band used Fender equipment: The clearest pictures show Phil using a Fender Bassman, Weir plugged into a Bandmaster, and Garcia already using his beloved Fender Twin Reverb. A small non-Fender speaker sits in front of Pigpen's Farfisa; evidently it was part of the organ setup.

Fender, as any self-respecting music aficionado knows, takes its name from the great electric guitar pioneer Leo Fender (1909–1991). Leo was born and raised in the town of Fullerton in Orange County, California, when the area was still mostly rural farmland. An inveterate tinkerer, he built an acoustic guitar while he was still a teenager, and in his early 20s he started making his own pickups and also brought in money by repairing radios. In the 1940s he hooked up with a musician and inventor named Clayton "Doc" Kauffman—Kauffman had patented a vibrato tailpiece in the late '20s and had also done work on early amplifiers. Their company, called K&F, built small amplifiers and electric lap-steel guitars. By early 1946, however, Kauffman had become concerned about Fender's relentless and expensive experimentation and bowed out of the partnership; shortly after that, the Fender Electric Instrument Manufacturing Company was born.

Though Fender said he had designed his first electric guitar as early as 1943 or '44, it was the introduction of the solidbody Fender Broadcaster in 1950 that put Fender on the map and changed the guitar industry's business landscape forever: The Broadcaster—which was renamed the Telecaster in 1952 after Gretsch complained that the guitar's name infringed on its Broadkaster line of drums—was specifically designed to be produced easily and quickly in large numbers rather than individually hand-crafted. No nimble-fingered Italian or Spanish luthiers were required—just workers who could screw the maple neck onto the simply designed ash body and mount the pickups, adjustable chrome bridge, and minimal controls. It had a crisp, biting sound unlike any other guitar on the market, and it immediately caused a sensation. In 1951, Fender introduced the similarly constructed but even more influential Precision Bass— the first commercially available electric bass. The incredibly popular Stratocaster guitar followed in 1954 (more on that later, too), and had Fender never developed another piece of gear, he still would have gone down in history as one of the immortals of electric music.

But the issue at hand here at the moment is Fender amps. As noted above, both Leo Fender and his partner Kauffman had worked on amps long before the Fender name became associated primarily with guitars. By the late '40s, Fender's tweed-covered, chrome-chassis "woodie" amps (so-named much later for their wooden cabinets of maple, walnut, or mahogany) were selling briskly to musicians. The first models included the Deluxe, Princeton, and Professional; next came the Dual Professional and the Champion 800 and 600. A year after the Precision Bass was introduced came the first Bassman amp, which housed a single Jensen 15P speaker. By the end of the '50s, the narrow-panel Bassman had been upgraded to include four 10″ Jensen P10R or P10Q speakers and had an impressive 40-to-50-watt output. The Warlocks' Bassman was the first of the "piggyback blackface" models, introduced in 1964. ("Blackface" refers to the color of the control surface; "piggyback" means the controls and preamps are in a smaller separate unit, or "head," from the actual speakers; often, but not always, the head was placed on top of the speaker cabinet.) With its silver sparkle grille cloth and script chrome "Fender" on the head and cabinet, this is the classic Fender amp look of the '60s and beyond. This version of the Bassman contained a pair of 12″ speakers—usually Jensen C12Ns—and was rated at 50 watts. It should be noted, too, that bass players weren't the only ones who bought Bassman amps; plenty of guitarists and keyboardists used them, too.

The Bandmaster was introduced the year after the Bassman, in 1953, and was designed to be a relatively high-output amplifier. The first models had a single 15″ Jensen speaker and could deliver 25 watts; that doesn't sound like much, but the Bandmaster was considerably more powerful than the Deluxe, Princeton, or Champion, which were only four-watt amps. Like the Bassman, the late-'50s Bandmaster switched from a single 15 to multiple speakers—in this case three 10s. The '61–'63 models went to a single 12 with a 40-watt output and a new tremolo control, but by the time the Warlocks were buying equipment, the blackface Bandmaster had the same silver sparkle grille cloth as the Bassman, but featured two 12″ Jensens and a 40-watt output.

The Fender Twin Reverb also came onto the market in 1963, but its lineage goes back to the early '50s. The 25-watt Fender Twin that the company sold beginning in 1953 was a combo amp with two 12″ speakers. Subsequent models stuck with the two-12s setup, but became increasingly powerful—the early-'60s blonde Twin could deliver about 80 watts. Meanwhile, in 1961, Fender started selling its own Reverb Unit, which was a small (16-pound) dedicated tube reverberation box that went between an instrument and an amplifier. The blackface Twin Reverb that Garcia favored was introduced in 1963; it effectively combined elements of the Twin and the Reverb Unit, hence the name. It still had the two 12s (Jensen C12Ns or Oxford 12T6s) and about 85 watts, but in addition to a "tremolo" switch (which was new on the earlier blonde), there's a "reverb" option, which gave it considerably more sonic versatility than many amps, and still within a reasonably small package. In 1978, Garcia said of that first Fender Twin, "I bought it in the first year they came out, around 1963 or 1964."

So that was the Warlocks' first arsenal. (It's unclear what microphones the group might have owned at that point, but popular budget-priced mics of the day included the Shure 545 and the still popular Shure SM57, which was introduced in 1965.) When they first started gigging regularly in the summer of '65, developing their unique repertoire, which combined blues, rock 'n' roll, and electrified folk and jug-band tunes, they were just getting to know each other as players, and truly learning how to play electric music for the first time. Long residences at Peninsula haunts like the Inn Room and the Fireside had them playing up to five 45-minute sets a night, several nights every week. It was in those settings that the band first started to experiment with stretching their songs through extensive improvisation between verses—as much as anything, this showed the influence of some of the preeminent jazz artists of the day: John Coltrane, Miles Davis, and others. There's also no question that pot and psychedelics made them looser and more willing to explore new musical ideas that came up in their improvisations.

At first, the band mostly used Billy Kreutzmann's gray 1958 Dodge station wagon to transport their mountain of equipment from place to place, but that quickly became inadequate, so they used the ancient International Harvester

MetroMite delivery van that Laird Grant—their very first roadie—had bought for next to nothing. In those days—and really for the next couple of years—the band members helped haul and set up equipment themselves. There was no money to hire the personnel required for that task, though as Grant told me, "a lot of times I could get someone to help me with the equipment in exchange for a ticket to the show."

Looking back from a time when sound equipment is so sophisticated and complex and venues big and small routinely have high-quality PA systems, it's difficult for many people to imagine a world when there were *no* PA systems in most clubs or auditoriums, and monitor speakers had yet to be invented. If a venue did have some sort of PA, chances are it was adequate only for speeches and perhaps singers, but certainly not for amplified rock 'n' roll. No, in 1965, the way most singers got heard was by plugging microphones directly into instrument amps and competing with the electric instruments that way. "Mixing" was something that happened (or not) onstage, by adjusting the volume of the different amps to create some sort of reasonable balance in the room. Drums were not generally miked at all; drummers just had to bash louder than the amps, which usually was not a problem because of the noise restrictions many venues put on bands. Drums would also bleed into vocal mics, so some amps might have an instrument, vocal, and drums pouring out of them. The sound was usually somewhat manageable in a club, but in any room that was high-ceilinged or deep or at all on the cavernous side, getting decent sonics was nearly impossible.

FIRST SESSION

In the fall of '65, the Warlocks decided to change their name after Phil Lesh supposedly saw a 45 RPM single by a band with the same name in a record store (this has always been a hazy part of the story). Around the same time, they decided to record their first demo tape, with an eye toward getting a record deal. The fact that they'd only been playing together for less than half a year didn't seem to matter; this band was never lacking in chutzpah. They went through a million silly, stoned suggestions for a new name but hadn't really settled on one by the time they entered Golden State Recorders in San Francisco on November 3, 1965 to cut some demo tracks for Autumn Records. A fledgling San Francisco label run by two influential local DJs, Bobby Mitchell and Tom Donahue, Autumn had hit the charts with a couple of songs by the local band the Beau Brummels, and Mitchell and Donahue were scouring the area looking for their next hit-makers. An interesting aspect of the Autumn Records story is that Sylvester Stewart—soon to become known far and wide as Sly Stone—was one of the label's house engineers. But he was not involved with the single session by the now *former* Warlocks, dubbed for this one occasion the Emergency Crew.

There wasn't much of a recording scene in the San Francisco Bay Area until the late '60s. Los Angeles was already well established as the West Coast's recording center, so most of the work done in San Francisco's few, mostly small, facilities involved radio and television commercials for local stations and occasional music recording dates for regional record labels. In the early and mid '60s, most of the business went to four studios: Commercial Recording, located in an old firehouse on Natoma Street downtown; Columbus Recorders, which began its life in North Beach's historic Sentinel building in the late '50s

Suggested listening: *Birth of the Dead*, released in 2001, contains tracks from the Dead's 1965 and '66 recording sessions, plus a live disc from '66.

as Trident Productions, owned by the Kingston Trio's manager, Frank Werber; Coast Recorders on Bush Street, which became the Northern California base for L.A. studio titan and equipment designer Bill Putnam; and at 665 Harrison Street, close to the downtown financial district, Golden State Recorders, which was owned by an engineer named Leo de Gar Kulka.

The Czech-born Kulka was new to the Bay Area when he first started recording bands for Autumn Records. All through the '50s and early '60s he'd worked at L.A. studios—first at Radio Recorders, then at his own facility, International Recorders, where he cut tracks with such artists as Frank Sinatra, Nat "King" Cole, Little Richard, Herb Alpert, Sam Cooke, and many others. "Golden State was a pretty big room," says Kulka's nephew David, who runs an L.A.-area business called Studio Electronics, which builds and services recording studios. "It was about 40 × 50, and the ceiling was quite high, because it was at least a two-story building and the studio went up to the roofline. In appearance it was sort of like an older studio. It was utilitarian, maybe with that perforated acoustical ceiling. The floors were probably linoleum.

"It had a custom console built by Mike Lerner, a tech who worked with Leo for many, many years. Later, Leo bought a Quad 8 [console] that came out of Wally Heider's. The studio had a good assortment of Neumann, AKG, and Sennheiser mics. Leo experimented a lot with miking techniques, and he was really into mic placement and capturing the sound of acoustic spaces. I think it's fair to say he was regarded as a very good engineer. If we're talking about 1965, I would guess that he probably recorded [the Emergency Crew] on an Ampex AG440 4-track and mixed it down to stereo. He also had a small live echo chamber he might have used, which was located near the back shop and the mastering room."

The Emergency Crew demo was done in a single afternoon—a typical session in those days lasted three hours—with the band laying down the instrumental tracks first, completely live with no overdubs, and then adding the vocals, and perhaps hand percussion such as tambourine, secondarily (but also live). They were mixed into what has become known through the years as "Beatles stereo" (after the stereo versions made for the American market of their early mono recordings), with nearly all the instruments in one channel and all the vocals in the other. They cut six songs at Golden State—four originals, including a Dylanesque number sung by Garcia called "I Can't Come Down," a Pigpen locomotive romp known as "Caution (Do Not Stop on Tracks)," and covers of Gordon Lightfoot's "Early Morning Rain" (lead vocal by Phil) and the old folk chestnut "I Know You Rider."

Within a week or two of the Autumn session, the group had found a new name: As has been oft-told, Garcia was over at Phil's house one day, high as a kite, and he poked his finger into a 1955 Funk & Wagnalls dictionary, and there it was: "Grateful Dead," which derived from a folk tale common to a number of old European cultures. It was strange and slightly menacing, and initially it was not that well-received even within the band. But it was also compelling and, as Garcia put it later, extremely "evocative... When I saw that phrase, 'Grateful Dead,' I went '*BONNNNNK!' What?! What?!*' It automatically moved into so many categories, it transcended being just those words and turned into something else entirely." It also turned out to be the perfect name for the next phase of the band's career: the Acid Tests.

ACID ANARCHY

It was only natural that the budding acid heads in the Grateful Dead (Pigpen excluded; he was a juicer from Day One) would at some point join forces with writer Ken Kesey and the Merry Pranksters, who lived over the hills from Palo Alto in the redwood-studded community of La Honda, a few miles inland from the Pacific. Kesey had been a willing guinea pig in the early-'60s government testing of psychedelics on the Peninsula; indeed, he had written part of his famous novel, *One Flew Over the Cuckoo's Nest*, under the influence. In Palo Alto, and then La Honda, he presided over a sort of free-form salon that periodically imbibed psychedelics obtained through various sources. In the summer of 1964, he and an unusual collection of psychedelically inclined fellow travelers, who came to be known as the Merry Pranksters, transformed a 1939 International Harvester school bus into a surrealistic, rolling party-mobile—painting it in the brightest, craziest, swirliest colors imaginable, tearing out the seats, and replacing them with mattresses and all sorts of audio and film equipment Kesey bought with the spoils from his hit novel. With Beat hero Neal Cassady at the wheel, Kesey and company tripped and goofed their way across the country, ostensibly headed toward the New York World's Fair and some promotional activities tied to Kesey's new novel, *Sometimes a Great Notion*. This was the bus trip famously described a few years later in Tom Wolfe's modern masterpiece *The Electric Kool-Aid Acid Test*, but long before that book came out, tales of The Bus and of Kesey's La Honda parties were circulating on the

If you could find the Acid Test through a poster like this, you were invited!

Peninsula and perking the interest of the Warlocks, and then...the Grateful Dead. Sometime in late November, the Dead and the Pranksters and whoever else was around agreed that it would be a blast to stage a series of multimedia LSD parties in different places. "Can *You* Pass the Acid Test?" was the challenge that went out on flyers and was tacked up in hip stores.

If there's such a thing as planned anarchy, this was it: At the Acid Test, everyone paid a buck at the door, took some acid (or not; it wasn't mandatory, but it certainly fueled every aspect of the proceedings), and then whatever happened, *happened*. The Dead would have their equipment set up somewhere, as would the Pranksters—though not really musicians themselves, Kesey and company still set up microphones and batteries of speakers and tape recorders and strobe lights...there were rivers of wires going every which way attached to God-knows-what, and over the course of the evening, folks would talk, sing, play hideous atonal flute and harmonica—whatever uninhibited urge or whim seized upon them at the moment.

"The groovy thing about the Acid Test," Garcia said in 1971, "was that we could either play as long as we wanted to, or not play at all.... Sometimes .we would play one or two tunes, and somebody would be just too stoned to move. So we'd stop in the middle of a tune, put everything away, and split." Since no one was going to an Acid Test specifically to see the Grateful Dead, "There was no pressure of any sort. We could either do it, or not do it." Years later, Garcia noted, "We had an opportunity to visit highly experimental places under the influence of highly experimental chemicals before a highly experimental audience. It was ideal. And that was something we got to do long enough to get used to it."

Bob Weir told *Guitar Player* in 1997, "We began turning up loud pretty quickly. From the start it was faster, looser, louder, and hairier [than what they'd been playing in clubs]. We were going for a ride. We were going to see what this baby'll do. It helped that we were playing in a completely uncritical situation. What didn't help was the fact that we were completely disoriented, so we had to fend for ourselves and improvise. When we would come around in a song to what should be a familiar chorus, it seemed completely unfamiliar... So we had to hang together. We got better and better at it as time went on, so we could take a pretty massive dose and hang in there for a while." Some of the group's early experiments using feedback for its own sake, almost as a compositional tool, came at the Acid Tests. And they were aided and abetted by the Pranksters, who always had their own bizarre audio trip going.

In a 1990 interview, Kesey described for me one of his favorite Acid Test sound experiments, the figure-eight: "By putting the Ampex [601] tape recorder on 'tape' instead of 'input,' you'd get a little lag on each channel. Then we'd put one speaker at one end of the hall and one at the other, and a microphone in front of each speaker so the sound would be going out of a speaker, into a microphone, back into the tape recorder and into the other speaker, and so on, until the sound just washed around in the hall."

Mountain Girl (née Carolyn Adams), who was a Merry Prankster and who became Garcia's girlfriend (and, much later, wife), added, "This short lag on your voice was just long enough to be really uncomfortable, and it would really fuck you up. It was exactly the length of time it would take you to form a thought, so just as your next thought was formed, you heard your voice speaking the previous thought. It was really hard to make progress through that."

In these stills, taken from a Merry Pranksters DVD called *The Acid Test*, we see Garcia (with his Starfire), Pigpen, Weir and Owsley (carrying equipment). In those days the band set up and tore down their own equipment, and in one sequence from the video, Garcia can even be seen sweeping the floors after an Acid Test!

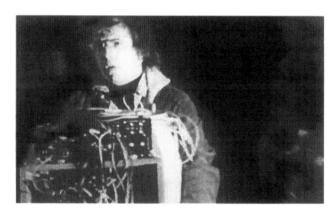
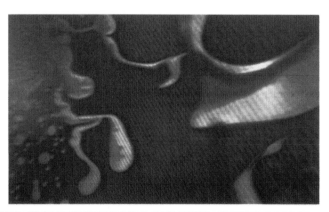
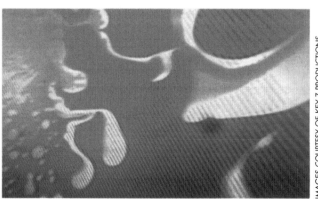

Kesey: "Even when the Dead were playing through their own equipment, that sound was washing around the hall. Nobody had ever heard anything like this—where they were part of the ambience of the sound."

Not surprisingly, the sound at an Acid Test was not always reliable, to say the least. Setting up and wiring equipment is difficult enough *without* being high on LSD. Dealing with cables that turn into cobras, boxes that seem to have phantom voices emanating from their dark recesses—even plugging in a simple connector could become a Herculean task under the influence of powerful psychedelics. And the result was sometimes scenes like this, which is transcribed from an Acid Test:

Weir: Hey, Ken! These microphones don't seem to be working.

Pigpen: They fucked up!

Weir: Nothing up here is working.

Unidentified: Excuse upon it friends, the electronic wasteland...

Pigpen: How 'bout a microphone? C'mon now!

Unidentified: Just keep a-playin', boys. She'll come through one o' these days ....

Pigpen: They ain't no power on the stage!

Unidentified: Just keep a...

Pigpen: All the 'lectricity on the stage—just fix it!

Kesey: This is the captain speaking. We have reached our first emergency, and we haven't even got by the boundaries of...

Pigpen: Well, why don't you rectify it pretty damn quick!

Kesey: Let's everybody put their worries and frets to mind to produce some e-lectricity for the stage....

Pigpen: It's about *time* to get it ready!

Kesey: There's wires all around here plugged into e-lectricity. Let's—

Pigpen: Hey, man, stop your babbling and *fix these microphones!* We need some *power!*

It was chaos on a grand scale. Sometimes the music was powerful and transcendent; other times it was disconnected, distracting, or just plum bad. As Bill Kreutzmann explained to me in a 1989 interview, "When you're high on acid you can't be expected to be too analytical about things; you're going more with the free-flow, and sometimes that would be synchronous with what the other guys were playing, and sometimes you'd just be in your own world playing. But we weren't examining what we were doing. I remember once when I was high on acid, it took me what seemed like 14 years to take my drums apart. It seemed like *lifetimes* had gone by," he laughed. "I'd gone gray, grown old, died, been reborn—all in the time it took to put one cymbal in the case!"

At an Acid Test on December 11, 1965, at Muir Beach Lodge, up the rugged Marin County coast north of San Francisco, the Dead first encountered the man who, more than any other, would inspire them to examine the audio side of playing electric instruments through amplifiers, and whose visionary (if unorthodox) theories would eventually help revolutionize the sound-reinforcement business: This was Owsley Stanley, also known as Bear.

Though his name would become synonymous with the production of the highest-quality LSD made in this country in the 1960s—much of it when the chemical was still legal—for our purposes in this book, it is Owsley the perfectionist sound guru that is of greater interest. (As we'll see later on, however, some of Owsley's concepts about sound were deeply influenced by his psychedelic experiences, and he also generously donated money made in the psychedelics trade to further the Dead's sonic aspirations.)

A little older than the Dead crowd, Bear was the grandson of a U.S. senator from Kentucky, and son of a Washington D.C. lawyer. He briefly studied engineering at the University of Virginia; he then joined the Air Force and was assigned to work at the Rocket Engine Test Facility at Edwards Air Force base, near Los Angeles. He told me in 1996, "I wound up teaching myself electronics, which I knew nothing about. I was reassigned to the salvage yard and took apart every piece of gear that came in—and there was some pretty high-tech stuff at Edwards." This training led to Bear working at a variety of radio and TV stations in Southern California, but he eventually moved north to Berkeley and went to the University of California for a couple of semesters before he dropped out of school for good. He said he discovered the Beatles and LSD in the same week in early 1964; both had a profound impact on him, and in short order he and his girlfriend began making their own acid in a lab they set up in a bathroom. It seems he, too, was destined to hook up with Kesey's already acid-fueled crowd, and that's why he was at the Muir Beach Acid Test that night. He was mightily impressed by the Grateful Dead's power and intensity—in fact, *ripped* on acid as he was, he thought they were even a little scary—but he came away thinking, "This band is going to be bigger than the Beatles." And though he didn't really connect with the individual band members that night (except cosmically, perhaps), this marked the beginning of a most unusual decades-long relationship.

It was also during this period that the Dead began their long association with Bill Graham, who put on his first benefit concert (for the San Francisco Mime Troupe, for whom he was acting as business manager) at the Fillmore Auditorium in San Francisco on December 10. Graham was initially reluctant to use the Dead's name; he found it much more repellent than the Warlocks, but the group prevailed, and so there they were on a bill with a host of San Francisco's finest young bands, including the already-popular Jefferson Airplane, the Great Society (with future Airplane chanteuse Grace Slick), local jazz great John Handy, and a couple of other bands. This was really the Grateful Dead's introduction to the burgeoning San Francisco freak underground, and it was a dazzling revelation: "Hey, there are *lots* of people like us!" By year's end, with the Acid Test still in full swing (if irregularly), the Dead had left the Peninsula behind and were poised to leap into the San Francisco scene. They would be welcomed there with open arms and, as important, open minds.

LOVE AND HAIGHT

DURING the first few weeks of 1966, the Dead made a couple of moves that proved they were serious about being a real working band. First, they enlisted Owsley to be their soundman. Then they brought onboard a pair of managers: Rock Scully, who had been part of the Family Dog, a loose collective of artists/musicians/freaks who had put on a few successful dances around San Francisco, and his friend Danny Rifkin, who, like Scully, had been a student at San Francisco State and was now managing a house in San Francisco's Haight-Ashbury district. The stately old Victorian at 710 Ashbury became the Dead's first office, and later that summer, home to three of the five band members, their girlfriends, and various other folks.

Say the number "710" to just about any Deadhead, and he/she will know what you're talking about.

Chapter Three
1966

The year got off to a bang when the Dead took part in the Trips Festival, which was like an Acid Test on a grand scale that took place at Longshoremen's Hall in San Francisco, January 21–23. A true multimedia event, it featured an incredible variety of performers, from poets to bands to light-show artists to radical theater groups to filmmakers—it was basically the San Francisco freak renaissance on parade in all its Day-Glo glory. The Dead was just a little part of the night helmed by Kesey and the Merry Pranksters, but everyone came away impressed that there was so much energy in—and such a big audience for—this burgeoning counter-culture.

In early February the Dead and friends headed down to Los Angeles for a series of Acid Tests (and a few semi-normal gigs). They lived communally in a big house on the edge of the depressed Watts ghetto, practiced their music at excruciating volumes until their neighbors rebelled, and generally spent time woodshedding and breaking in new material. After the band had been in L.A. for a few days Owsley jumped into the fray, with a head full of ideas about lifestyle (acid, meat: good, though probably not recommended together) and, more important, sound.

Though Bear did have his self-taught electronics background, he had no experience working with electric musical instruments and amplifiers, "and I didn't consider myself a design engineer in any way, shape, or form," he said. Still, he was convinced that what the Grateful Dead needed—what rock 'n' roll needed—was a better, more reliable sound delivery system. As he told David Gans in 1991, "I knew we had to do something, because the technology was so primitive that it seemed like it was holding the music back—that we could go to another level if we had better instruments. Half the time they'd crackle and pop and hum and there would be distortion out of the speakers."

In a 1993 interview, Bear noted, "When I first started with the Grateful Dead, I was concerned because America was obviously on its way into space, which seemed to be the pinnacle of our technology. I thought about back in the days of Bach, the highest, most technologically superb things that were being built were the great organs. Music was the height of technology.

Primal Dead at the Santa Venetia Armory in San Rafael, Calif., fall '66 or winter '67.

PHOTO: BOB CHEVALIER/GRATEFUL DEAD

I felt it was absolutely disastrous that we were shooting rockets, building rockets that could deliver atomic bombs to destroy entire cities, and musicians were playing on something that looked like it was built in a garage in the 1930s. You took a Twin Reverb apart and it looked like the radio I had as a kid, except instead of having a tuner, you plugged a guitar in…I thought the [sound reinforcement] technology was a disaster, and nobody seemed to care. I figured it was worth caring about. I figured 'good enough for rock 'n' roll' should be better than good enough to go into space."

So what's a conscientious neophyte soundman to do? "A few months before I met the Grateful Dead," Bear told Gans, "I tried to figure out what was the best hi-fi. I had a pretty good-size place [in Berkeley]—must've been a 55-foot-long room, about maybe 35 feet wide; just a big single room. I wound up going around and listening to a lot of stuff, and I decided to buy a Voice of the Theatre system, which was about the ugliest hi-fi system you could possibly conceive of. It had a cabinet on the bottom with a 15″ speaker in it, and it was in a large box about the size of a small fridge. It had a little horn mounted on top. The driver was maybe 4″ in diameter; it was a relatively small horn. It looked like something that someone had rescued out from behind a screen at the local movie theater… When I started out with the Grateful Dead, that became the Dead's PA system," he added with a laugh. "My stereo became the Grateful Dead PA. It had a McIntosh amp, two channels, 40 watts per channel."

The reason Bear's speakers looked like they had been lifted from some old movie house is that's precisely what Altec Lansing's Voice of the Theatre line was designed for. The company's roots go back to the earliest days of movie sound. It was engineers from Western Electric—the AT&T division that originally developed the technology for "talkies" through its Bell Labs research group—who formed the All Technical Products Company in 1938; a year later the name was changed to the Altec Service Corporation. In 1941, Altec bought the Lansing Manufacturing Company, whose head, James B. Lansing, had been instrumental in the design of the loudspeaker components (cones and drivers) of the MGM-Shearer two-way system that became popular in movie theaters beginning in the mid '30s. Lansing's Voice of the Theatre speakers were introduced in 1944 and caused an immediate sensation. With improved bass response, front-loaded 15″ speakers, and single-driver high-frequency horns (the driver magnets were made of the then-new Alnico V aluminum-nickel-cobalt alloy), the VOTT line was scaled from huge one-ton-plus systems that could disperse high-quality audio in the enormous movie palaces of the day (many Deadheads can fondly recall various venues in the Fox theater chain), or fit comfortably in smaller theaters and screening rooms. Lansing's most successful model was the modest A4, which had a solitary bass horn; the A1-X, by contrast, contained two large bass horns and six 15″ woofers and four compression drivers.

The modern Legacy Edition of the Altec A7 is similar to ones the Dead used in the '60s.

Lansing also helped develop one of the most popular recording studio monitors of all time, the model 604 coaxial loudspeaker. Lansing split off from Altec Lansing to form his own company, Lansing Sound, in October 1946. Shortly after that, it became known as the James B. Lansing Sound Company. Despairing over financial troubles, Lansing killed himself in September 1946. However, the company he started continued to grow without him, and by the mid '50s it had adopted the familiar name JBL, which would also figure prominently in the Dead's history.

As for McIntosh, whose superior amps formed the backbone of the Dead's live sound systems throughout much of the band's history, that company, too, has links to the intrepid audio pioneers of Bell Labs in Murray Hill, New Jersey. Frank McIntosh worked at Bell Labs for a decade before starting his own business in 1942 designing radio stations and sound systems out of offices in Washington D.C. Frustrated by the quality of the amplifiers he encountered, in 1946 he teamed up with an engineer named Gordon Gow and started to develop a new kind of high-powered, low-distortion amplifier. "The necessary materials to build the Unity Coupled transformer were just becoming available," Roger Russell wrote in his definitive history of McIntosh. "By 1948, the component parts of the Unity Coupled circuit were assembled into a symmetrically driven balanced output stage." McIntosh was granted his first patent in 1949, the same year that McIntosh Engineering Laboratory (later just McIntosh Laboratory) was incorporated. The company's first product was the McIntosh 50W1 Unity Coupled Amplifier, which had 50 watts of output power, a bandwidth of 20Hz to 20kHz, and distortion of less than 1%. The following year, McIntosh's first preamp, the AE-2, was unveiled. Shortly after that, the company moved north to Binghamton, New York, where it continued to grow for many years. The MC-30 and MC-60 became cornerstones of McIntosh's amplifier line, and McIntosh also expanded into the home loudspeaker and consumer amplifier/tuner market, with varying degrees of success. By the early '60s, the brand was widely adopted by audiophiles, Bear included.

To aid him in trying to develop better equipment for the Dead, Bear took on a young charge with considerable electronics aptitude of his own, Tim Scully (no relation to Rock). Scully, who was born in Berkeley and raised in nearby Pleasant Hill, was a genuine science prodigy. In his mid teens he developed a "small linear accelerator to produce a neutron flux by a deuteron-deuteron interaction" (don't ask me; look it up). At the end of his junior year of high school, he was admitted to U.C. Berkeley to study math and physics. He worked as an assistant at the Lawrence Radiation Laboratory, and by age 20 he was working as an electronics-design consultant for such companies as Atomic Laboratories, Quantum Electronics, and General Radioisotopes. Even with that impressive background, "I certainly couldn't claim to have been any kind of audio expert," Scully said. "Bear had much more audio background from his work in radio and TV, but he was less versed in electronic-circuit design."

Mysterioso electronics man and psychedelics pioneer Tim Scully in his 1966 passport photo.

Together, Bear and Scully patched together the Dead's first sound system and immediately looked for ways to improve on the existing components. This was more difficult than it seemed: "Hi-fi stuff wasn't heavy-duty enough, and the Voice of the Theatre speakers weren't strong enough," Bear told Gans. "I went down [to L.A.] with Tim and talked to the engineers at Altec Lansing, and they weren't interested. They said, 'Well, you want power here, use this driver'—and that driver rolled off at 3,000 Hertz. 'Oh, you want it to go higher? We have this one: It goes to 9,000,' but it would take only two-and-a-half watts. I said, 'No, we want one that's this powerful that will go twice as far out as that; we want to go to 15,000 [Hertz].' [They said,] 'Well, you can't do that. We don't want to; we're not interested. Besides, we sell all the speakers we make, anyway. Get lost!'" So that forced Scully and Bear to improvise. At Bear's urging, Scully devised a central preamp and distribution system: "All their amplifiers—everything, the guitars—all plugged into this black box that Tim had. *Everything* went into this box. And then out of the box it went into the amplifiers and then it went into the speakers." Unlike today's mix stations, which are located in some ideal central location out in the audience, the Dead's setup was usually hooked up on the side of the stage.

While down in L.A. in early 1966 with the Acid Test, Owsley/Bear bought the Dead a considerable amount of equipment, including McIntosh amps and Altec drivers and diaphragms. The California Sound receipt shows the address of the Dead's house in Watts.

COURTESY OF TIM SCULLY

"It served several purposes," Scully explained. "One, Bear wanted to do direct recording of the electric instruments, and he bought a decent ¼″ stereo Ampex tape deck [a 354] with 10½″ reels for this purpose. Since this was only a stereo tape deck, I had to build a preamp/mixing board to produce a mixed stereo signal from all the electric instruments, plus the drum and vocal mics. [Bear also owned an Ampex 602-2.]

"Two, he wanted to provide monitor speakers, which would let the band hear this mixed sound as they played.

"Three, he wanted the audio to be as clean and undistorted as practical. For example, we wanted to avoid unintentional clipping, and I brought along my Tektronix scope, which we used to monitor the signals to ensure that we weren't clipping.

"Four, he wanted to reduce the hum and noise picked up by cables from the instruments to the mixing board. We put good-quality audio transformers in each instrument, mounted close to the pickup, which reduced the high-impedance signal to a 600-ohm balanced line, and used good-quality rubber-jacketed microphone cable and XLR connectors at the mixing board end to connect each instrument to the mixing board. Another audio transformer was at the mixing-board end of each instrument's line, bumping the signal back up to high impedance before going to an FET input circuit.

"Finally, the box had a preamp for each channel—each instrument—with volume and crude bass and treble controls. There was an output to a McIntosh power amp for each instrument, and a mixing pot for composing the mixed stereo signal for recording. There were preamps and mixing controls for the PA mics, too."

The intrepid duo also took a stab at designing a short-lived "super bass" setup for Phil. According to Scully, "This was a large loudspeaker Bear found that had extreme low-frequency response and was driven by a several-hundred-watt—400 is the number that comes to mind—amplifier. It coupled powerful sub-100Hz audio into the ground or floor. You could feel it in the ground some distance away. We first hooked this up for the Watts Acid Test."

When everything was working right, the Scully-Owsley system produced what nearly everyone agreed was some of the cleanest and most powerful sound that anyone had heard from a rock 'n' roll band. Unfortunately, it proved to be difficult and extremely time-consuming to set up and tear down, and unreliable on a number of levels. Some smaller venues the band played back then couldn't adequately handle the power requirements. And, "I don't think any of us understood the abuse the equipment would have to withstand," Scully said. "We learned over time that it needed to withstand immersion in Coca-Cola, getting dropped in stairways, etc. And some of the reliability issues may have been related to being stoned on acid while setting up and operating the equipment." Scully and Laird Grant would haul the huge, heavy system—the McIntosh amps alone, mounted on a thick sheet of plywood, became known as the "lead sled"—in a 16-foot GMC van that had once been a Sunshine cookie truck.

There were a couple of changes on the musical instrument front during this period, too. Bob Weir switched from the Gretsch guitar to a red Gibson ES-345. "I don't remember exactly how the transition happened," he says, "but I think that when we hooked up with Owsley, he decided he was going to fix us up with better equipment. Somehow it was deemed that a Gibson was going to be a better choice than the Gretsch. I might have been in on that decision; I don't recall. But part of it was that Owsley wanted to get inside the guitar. So I got a 345, he and Tim cut a hole in the back, and I guess they re-wired it to be low-impedance and all that kind of stuff, which was actually the wrong move.

"They totally discounted the fact that the electric guitar was evolving as an instrument in connection with the electric guitar amplifier. They figured it was going to be a hi-fi deal, because they were hi-fi purists. So they were going to have the guitars sounding sparkling and tinkly and all that, which was certainly not what rock 'n' roll was all about. In the 40-some years since that era, if someone was going to make a go at that kind of sound, it would've been done by now," he adds with a laugh.

Electronic legerdemain notwithstanding, the 345 was an instrument with a solid track record and a great reputation. It was introduced by Gibson in 1959, a year after the similar but more famous 335; both were attempts to fuse the best elements of Gibson's great hollowbody jazz line with the popular solid-body Les Paul. The revolutionary element of both models (Weir would play a 335 later) was that its thin, hollow cavity was bisected by a solid block of maple that stretched from the base of the glued-in neck to the strap button. The pickups, bridge, and tailpiece were all attached to this block, which is what gave the guitar some of the sonic characteristics of a solidbody electric, while the side acoustic chambers, each with sizable *f*-hole, contributed to its woody, resonant qualities. The body was constructed from a four-ply maple laminate; the neck was mahogany with a rosewood fingerboard. The double-cutaway design proved to be extremely popular with guitarists because it provided such easy access to the top frets, and in no time the style was copied by a number of other guitar manufacturers. The two Gibson humbucking pickups were selectable by a three-way switch, with each also having its own tone and volume control. The bridge was the all-metal Gibson adjustable "Tune-o-Matic" variety, and it had a rotary "Varitone" six-way tone-control switch. "It was great," Bob says. "You could sort of selectively hollow out the middle of the sound." Weir's model also had a Bigsby vibrato tailpiece. (Weir couldn't remember what year his 345 was from, but the Bigsby places it pre-1965.)

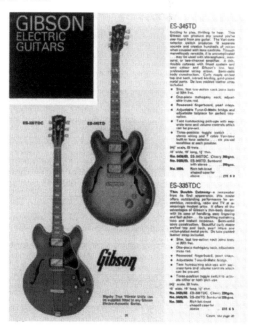

A 1967 Gibson catalog shows versions of the 345 and 355, both of which Weir played.

ENTER THE CONTINENTAL

Pigpen switched from a Farfisa to a Vox Continental organ during this period, a definite (and relatively costly) upgrade in terms of sound quality. Vox was a British brand manufactured by Jennings Musical Industries. Though owner Tom Jennings started his company as a maker of hand-built valve church organs in the early '50s, by the end of the decade it was renowned for its Vox line of amplifiers: the AC-30 guitar amp, in particular, became very popular with rock bands. Once again, the Beatles were responsible for transforming the company from a moderately successful regional operation to a worldwide phenomenon. Early on the Beatles struck a deal to use only Vox amps onstage, and they were true to their word. Vox even developed equipment especially for the group, including the powerful AC-100 guitar and bass amps (renamed the Super Beatle in America by Vox's U.S. agent, Thomas Organ). The Continental organ, which was introduced in 1962, also benefited from Beatles exposure: John Lennon played one on "I'm Down" (the B-side of "Help") and also brought it on tour with him in 1965. Meanwhile, the Continental was also getting a workout from various other British and American bands, including the Animals (who featured it prominently on the smash "House of the Rising Sun"), the Zombies, the Dave Clark Five, Paul Revere & the Raiders, and the wonderfully trashy group Question Mark & the Mysterians, of "96 Tears" fame. The Continental would also form the basis of the Doors' early sound.

Continental organs looked striking: Most had a charcoal-grey base and a bright orange top, and the key colors were reversed. The early models had wooden keys; later ones had plastic keys. The organ had a four-octave range. It had germanium-transistor circuitry (like the Farfisa Combo Compact) and six drawbars for tone setting, apparently inspired by the Hammond organ. According to Ron Lebar, who used to build organs for Vox, "The four-tone harmonic mixture, together with the reed timbre, enables this instrument to cut through a mix. Even a screaming, distorted guitar can't drown it out. Definitely the ultimate group organ."

Pigpen was a rudimentary player at best—certainly no virtuoso—but his organ work in the Dead's early days was mostly quite effective, a nice complement to Garcia's fast lines and Weir's chordal attack. Only when the band started playing longer, more improvisatory pieces did his limitations become a liability, and that *was* always more apparent when he was playing the Continental—which really could cut through a mix, for better or worse—rather than the Hammond B-3, which he added to his arsenal a little later.

In June 1966, the Grateful Dead went into the studio a second time, in an attempt to create a demo that reflected their steady improvement as a band since the Autumn Records sessions nearly a year earlier. Buena Vista Studio had been built by a man named Gene Estribou in a beautiful 60-year-old Victorian house once owned by writer Ambrose Bierce, just a few blocks from the heart

PHOTOS: BOB CHEVALIER/GRATEFUL DEAD

Phil and Jerry at the Santa Venetia Armory, late '66 or early '67. Jerry still has the Starfire; Phil started playing a Fender Jazz Bass around this time (see next chapter).

of Haight-Ashbury. At the time, however, the Dead were living for a short spell in Lagunitas in northern Marin County, about an hour away. The band liked that the atmosphere at Buena Vista was looser than at Golden State Recorders, but there was one serious drawback: It was located on the fifth floor, which meant that a whole mess o' equipment had to be lugged up multiple flights of stairs—the "lead sled" really earned its sobriquet in those days! Estribou had already recorded demos for several other local bands, including Big Brother & the Holding Company, so he had a good reputation, and decent equipment to boot—an Ampex 3-track was at the heart of his operation, "and we had good condenser mics and spent a lot of time optimizing the [custom] board," he told John Dwork.

Once again, the group chose to record a combination of traditional, electrified folk tunes and group originals: They'd swiped "Stealin'" from the Memphis Jug Band; "Don't Ease Me In" was a lively Texas blues from the '20s; "Cold Rain and Snow" was an old-time Appalachian tune; "I Know You Rider" was another evergreen folk song—it was the only track repeated between the Golden State and Buena Vista sessions. The original songs were a peppy rocker called

"You Don't Have to Ask," a slow blues by Pigpen known as "Tastebud" for some reason, and a rather convoluted Phil Lesh composition, "Cardboard Cowboy." None of the group-penned songs would survive even into 1967—but with the exception of "Stealin'," the cover tunes would still be in the group's repertoire nearly 30 years later. In *The Deadhead's Taping Compendium, Vol. I*, Gene Estribou claimed that besides recording the band at Buena Vista, he took the Dead "down to Western Recording and used their studio for doing some tapes that ended up being on their first [and only] single from Scorpio [Records], 'Don't Ease Me In' and 'Stealin'.'" What's troubling about this anecdote is that Western Recording was located in L.A., where the Dead did not record until their first album. More likely, Estribou is confusing Western Recording, which was owned by Bill Putnam, with Putnam's San Francisco studio, Coast Recorders. It's interesting to note, though, that for whatever reason, Estribou's Dead recordings from Buena Vista sound much better than the reverb-drenched Scorpio single. In the end only about 150 copies of that single were pressed, the bulk of them being sold at the newly opened Psychedelic Shop on Haight Street, or given away to local radio stations and to friends.

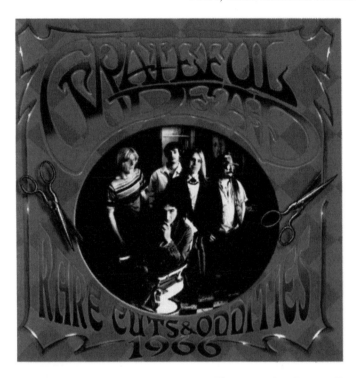

Suggested Listening: *Rare Cuts and Oddities 1966*, released in 2005, compiled never-before-heard rehearsal tapes recorded by Bear along with a number of fine live cuts.

The great Owsley-Scully sound experiment sputtered to a close in August '66, when the Dead finally decided they'd had enough. "The thing was, there was so much paraphernalia we needed in order to make [the system work] that we spent five hours setting up and five hours breaking down every time we played," Garcia said in a spring 1967 interview. "Our hands were breaking and we were getting miserable, and the stuff never worked. Sometimes it was so weird; we got some far-out stuff on that system. It had its ups and its downs, and we thought that if Tim was able to work on it long enough and get enough parts made, we would be able to have a working system....

"Then we went to Vancouver [at the end of July '66], and that was the downfall. Laird, who drives our truck, was stopped at the border because he had a record [a pot bust] and they wouldn't let him into Canada. So the equipment finally got there somehow, and it was set up there and we played through it without too much hassle, but it was lousy; it was just bad, and it brought us down. Then we had to work until dawn to pack it up. It was uncomfortable and it was very bad, very down; very unfortunate." When they got back to the Bay Area, "we decided to disassociate from his benevolence and [Bear's] experiment."

"We called it the 'Owsleystein' system," Weir recalled with a laugh in 2005.

"Nobody could define what it was that [the system] had to do," Bear explained to David Gans. "The musicians themselves couldn't—they'd say, 'Well, I play the guitar and I want to hear a sound.' 'What kind of sound?' 'Well, you know, the right sound.' The musicians couldn't talk about it, and I hadn't a clue. I just knew that what [existed] was too primitive, and Tim didn't have a clue what to do. So we were constantly changing things, wiring stuff, trying to find out how to make it do whatever it was that everybody in their own way knew, but nobody could communicate about. It was not something that could be defined….

"It finally got to the point where it was just not working and everybody sat down and said, 'Hey, it's not working,' and I said, 'I agree with you.' And they said, 'Well, we want to do something different. I said, 'Fine, go to the music store and pick out what you want. I'll buy all the stuff you have now, for the amount of money it takes to buy all this stuff you need.'" In the end, Bear sold some of it to the Straight Theater in Haight-Ashbury, traded more to one of the local music stores, which then turned around and sold it to the Fillmore Auditorium, and gave the rest of it away. "A few weeks later I walked into the Fillmore, and there's my old hi-fi on the stage!" he said.

In the early '67 band interview quoted above, Billy noted, "We got $4,000 and bought some Fender equipment." Garcia added, "Good old reliable Fender equipment, and some Sunn equipment."

"The time when the band went back to more conventional gear for a while coincided with the time when Bear and I went off to make more LSD," Tim Scully recalled in 2005. "He and I remember this differently. My memories are that the band was uncomfortable with having us too involved with them while [we were] actively making acid [which was about to become illegal], while Bear remembers the parting being more over equipment."

Wait, you're both right! The sound system wasn't working out, *and*, as Weir put it recently, "With Tim and Bear with us, we were a bust waiting to happen, so it was a good idea we went our separate ways when we did."

Owsley re-enters our sound story a few years up the road, but even in this relatively brief first tenure with the band, he made a significant mark. He got them thinking about the inadequacy of the prevailing live sound systems of the day, while pointing at possibilities for improving the state-of-the-art. He also was the first person involved with *any* rock band to routinely record tapes of rehearsals and performances as a way to understand how the band was developing.

"I think we listened from the beginning," Bear told John Dwork. "'What was it like?' We thought it might be good to hear what it was really like…. The only way to find out what you had done was to listen to it later. In the heat of a show, no one can tell."

As for the acid he provided to the Dead (and all of hip San Francisco), well, that proved to be creatively formative as well, though less definable (and out of the purview of this book).

At the end of the summer, Garcia, Weir, and Pigpen all moved into 710 Ashbury, along with various friends and "old ladies" (as hippie girlfriends were invariably labeled), and Phil and Billy and their mates moved into a pad around the corner on Belvedere Street. This was when the Haight scene was really coming into full flowering—a year before the vaunted Summer of Love. The Dead were now playing regularly at the Fillmore Auditorium and the Avalon Ballroom and starting to cement their reputation as one of the best live bands in San Francisco. Jefferson Airplane was the first of the local groups to ink a major record deal (with RCA), and as the scene began to attract national attention, it was no surprise when the major record labels—all of which were based in either New York or Los Angeles—came sniffing around the ballrooms, trying to find the Next Big Thing. The Dead attracted a number of A&R scouts to gigs that fall; by year's end they had signed with Burbank-based Warner Bros. Records—despite the fact that label honcho Joe Smith refused to take acid with them. The nerve of him!

HEALY HEROICS

Sometime that fall, too, the Dead hooked up with another key figure in their story—soundman Dan Healy. A self-described "tech nerd" who grew up in the redwoods of Humboldt County, far north of San Francisco, Healy was already tearing apart radios in elementary school and had even set up a primitive radio station by the time he was in sixth grade. "I was always a tinkerer," he told me in a 1985 interview. "While other kids were playing cowboys and Indians, I was learning how to use a soldering iron." Anxious to escape the fate of so many kids growing up in that part of California during the '50s and early '60s—"working in the saw mills or the forests"—he quit high school during his senior year and moved down to San Francisco, landing a job doing part-time maintenance work for one of the major radio stations in the city, KSFO. Later, a contact at the station helped him get a janitorial/maintenance position for a leading San Francisco recording studio, Commercial Recording. By 1964, he'd moved into an engineering position at the studio, which, as the name implied, was mostly devoted to cutting radio and television commercials. Healy wasn't such a nerd that he was deaf to the exciting music that was starting to pop up around town, however, and his friendship with one of the first-wave S.F. bands led to his hooking up with the Grateful Dead.

"I was living over in the Corte Madera area [Marin County] on the Larkspur slough on a houseboat—there used to be a great houseboat scene there," he told me in 2004. "The next houseboat over from me was owned by [promoter]

Bobby Collins, and the guys from Quicksilver Messenger Service were living there. I knew about recording and I knew about electronics, and in those days nobody had any money, so when the Quicksilver guys found out I knew about all that stuff it became, 'Hey, Dan, will you fix my amp?' In those days, if you broke a string you were in trouble! Nobody had any spare parts for anything. A broken amp could end a show! And Quicksilver was always after me to come to one of their shows, especially [guitarist] John Cipollina, who became a lifelong dear friend of mine.

"So one night I went to a gig at the old Fillmore. Quicksilver was the head-lining act and the Grateful Dead was the opening band. I think we got there about two-thirds of the way through the Grateful Dead set, and the music had *stopped*. Somebody's amp had just broken; I believe it was Phil's. So it became one of those, 'Is there a doctor in the house?' situations. And John [Cipollina] pushed me forward and volunteered me. So I went up onstage and did something and got everything working again. Then, at the end of the set, Jerry came up to me and introduced himself and thanked me for lending a hand.

"At that time, I'd been mixing in the studio, so I knew what good sound was, and what was coming off that stage was not good sound," he added with a laugh. "In those days, the sound systems were called public-address systems, and if I remember correctly there was just one little speaker box on each side of the stage. Pigpen would be singing and there would just be this garbled stuff coming out of the speakers; the instruments would drown out the PA. And I remember saying something to Phil and Jerry to the effect of, 'God, this sound system really sucks!' And they basically challenged me to put my wherewithal where my mouth was. So I did.

"Within a couple of weeks there was another Grateful Dead gig there, so I went and dealt a bunch of weed around town to get some money…. Now, in those days, there were only a couple of sound companies around. In the East Bay [Oakland/Berkeley] there was Swanson Sound, and then there was McCune [Sound] in San Francisco; those were the best in the Bay Area. So I rented all the equipment I could get. Unfortunately, the equipment these places had was not mutually compatible. I used to know the lady who was the secretary in the office for the Fillmore, so I conned her into letting me into the Fillmore a day or two in advance, and so I piled all this equipment in there and rearranged all the connectors and made this huge sound system. It was a monstrosity, but it worked. And we played the gig and it sounded great—you could actually hear the vocals. I guess you could say the rest is history. That was really my entrance into the whole live sound thing."

UP AGAINST THE WALL, DAVE!

PEGGING the exact dates when certain transitions occurred during the Grateful Dead's early history is a hazardous enterprise. Memories are unreliable, and the photographic record is scant. That said, it would appear that there were two more instrument switches in the band toward the end of 1966, or very early in 1967.

Chapter Four
1967

Bob Weir, who would prove to be the band member who changed axes most often during the Dead's history, didn't stick with the Gibson 345 very long (though he would return to it, as well as a 335 later), opting to switch to a Rickenbacker. That's the guitar Weir played at the historic Human Be-In on January 14, 1967, when 20,000 people showed up in Golden Gate Park to hear the top San Francisco bands and various poets and leading lights of the counter-culture, in what was billed as a Gathering of the Tribes. And it's what Weir was playing in Gene Anthony's famous series of early-1967 photos of the Dead rehearsing at a space they rented at a heliport in Sausalito. When I showed the photos to Weir in 2005, he sounded positively wistful: "Oh, there's that thin-body Rickenbacker! That was one of my favorite guitars of that era. In fact, I'd love to get another one of those."

Try as he might examining the pictures, he had to admit, "I have *no* idea what the model was. Of course I'd seen them being used by the Beatles and the Byrds by that point. I liked that they looked and sounded pretty distinctive. I remember it did a couple of tricks that were cool, like it had a blend switch, and I'd turn up the treble pickup about halfway and then rhythmically click into the forward pickup and you'd hear this great *chang! wop-wop-wop! chang!* It was great fun."

The Dead rehearse at the heliport in Sausalito, early 1967. Weir's playing a Rickenbacker, Phil has a Fender, Jerry his Starfire, Pigpen the Vox Continental and Billy a Ludwig kit.

These days, Adolph Rickenbacker doesn't get nearly the credit for electric-guitar innovation as Leo Fender and Les Paul, yet the Rickenbacker "Frying Pan" lap steel manufactured by his Electro String Instrument Corporation beginning in 1932 was the first commercially produced electric guitar with magnetic pickups. Actually, though, that instrument was mainly designed by a steel player named George Beauchamp (pronounced "Beech-um"), who'd previously worked with National Guitars, developers of the Tri-cone resonator guitar and Dobro. Rickenbacker's Los Angeles-based tool and die company had made metal bodies for National, as well. By 1935, Rickenbacker had added the Electro Spanish Model B solidbody (bakelite) guitar to the line, but it wasn't until the mid to late '50s that Rickenbacker electric guitars started to acquire their distinctive look and sound. The original horseshoe magnet pickups were replaced by new, brighter-sounding "toaster" pickups (so named because they resembled a toaster). The main Rickenbacker John Lennon played throughout the '60s was an extremely rare model 325, while George Harrison played a 360 12-string on "A Hard Day's Night" and several other songs. Roger McGuinn of the Byrds most often played a 370/12, but he also occasionally used a 360/12. (He even owned a Rickenbacker Bantar, which was a cool-looking two-pickup electric banjo the company made for a while. McGuinn's Bantar had originally been given by the company to Bob Dylan, who apparently was not interested, thank you.) One other prominent Rick user in the mid '60s was Pete Townshend of the Who, who played a 360 and a 1997 (which may have been the first guitar he ever smashed!).

It is likely that the guitar Weir is playing in the heliport photos is a thin, hollow-body red sunburst Rickenbacker 335, which was almost exactly like the popular 330 (introduced in 1958), but with an added vibrato tailpiece. The guitar had a maple body and neck, rosewood fretboard, two chrome "toaster" pickups, a single "cat-eye" soundhole, and a white plastic pickguard.

Phil practicing alone at the band's Sausalito heliport rehearsal space. That's Garcia's Guild Starfire in the foreground.

Meanwhile, Phil switched from his Gibson EB-0 to a Fender Jazz Bass. That model was the second one developed by Leo Fender (after the Precision Bass)—it was introduced in 1960 as the "deluxe model." It differed from the P-Bass in that the maple neck was narrower toward the nut (designed that way to make the transition from upright bass to electric bass easier, Fender claimed), and it had three controls—two for pickup volume, one for overall tone—rather than two. It had two bi-polar single-coil "jazz" pickups. Both the P-Bass and the Jazz Bass were widely used in rock 'n' roll. Jefferson Airplane's Jack Casady played one during his first couple of years in the group—which may have influenced Phil somewhat, as Casady, from the outset, was widely regarded as a fantastic bass player. Another notable Jazz Bass user in that era was the Who's John Entwistle, who used it on "My Generation," with its monstrous bass sound.

THE FIRST ALBUM

In late January 1967, the Dead piled into a few cars and shot down to RCA Studios in Los Angeles to record their debut album for Warner Bros. Records. Why not stay in San Francisco? Well, even though there were a couple of decent studios in town (Coast Recorders and Columbus Recorders probably being the best), the major labels routinely brought bands to New York or Los Angeles to make albums. Jefferson Airplane recorded its first several albums in Los Angeles. The first Big Brother & the Holding Company and Moby Grape albums on Columbia were cut in New York. Quicksilver's debut for Capitol Records (cut a number of months after the Dead's) was recorded at Capitol Studios in Hollywood. Warner Bros. was based in Burbank and at that point didn't have its own studio, so the label sent its artists to various other facilities around town, including Goldstar, Western, and RCA.

Actually, this marked the second time that Garcia had been to RCA Studios. In November 1966, the Jefferson Airplane had asked him to join them in L.A. during the recording of their second album for RCA Records, *Surrealistic Pillow* (the title was Garcia's idea). According to the Airplane's Paul Kantner, "Our first album had been made rather restrictive by RCA and we were sort of unhappy with the results, and we needed to get more communication between us and the studio—and in some idiotic fancy of mine, we figured Jerry Garcia would be the person to communicate some of the things we were trying to accomplish in the studio. So [the engineer] would know that Jack [Casady]'s bass should make the board *smoke*. Smoke comes out of the board, put another fuse in; don't try to damp it down.

"[Also] we would be rehearsing something out in the studio, and [Garcia] would say, 'I have a nice little part that would work in there; maybe you should play this.' And he would pick up his guitar and go *boom*—'Why don't you play that?' and he would play it so good that we'd say, 'Why don't *you* play it? It sounds really good and we can't play it better than that. Come on, help us out here.'

"But mostly he was there to serve as sort of a buffer zone between us and the other side of the window [the producer and engineer in the control room]. A lot of what we were trying to do, both sound-wise and lyric-wise, was eased quite a bit by his very gentlemanly manner. He was not harsh, not abrasive," as the somewhat volatile members of the Airplane could be.

In the end, Garcia contributed acoustic guitar to several tracks (uncredited) and also helped arrange "Somebody to Love," which became the Airplane's first hit. It was through those sessions, too, that Garcia met the man who would produce the first Grateful Dead album, Dave Hassinger.

Suggested listening: The first album, recorded and mixed in a week at RCA Studios in L.A. The remastered version also contains some studio outtakes and live tracks.

Before he produced the Dead, Hassinger had been an engineer exclusively, working out of RCA Studios. The greatest achievements of his early career are the work he did with the Rolling Stones in the mid '60s: He cut a number of tracks that appeared on *December's Children* and *Out of Our Heads*, and also the entire *Aftermath* album, which was the first Stones LP consisting entirely of original material. He was behind the board for such tracks as "Satisfaction," "It's All Over Now," "Lady Jane," "Under My Thumb," and "Paint It Black"—classics all. A little later he recorded *Jefferson Airplane Takes Off* and *Surrealistic Pillow*.

The reclusive Hassinger was very rarely interviewed, but I managed to track him down in Palm Springs in 1985 to talk about his experiences with the Dead. He noted that on *Surrealistic Pillow*, Garcia was around mostly to help the Airplane "get some of their ideas into focus. Actually, though, he'd been down there [in L.A.] quite a while before I even met him. I spent most of my time in the control room working on the sound. Finally, it came to me from [Airplane singer] Marty Balin, I think, that Garcia wanted me to work with the Grateful Dead. Shortly after this, I joined Warner Bros. full-time as a producer and engineer, and that's how I ended up working on their first album.

"We went in and did the first album very, very fast—less than a week in RCA Studio A. At that time I didn't know them, and looking back I wish I could have had more time and done some things a little differently. But my understanding was that these were songs they'd played a lot and they essentially wanted to get them down like they played them live. I'd made two or three trips up to the Bay Area and seen them at the Fillmore, and I thought they were dynamite. What I was after on the album was to capture as much of the energy as I could."

According to Dick Bogert, who engineered the album, "RCA Studio A was *huge*. I once did a Jerry Goldsmith score in there with 93 musicians, and there was room for more. It was like a barn, really, and back then it didn't sound that great, either. [RCA] didn't really straighten it out [sonically] until the '70s. So we used a lot of baffles to try to close it down, contain the sound."

The control room was equipped with a custom console built by RCA technicians, and a still relatively new Ampex 4-track recorder. (*Jefferson Airplane Takes Off*, recorded in the same room, had been 3-track; *Surrealistic Pillow* was 4-track.) Signal processing was extremely limited. Besides the ubiquitous EMT plate reverbs of the era, RCA Studios also had its own live echo chambers on the roof, "which were okay if you were working at night," Bogert says, "but during the day you'd hear tires squealing on the street below; all sorts of noise got into them. Then they took the original metal boxes and plastered them, and that helped a bit.

"RCA didn't have a great selection of mics in those days," Bogert adds. "They used mostly their own [RCA mics], some of which were really good, but not all of them. The 77s and 44s [both RCA ribbon mics] were good for certain things, but necessarily for rock 'n' roll. So we went to 10001s, which are horrible mics—really ugly microphones." Also called the KU-3A, the 10001 was a unidirectional mic used mostly for production recording on film sets. "And we had BK-5s, which were also ugly mics [used mostly as boom mics for broadcasts]. RCA was so corporatized in those days that if it wasn't RCA or Telefunken, they didn't buy it. But in those days you wouldn't think of using a Telefunken on a rock 'n' roll date—you'd crunch the front end of the preamp and it wouldn't survive! So there really weren't any great rock 'n' roll mics there. We probably used 10001s and 44s and 77s on the Grateful Dead."

As Hassinger noted, the album was basically cut live, with all five band members playing at once; vocals were added later. Typically, there would be several takes of each song. The best take would be chosen, and then the lead and backing vocals would be added to that take, as well as any percussion overdubs (such as tambourine). In keeping with record-industry practices of the day, most of the songs were kept to under three minutes, in some cases by fading abruptly during a hot jam. There were exceptions, however: Pigpen's workout on "Good Morning Little Schoolgirl" was allowed to blossom with some nice jamming; "Morning Dew" clocked in at nearly five minutes; and the group's epic jam tune of that era, "Viola Lee Blues" (originally by a 1920s Memphis jug band called Canon's Jug Stompers), stretched out to ten minutes. Still, the nine-song LP clocked in at just under 35 minutes. (When the album was remastered in 2001 for a box set called *The Golden Road*, some of the tunes that had been truncated at first—"Schoolgirl," "Morning Dew," Garcia's "Cream Puff War," "Sitting on Top of the World"—were presented in fuller versions for the first time, a great improvement! The box set also included several unreleased bonus tracks from the same sessions, including "Alice D. Millionaire," "Overseas Stomp," "Tastebud," and an instrumental take of the old blues "Death Don't Have No Mercy.")

Upon the record's release in the spring of 1967, Garcia was fairly positive about it and the experience: "I think our album is honest. It sounds just like us. It even has mistakes on it. But it also has a certain amount of excitement on it. It sounds like we felt good when we were making it ... . It's the material we've been doing onstage for quite a long time. It sounds like one of our good sets."

However, a few years later he'd changed his tune a bit. "At that time we had no real record consciousness," he told *Rolling Stone* in 1971. "We were just going down to L.A. to make a record. We were completely naïve.... So we went down there and, what was it we had, Dexamyl? Some sort of diet-watcher's speed, and pot and stuff like that. So in three nights we played some hyperactive music. That's what's so embarrassing about that record now—the tempo was way too fast.... It has a sort of crude energy."

And in the '80s, Dave Hassinger reflected, "I wish I could have taken them someplace other than RCA, someplace where I could have engineered it. But at RCA Studios, once you started using their facilities as an outside producer, you had to use their engineers. It came out later that that upset the band, because I had been primarily an engineer and that's what the band wanted from me. I was new to production, and the Grateful Dead didn't really need a producer to tell them what to play or how to play it. They needed someone to help them get the record to sound the way they wanted it to sound, and that's what I would have liked to have done." As for the band's vibe during the sessions, "They had a good time certainly," Hassinger said, "but they were very workmanlike at the same time."

Engineer Bogert didn't remember many specifics about working with the Dead, but offered, "I liked them as people; they seemed like pretty down-to-earth cats—especially compared to the Airplane, whom I'd worked with. They were assholes. But you know, we were all working so much, a lot of it is just a blur. Back in those days you might be working 100 hours a week, so you might easily do a commercial in the morning, a religious session in the afternoon, and then the Grateful Dead in the evening. A lot of my days were like that."

It is worth noting, too, that the album's leadoff track, "The Golden Road (to Unlimited Devotion)"—the most complex piece on the LP from a recording standpoint, with its overdubbed acoustic guitar and dense backup vocal arrangement—was cut at Coast Recorders in San Francisco in an attempt to find a "single" the Dead might land on radio. It didn't work, but it's still a strong track.

On June 1, 1967, the Dead played their first shows outside of the West Coast. In what would become the most fertile breeding ground for Deadheads within a couple of years—New York—they put on a free concert in Greenwich Village, rocked the trendy Café Au Go-Go and Cheetah clubs for several nights, and gigged at a state college on Long Island.

A NEW AXE FOR JERRY

Sometime between the recording of their first album and these shows, Garcia switched guitars for the first time in the group's history, leaving his Guild Starfire behind and picking up a black 1956 Les Paul Custom, the first of several Les Pauls Garcia played during the late '60s.

The Les Paul, of course, was the proud creation and namesake of the great guitarist, bandleader, and inventor Les Paul (born Lester Polsfuss, in Waukesha, Wisconsin, in 1915). He took up the guitar at about age ten, and within a few years had figured out a way to amplify it using a phonograph needle and the family radio. Early in his musical career he played a Gibson L-5 archtop (picked directly from the company's factory in Kalamazoo, Michigan), but by 1934 he was looking ahead: He commissioned Chicago instrument makers the Larson brothers to build him a guitar with just a ½″ maple top and no *f*-holes. "They told me I was crazy," he told *Guitar Player*'s Jon Sievert in 1977. "They told me it wouldn't vibrate. I told them I didn't *want* it to vibrate, because I was going to put two pickups on it. As far as I know, I was the first guy to put two pickups on a guitar." By the late '30s he was playing both an L-5 with a pickup and the Larson Bros.' guitar with Fred Waring's band, spreading the electric-guitar gospel wherever he played.

The first guitar Paul built himself was "the Log," which he constructed in 1941 out of a 4×4 fencepost fitted with a bridge, neck, and pickup attached. To give it the "regular" guitar appearance that people seemed to demand, he put the body of an Epiphone guitar around it. In 1946, after several years of playing the Log on the road and on records, Paul approached Gibson about the idea of manufacturing a solidbody electric guitar based on the Log, but the company turned him down. (Today, the Log resides in a case in the Smithsonian Institution in Washington, D.C.) Meanwhile, Paul had also been dabbling in various recording experiments, bankrolled in part by singer Bing Crosby (who would fund many early technological projects...thank you, *Der Bingle*!). Paul built his first garage studio in 1946 and started experimenting with what was, in effect, early multitrack recording—he'd record a part on an acetate disc, then play back the disc while recording another part on a second recorder, and so on, building songs that way; his hit "Lover" had 24 parts on it!

Though his right arm was nearly shattered in a 1947 car crash, Paul continued to play (the 1950s were the heyday of his partnership with his wife Mary Ford, née Colleen Summers)—and to work on recording and sound innovations.

He was a pioneer in the use of echo, delay, and phase shifting, and in 1949 he modified an Ampex 300 tape deck to allow for sound-on-sound recording, which freed him of some of the technical challenges of his old two-disc-recorder bouncing method. Paul was also the first person to close-mic a vocalist—his experiments with Mary Ford immediately influenced how future generations of engineers cut vocals. In the mid '50s, he commissioned Ampex to build the first 8-track recorder, at a time when even *stereo* records were rare. (Let's face it, the guy deserves his own book!)

Electric guitar and recording pioneer Les Paul in his home workshop in the late '40s, mastering a record. That's a Lansing Iconic speaker on the wall behind him.

The Les Paul guitar, introduced in 1952, was Gibson's response to the success of Leo Fender's solidbody Broadcaster/Telecaster, introduced two years earlier. However, in keeping with Gibson's design standards—and to avoid what some at the company viewed as Fender's mass-produced "slab" look—a bit more craftsmanship went into the Les Paul than the Fender. In looks, the single-cutaway Les Paul somewhat resembled two Gibson electric archtops already in production, the ES-175 and the ES-295. It had a solid mahogany body topped with a carved maple top, and a mahogany neck which was glued in (rather than screwed on, like the Fender). The fingerboard was rosewood. It had four knobs for the two Gibson P-90 single-coil pickups' volume and tone, and an easily accessible toggle pickup selector. Garcia's 1956 axe was a Les Paul Custom model, all black with white outline piping, black "top-hat" knobs, black plastic pickguard, and a Bigsby tailpiece with whammy bar. There were certainly many other rock and blues players who had adopted the Les Paul at one time or another, including Eric Clapton, Jeff Beck, and Pete Townshend.

Garcia's Guild Starfire still had a prominent role in the band during this period, however: Bob Weir played it on and off during the summer of 1967. "Somehow my Rickenbacker got broken, and I think it might have gotten sent away to fix; I don't know what happened to it," Weir recalls. "So I was playing Jerry's old guitar for a while, and then I went over to a Gibson again."

Mark Dronge, the son of Guild Guitars founder Al Dronge, recalls the Dead's first trip to New York: "Nobody really knew who they were when they came and played the Café Au Go Go. But I used to live in the Village on 12th St. One night the Dead were onstage, and actually Bob was playing a Starfire; maybe it was the same one Jerry had played. Jerry was playing a black Les Paul. All the way from the back of the room I could see that the neck of the guitar Bob was playing was warped, so I walked up to him afterwards and introduced myself and said, 'I'd like to straighten out your guitar.' Our factory was in Hoboken [New Jersey] at the time, which was about 20 minutes away, and I said, 'I'll pick you up tomorrow and take you out there.'

"So the next day I went to pick him up, and Phil and Jerry and Bob all piled into the car and we went out to the Guild factory and poked around, and that was the start of our relationship. It's funny—they were smoking dope in the kiln, or Jerry and Phil were, anyway; Bob wasn't. They disappeared at one point and we couldn't find them. The kiln was about a 6-foot-by-5-foot room filled with ebony and rosewood fingerboards—very pungent. It was where we'd dry out fingerboards, because they have oil in them. It takes a long time before they're ready to put on a guitar. So, they were in there smoking away, which was pretty bold for that time, I guess.

"Anyway, we all sort of hit it off, so we talked about making various guitars for them, and we did end up making a couple for Bob and a bass for Phil, and we were working with them fairly closely for a while. I remember someone we knew offered them some studio time at a place called Gotham Studios, but I don't think they ever went there."

In mid June, the Dead played the Monterey International Pop Festival, a hundred-plus miles south of San Francisco. Initially suspicious of the three-day event because it was put on by L.A. promoters, the Dead ultimately joined the other top names from the San Francisco scene, but refused to allow themselves to be filmed for a documentary that was being made of the event by D.A. Pennebaker. Besides the S.F. bands, acts included Simon & Garfunkel, the Mamas & the Papas, Eric Burdon & the Animals, Otis Redding, Ravi Shankar, Canned Heat, the Association...it was quite a lineup of hip and commercial bands. The Dead had the unenviable task of performing between two of the most sensational acts on the bill: the Who, who ritually destroyed much of their equipment during their final number, "My Generation," and a little-known guitarist who was making waves in England: Jimi Hendrix, whose performance at Monterey is one of the most famous moments in rock history, thanks to Pennebaker's *Monterey Pop* film, which hit American theaters on New Year's Day in 1968.

From an equipment standpoint, the Dead's weekend in Monterey is interesting mostly because of what happened after the festival: Manager Rock Scully and various others drove a van up to the backstage area at the end of the last concert and "liberated" thousands of dollars' worth of amps and other equipment that had been provided by Fender for the event. In that oh-so-noble 1960s spirit, their theft ("appropriation" was usually the term used) was allegedly for a

Jerry with his black Les Paul at a free concert in San Jose, June 1967. Note that Billy has a new Ludwig kit and that both Sunn and Kustom amps are visible.

good cause—a guerrilla, no-permits free Summer Solstice celebration concert in Golden Gate Park. Music for the people and all that. A groovy time was had by all, and a few days later, the equipment was returned to a neutral spot—the Ferry Building in downtown San Francisco—and Fender (and its new corporate parent, CBS) was none the worse for it.

It was around this time, too, that Phil Lesh first picked up a Guild Starfire II bass, a move away from the solidbody sound of the Fender and back to the warmer, "woodier" hollowbody style. (Photos from the Solstice concert on June 21 show Phil playing his Fender bass. At an outdoor concert in San Jose, probably a little later, he's playing the Guild. However, Phil told me, "My first Starfire was stolen from a gig in L.A. just before Monterey Pop. I played a Fender Jazz at the festival and for some time afterward, until I could afford a new Starfire." So it's unclear when he really started playing the Starfire regularly.) Like Garcia's Starfire, the bass had two *f*-holes and a mahogany top, back, sides, and neck, with a rosewood fretboard. Unlike Garcia's Starfire, the bass had two cutaways. It was considerably lighter than a Fender, had a thinner neck (which, at 30 1/2″, made it a short-scale bass), and—a key to its sound—two big Hagstrom single-coil "Bi-Sonic" pickups, noted for their wide frequency range. (Hagstrom is a Swedish company that got its start importing German and Italian accordions in the 1920s, began manufacturing its own in the '30s, and by the late '50s was making its own electric guitars, featuring a patented pickup design using Swedish blue steel magnets.) The strings on the Starfire II were flatwound Pyramid Golds. As we'll see shortly, the Starfire II—which was also adopted by Jack Casady sometime during this period—became the breadboard of sorts for a number of bold experiments in instrument sonics.

Phil's Guild Starfire bass was brand-new at the San Jose gig. Bob's playing a Gibson 345.

PHOTO: LEO HOLUB

PHOTO: LEO HOLUB

Pigpen noodles on the Vox Continental before the San Jose show, while Jerry messes with his amp.

By that summer the Dead had finally settled their sound-reinforcement issues by augmenting their Fender gear with some amplifiers/speaker cabinets made by two leading companies of the day, Kustom and Sunn.

Kustom gear is instantly recognizable: Its amp coverings were famous for coming in seven different colors of Naugahyde tuck & roll—you know, they look like they were made from seats in a diner! The company was founded in the mid '60s by a fellow named Bud Ross in Chanute, Kansas, of all places, and quickly became a major player in the highly competitive rock 'n' roll amp and PA market. Most of Kustom's solid-state amps had volume, bass, treble, reverb, and tremolo controls and Jensen or JBL speakers. In photos from the summer of 1967, it appears that the Dead are using two Kustom 4-15Ls, which featured two 15″ JBL speakers per cabinet. And though the look is a bit dated now, the tuck & roll actually proved to be fairly durable, if not completely practical for stacking with other equipment in a tight truck pack.

Kustom made a popular line of Naugahyde tuck & roll amps.

Sunn was also a relatively new player on the scene. The company was started in 1964 by Norm Sunholm, the bass player of the Oregon group the Kingsmen ("Louie Louie"). Unhappy with the sound he was getting from his touring bass amp, he and his brother Conrad took it upon themselves to design a better piece of gear (literally in their garage), and the Sunn Musical Equipment Company was the ultimate result. The Dead used several Sunn amps in the late '60s, including the Sonic II, which contained a pair of JBL D-130-F speakers, and the 2000S, which was favored by many rock bass players, including Phil and Jack Casady.

With the Summer of Love bringing an unprecedented inundation of (mostly) young people into Haight-Ashbury in 1967, the Dead had the good sense to get out of town. In August they played shows in Toronto, Montreal, Detroit, and Ann Arbor, Michigan, then went up to the funky Russian River resort community of Rio Nido (a couple hours north of S.F.) to work on new material and get in a little rest and relaxation. The band's music had been evolving steadily as the year progressed, and increasingly their new songs reflected their growing sophistication as players and songwriters. The short rock ditties of '66 were long gone; their newer material was darker and more complex, with changing rhythms and more room for improvisation. In the spring of '67, Garcia's old friend Robert Hunter had sent him some song lyrics he'd written while traveling around the Southwest, and it wasn't long before the Dead started setting them to music. Beginning with "Alligator" (music by Phil and Pigpen), the first batch also included the future Dead classics "China Cat Sunflower" and "St. Stephen." Phil wrote a song with his poet-friend Bobby Peterson called "New Potato Caboose." Bobby penned a strange number called "Born Cross-Eyed," and he collaborated with Bill Kreutzmann on a propulsive tune that eventually became known as "The Other One." That song became joined at the hip with Garcia's "Cryptical Envelopment" under the über-title "That's It for the Other One," which marked Garcia's last attempt at writing lyrics. By the time the band was encamped in Rio Nido, Hunter had returned to the Bay Area and had become "The Writer." His first stab in Rio Nido proved to be one of the band's most enduring numbers: "Dark Star."

In mid September, work on the Dead's second album began in Los Angeles, with Dave Hassinger once again in the producer's chair. During the eight-plus months since their first album sessions, Ampex's new 8-track recorder had crept into a lot of the better New York and L.A. studios, and Hassinger and the band agreed 8-track was the way to go for this album. On that first trip down to L.A., very little got done at RCA Studios—the Dead attempted basic tracks on "Alligator" but couldn't nail it. It was clear from the outset that things were not going to go as quickly as they had with the first record. The Dead, inspired by the Beatles' *Sgt. Pepper's Lonely Hearts Club Band* and the Beach Boys' *Pet Sounds* and other carefully crafted records, wanted to take their time with their second LP. Hassinger didn't want to rush, either, but he didn't really know at this early stage what he was getting into.

MICKEY JOINS THE FRAY

Then, in late September, the band added a sixth member, drummer Mickey Hart. This move would fundamentally change the group's sound and usher in an era of relentless musical experimentation and growth. A native of Long Island, Hart was the son of a drummer who abandoned him and his mother early in life. Curiously, once he discovered his father's musical past, Mickey started taking drum lessons, and from about age ten on, he was completely obsessed with playing: As he once said, "When I had my drum I was the prince of noise." Mickey played drums in high school and in the Air Force, and while he was stationed in Southern California, he saw a photo of his dad, Lenny, in a brochure for Remo drums. Company founder Remo Belli himself helped Mickey reconnect with his father, and once Mickey was discharged from the Air Force, he moved to San Carlos, south of San Francisco, to help Lenny run a drum store, Hart Music. It was only a matter of time before Mickey tried LSD and became wrapped up in the burgeoning local music scene. In fact, it was at a Count Basie show at the Fillmore Auditorium that someone introduced Hart to Bill Kreutzmann. The two hit it off and decided to go see Big Brother & the Holding Company over at the Matrix club, and that performance, as much as anything, convinced Mickey that he wanted to play this kind of music. The two spent hours after the show banging on garbage cans, cars, anything in their path as they roamed the city.

Then and there, Billy extended an invitation to Mickey to come jam with the Dead at one of their rehearsals at the Potrero Theatre, but it would be nearly a month before they'd hook up again. On September 24, the Dead played at the Straight Theater on Haight Street; Mickey brought his drums down, and immediately he and the band clicked. By the end of the night, there was no turning back. The Dead had a second drummer.

Mickey's first kit with the Dead was a standard Rogers set, and he stayed with that for a few years, replacing a drum or two and adding more cymbals and a second floor tom along the way. Like Kreutzmann, Mickey says that in that era, there wasn't much of a difference between the top brands of drums. "They were pretty much interchangeable," he says. "Ludwig, Rogers; Rogers, Ludwig... I'm not sure it mattered."

As a company, Rogers dates all the way back to 1849, when Richard Rogers, an Irish immigrant, started a drum-head factory north of New York City in a town called Brewster's Station. Over the next few decades, he and his son (and various other members of the Rogers family and in-laws) would move around the Tri-State area, finally settling in Farmingdale, New Jersey, in 1909. At a time when most drum heads were made of sheepskin, Rogers & Sons helped establish the more expensive (but also more durable) calfskin as the best material for drum heads, and, during the teens and 1920s particularly, banjo heads. (Jerry's Weymann banjo likely had a Rogers calfskin head.) Rogers had its own tannery and also made other leather products, including book bindings and even coverings for artificial limbs! It wasn't really until the early 1950s, however, when the company was sold to Grossman Music, that it became a major manufacturer of drum *kits*. Under Grossman, Rogers moved to Covington, Ohio, and began to actively compete against Ludwig, Slingerland, Leeds, and others drum makers of the day. Rogers became famous for its Dyna-Sonic snare drum, as well as its reliable hardware. In fact, John Auldridge, editor of *Modern Drummer* magazine, called Rogers drums "the Cadillac of the 1960s...[Rogers's] innovations in hardware design have been copied by almost every drum manufacturer in existence." Mickey says simply, "They sounded good; I didn't care what name was on them."

Around this time, too, the Dead first leased a Hammond B-3 organ for Pigpen. Though the Vox Continental would continue to be part of the Dead's sound through 1969, the B-3, which would figure prominently in the sound of their second album (later named *Anthem of the Sun*), brought a new richness and—dare I say—gravitas to the keyboard underpinnings of the Dead's sound. This was a serious instrument: At more than 300 pounds, it was a bitch to carry around from town to town (and perhaps for that reason it didn't go out on every tour), but it represented a quantum leap in the sheer quality of the organ sound.

The popular organ was invented by an engineer named Laurens Hammond (b. 1895 in Evanston, Illinois), who originally made a name for himself by developing one of the first electric clocks, then worked on such disparate technological miracles as 3-D movies and missile guidance systems. Then, using the same kind of steady, synchronous motor he'd invented for the electric clock, he worked toward inventing an organ that would make sounds generated mechanically. As Allen Sears explained in his 1994 missive "A Walk on the Wild Side: The Story of Jazz Organ," "Hammond's ingenious idea was to use this motor to turn small metal wheels with accurately grooved edges. Each wheel had a corresponding pole magnet wrapped with a coil of wire at the tip, which was pointed at the edge of the tone wheel. When the wheel rotated, it disrupted the magnetic field, thus inducing a current in the coil of wire. By adjusting the number of grooves on the tone wheel, the frequency of the current could be adjusted. The tone wheels were engineered to rotate at the correct speed and with the appropriate number of grooves to produce audible frequencies which then could be amplified and fed to a speaker system. Perhaps the most practical result of this method is that a Hammond organ never goes out of tune; the motor will always rotate the wheels at a constant speed."

Hammond's organ design was patented in 1934, and production began the next year. It caused an immediate sensation, particularly in churches, where it was quickly adopted as a much more inexpensive and compact alternative to pipe organs—the reigning technology in that field of music for the past several hundred years. Fats Waller was among the first major artists to adopt the Hammond organ and take it on tour, but it was mostly little-known black gospel acts that brought it into the studio for recording during the 1940s and '50s. It would be the ascendancy of a jazz player named Wild Bill Davis in the late '40s, followed close behind by the young Philadelphia keyboard titan Jimmy Smith, that really gave the Hammond "street cred." Hammond introduced the B-3 in 1955, a year before Smith burst onto the scene. Indeed, Smith's dominance as a jazz organist would span decades. On the rock/soul side, Booker T. Jones of Booker T. & the MG's helped bring the Hammond sound to millions on "Green Onions" and a slew of other hits. (Booker played an M-3.) The unforgettable organ sound of Procul Harum's biggest hit, "A Whiter Shade of Pale," came from a Hammond 102 played by Matthew Fisher. And by 1968 a slew of other players were favoring Hammond organs, including Rick Wright of Pink Floyd, Al Kooper of the Electric Flag, Felix Cavaliere of the Young Rascals, Jon Lord of Procul Harum, Steve Winwood of Traffic, and Keith Emerson of the Nice. (The B-3 would play an even bigger role in the Dead's sound in the 1980s, thanks to Brent Mydland.)

With two levels of keys and controls, the B-3 offered many more sonic possibilities than the Vox. Each level had 61 notes and two sets of nine drawbars for each. Additionally, there were two drawbars for bass pedals, percussion attack and decay switches, two sets of preset keys, volume, vibrato speed, and chorus functions, and a Leslie-speaker speed switch. The Leslie's swirling sound has become practically synonymous with the B-3, but early on, Laurens Hammond and Don Leslie, who developed the rotary tremolo speaker that bears his name with his brother Bob in 1940, were practically enemies. Leslie approached Hammond about using his speaker with the organs, but he was rebuffed. Instead, Hammond engineers came up with their own (inferior) rotary tremolo system, and the company's literature of the day even took swipes at Leslie's invention (which was originally dubbed the Vibratone). The rivalry went on for decades, yet almost from the start, Hammond users sought out the Leslie speakers to go with their organs. Even Hammond dealers defied the wishes of their boss and carried the Leslies. Leslie sold his Electro Music company to CBS in 1965 but stayed on as a consultant until 1970. In 1966, Hammond finally gave in and started incorporating Leslie speakers as part of its organs, despite the objections of the company's retired founder, who stubbornly never embraced Leslies. Ironically, Hammond bought Electro-Music and the Leslie name from CBS in 1980—seven years after Laurens's death. The last B-3 was produced in 1975, but other Hammond models continued to draw acolytes. Now, of course, there are electronic plug-ins that can ape the B-3 and Leslie, though for my money none can match it for depth and character of sound.

Laurens Hammond, inventor of the famous organs that bear his name. Here he is shown in the mid-'30s with the Hammond A, predecessor of the B-3.

WEIRD TIMES IN THE STUDIO

The Dead, with Mickey in tow, returned to RCA Studios in October to continue sessions on the new album, working on "Alligator" some more and also dipping into "Cryptical Envelopment" and "The Other One." There was no question that adding the second drummer took these songs to new and exciting places, but things still progressed slowly in the studio, and increasingly there was friction between the band and Hassinger. Believing the Dead might do better in a different studio, Hassinger shifted the action to American Studios in North Hollywood (which was "as tiny as RCA was big," Phil remembered) when the band came down for more studio work in November. They tackled "Born Cross-Eyed" and "New Potato Caboose" at American, but Hassinger was not pleased with the way the sessions were progressing. The Dead had been smart enough to put a clause in their Warner Bros. contract granting them basically unlimited (though *not* free) studio time to make their albums, but this clearly went against Hassinger's instincts.

With Warner Bros. pushing for the Dead to complete the album sooner than later, Hassinger decided to try his luck in New York, booking time at various Manhattan 8-track studios while the band gigged in the area, and lugging 8-track reels across the country to work on vocals and more basics. They spent a couple of days working at Olmstead Sound in midtown Manhattan, which had a solid reputation as a good "live" room, having hosted scads of jazz sessions through the years for the likes of Jerry Mulligan, the Modern Jazz Quartet, Buddy Rich, Jimmy Guiffre, and other acts ranging from the Four Seasons to Richard & Mimi Fariña. The Dead also tried their luck at Century Sound, which was co-owned by the fine engineer Brooks Arthur, who'd worked on hits by the Chiffons, the Dixie Cups, Marvin Gaye, Neil Diamond, the McCoys, Astrud Gilberto, and others.

"We'd work at Olmstead during the day," recalls Bob Matthews. "Then I'd pack all the equipment, go down a narrow staircase, put everything into the GM Metro van, and go over to Century, where we had a helluva time double-parking; you'd have cops all over you. Then we'd set up at the other building, where at least there were elevators. Plus they were playing shows at night. There was a lot of tension between Hassinger and [Dan] Healy, but it was Bobby who eventually sent him over the edge."

Engineer Brooks Arthur, who co-owned Century Sound, remembered, "Working with the Dead was my first experience with what I can only call pre-Woodstock Woodstock. I'd worked with Neil Diamond, I'd worked with Van Morrison, and I'd never seen anything like the Dead before. The Dead moved in there lock, stock, and barrel—guitars, drums, and family and children and friends and roadies and breastfeeding ladies and people sitting on the floor. It was flowers, peace symbols, beads, bells; the whole thing. Pot was everywhere. There was so much pot, the accountants upstairs would get high from the smoke going up through the air-conditioning system.

"Although I was helping Dave Hassinger, I didn't really hang out much with the group," Arthur continued. "What I remember most about those sessions was that everything took forever to do. I think Dave and I spent 48 hours just on the drum sound, getting the cymbals right, getting the imaging right for those guys. That was their M.O.; that was their style. Normally I could get an orchestra recorded—I could get two albums done in the time it took to get a drum sound for the Dead. But I understood their logic. It was a different room for them, and they wanted to get a certain sound that was a departure from their old sound, so they took time with their bass and drum sounds. Which microphone sounded better with this cymbal? What does it sound like when we stuff the kick drum, or unstuff the kick drum, or pop a hole in the head of the kick drum? You try a microphone in-phase, out of phase. Then you take a long coffee break, get high, and then there's lunch.

"Actually, the way the Dead worked then was more the way people did it in the mid and late '70s. I had seen this a little bit working with the Lovin' Spoonful, who really cared about how their sounds went down to tape, but the Dead took it to a new extreme for me. This was also my first experience of a studio lockout—where the room was booked by only one group for a [while]. I actually had to go and book time for myself at other studios around town to complete my own work while the Dead were there."

This East Coast jaunt was also notable because it was the first to include the roadie who would become the solid foundation of the Dead's road crew for the rest of their history: Larry Shurtliff, known and loved by everyone as Ram Rod. Raised in Oregon, Ram Rod connected to the Dead through Kesey and the Pranksters (who had gravitated up to Oregon following the Acid Tests). A number of other Oregon folks would become part of the crew at different times.

By the end of their East Coast stay, relations between the band and Hassinger had deteriorated to the point where he wanted off the project. "I gave up in New York," he recalled. "We'd been working for a long time on that second album, and they had put down some new tracks in New York, and nobody could sing them [reportedly "Born Cross-Eyed"], and at that point they were experimenting too much in my opinion. They didn't know what the hell they were looking for. I think if you experiment you should have some sense of what you're ultimately going after, but they were going from one end of the spectrum to the other.

"One time during the making of the record, I went into American Recording [in L.A.], and the Dead had ordered so much equipment from Studio Instrument Rentals and other places you literally could not get into the studio! The whole album was that way. It was like pulling teeth, until finally I couldn't take it anymore. When I came back to L.A., the head of Warner Bros. asked me, 'Have you had enough yet?' and I said, "Yeaaaah!'" Hassinger laughed.

In 1977 Dan Healy, who was the Dead's live mixer on the tour and was assisting in the studio, said, "The whole matter of having to compromise the music to fit within the production ideas of Dave Hassinger and the record industry was really hanging everybody up. So there was going to be friction between the band and Hassinger—hassle, hassle, back and forth. We were at the session one afternoon when we got into an argument with Hassinger about something he was doing in the mix. He jumped up, freaked out, and stomped out of the studio. Everybody just sat there. We were left there, halfway through finishing the record."

In Bob Weir's telling of the Last Days of Hassinger, the end came after he asked the producer to figure out a way to record the sound of "heavy air." But Hassinger remembers, "That did come up, but that was earlier. That might even have been in Haight-Ashbury. I just looked at him when he said it. But he said it in such a serious way I didn't really know how to react. Actually, a little later, we did seriously look into trying to get a certain quality of sound like I suppose he was talking about. We were going to take all the equipment out to the desert east of L.A. and record out there, but it never happened.

"But that wasn't the cause of our split. That was over those two dynamite tracks that nobody could sing [the other was "New Potato Caboose"]. I wanted them to sing as a group because they weren't making it as individual singers, and they just thought that was ridiculous ... What really brought it to a head was when we were in Century Sound in New York City and the road manager and I got into an argument about something. And of course with that band, if you argued with anyone in the entourage, you were taking on the group—at least that's how they saw it. So that was the first big fracture. Basically we just couldn't see eye to eye. I still think they were a fantastic group, and despite the ending, I enjoyed working with them."

Hassinger thought Garcia was "just a super guy—I really liked him a lot. But they were all in on the decisions ... I got along with them all pretty well, except for Phil Lesh. He was worrying about the sound of his bass to the point where it got almost ridiculous, I thought. But one of the things you have to remember is that I was very straight, and it wasn't too easy for me to deal with people during that era. I knew I was dealing with people who were probably heavy into acid, and I knew that at times our conversations weren't going to make a lot of sense. I always felt that it was hard to do real constructive work with musicians on acid, but I guess there were some great records made that way."

Hassinger relayed all his negative feelings about the Dead to Warner Bros. president Joe Smith (who had signed the band originally), and in late December 1967, Smith fired off a letter to Dead manager Danny Rifkin that read, in part: "The recording in New York turned out to be very difficult. Lack of preparation, direction, and cooperation from the very beginning have made this album the most unreasonable project with which we have ever involved ourselves.

"Your group has many problems, it would appear, and I would believe that Hassinger has no further interest or desire to work with them under conditions similar to this last fiasco. It's apparent that no one in your organization has enough influence over Phil Lesh to evoke anything resembling normal behavior. You are now branded an undesirable group in almost every recording studio in Los Angeles. I haven't got all the New York reports in as yet, but the guys ran through engineers like a steamroller.

"It all adds up to a lack of professionalism. The Grateful Dead is not one of the top acts in the business as yet. With their attitudes and their inability to take care of business when it is time do so would lead us to believe that they never will be truly important. No matter how talented your group is, they're going to have to put something of themselves into the business before they get anywhere."

The letter also urged the band to finish the album during three days of sessions the label had set up for them in early January '68, but by this time the Dead had a new vision of what their record should sound like, and it wasn't about to be completed in three days.

INDEPENDENCE

CONSIDERING Joe Smith's damning criticisms of the Grateful Dead, it's nothing short of miraculous that following Hassinger's departure, Warner Bros. then allowed the group to produce themselves—in that era a privilege rarely granted to bands, even those with considerably more status than the Dead. The label could have easily just installed a new producer, but perhaps sensing that these San Francisco crazies didn't really mesh well with conventional studio types, they took the gamble that, left to their own devices, the Dead might come up with something interesting on their own. And they did: *Anthem of the Sun*.

Chapter Five

1968-1969

"It was our springboard to weirdness," Mickey Hart said three decades later. "We thought, 'Now we're not tethered by the engineers or the technology of the day! We can fly the lofty peaks, man...let us go together!' And of course we knew *nothing* of the studio. It was very startling, it was new, it was invigorating...it was the edge."

Actually, Dan Healy, who was mixing the band's live sound, was also a seasoned studio pro, so at least *someone* in the organization knew his way around a console and multitrack.

What Warners probably didn't fully comprehend, however, was that the Dead were no longer interested in making a conventional studio record. Instead, Phil and Jerry, with Healy egging them on, decided to create an album that would combine live and studio tracks into a psychedelic audio collage—it would, ideally, capture the group's incredible live energy and fuse it to polished studio recordings. The fact that no one had ever done this before didn't seem to be a deterrent; indeed, it provided some of the impetus. Whatever studio work still needed to be done would transpire at Columbus Recorders—the Kingston Trio's old place—which was wedged between the financial district and North Beach; Healy had used the studio before and liked it.

"We began recording [shows for *Anthem*] with a small ¼″ 4-track machine," Healy recalled in the late '70s. "Four-track was big time in those days, and ¼″ meant that we could afford to buy tape. The machine was an old Viking deck that [had been] made by splicing two stereo machines into one machine. It was a real funky machine. You had to set it down and have a talk with it, warm it up, and if you got it in just the right mood, it would record for you, and cease to stop and warble." Quarter-inch stereo recordings were also made at each stop along the way.

The first live recordings for the album were made at a new venue in town: the Carousel Ballroom on Market Street, upstairs from a Honda dealership, had been through numerous incarnations through the years, most recently as an Irish dance hall. It would fall into hippie hands that winter, being booked and run by a loose consortium of "heads" (supported by financial backing from the Dead, Quicksilver, and Jefferson Airplane) who were interested in providing an alternative to Bill Graham's shows. Owsley (who had been busted in December 1967 and was looking for some honest work) and Bob Matthews did sound for the hall, and that's also where we encounter another member of the Dead's future sound team, Betty Cantor. She had done some recordings and stage-setup work at the Avalon Ballroom, then worked briefly for the Denver Family Dog, where she was spotted by Matthews, who brought her into the Carousel scene—originally she worked the drink concession. Laird Grant, the Dead's original "kwippie" (as they called equipment crew folks), had come back from New Mexico and was stage manager.

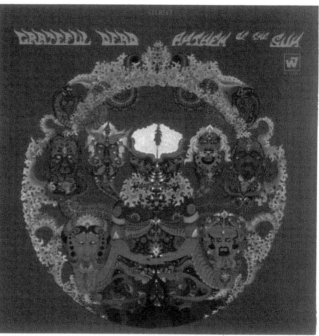

The house system at the Carousel, Betty recalled in 2005, "consisted of a couple of scrounged [Altec] A7s that had been converted to what the McCune hot-rodded version was, which was to seal up the port, replace the Altec [speaker] with the JBL D-130, and use a whole other horn system on top."

A few days after that first Carousel show, the band packed up their gear and headed to the Northwest for shows in Eureka (in northernmost California), Seattle, and Portland, Eugene, and Ashland, Oregon. Mid-February and mid-March shows at the Carousel, and February gigs at a defunct bowling alley near Lake Tahoe, were also recorded with a ½″ Ampex 4-track the group acquired (as well as ¼″ 2-track).

"We got all these tapes and they were all recorded on different machines in different cities," Healy said. "The speeds were all different and weird and variable. There would be things wrong: The performance would be going along real good and suddenly somebody would kick out a plug, or the power would go off and the performance would end prematurely…．

"We got back to the studio, and it turned out there wasn't one performance that played all the way through and did anything. We decided to just devise a way to be able to play them *all* by aligning and starting two different performances in the same place, and comparing the different meters and rhythms."

Garcia added, "[We'd have] four stereo pairs of completely different shows that all started in the same meter and had about the same tuning." The eventual methodology in the mixing process, then, was to fade different performances in and out, sometimes playing two or more with similar (but not exact)

Suggested listening: *Anthem of the Sun* was the product of hundreds of hours in the studio and combining live tracks with studio recordings. The tapes that eventually became *Dick's Picks Vol. 22* (released 2001) were recorded in February 1968 and were part of the raw material used for the live-studio collages on *Anthem*.

passages simultaneously, building the track in layers that way. For instance, in the fine British documentary about the Dead called *Anthem to Beauty*, Phil sits at a console with the finished 8-track *Anthem of the Sun* master and discusses the passage that would later be known as "The Other One": "On tracks 1 and 2 we have the Grateful Dead from Kings Beach, California; on tracks 3 and 4 we have Eureka, California; and on 5, 6, 7, and 8 we have two different performances from Portland, Oregon—one was Friday night, the other was Saturday night. It must have been smokin', because all these performances are really high-energy."

STUDIO EXPERIMENTATION

Meanwhile, on the studio side, the band worked on "Alligator" at Columbus Recorders, and also finished up a striking, *moderne* transitional passage between "That's It for the Other One" and "New Potato Caboose" featuring contributions from a keyboardist and composer named Tom Constanten. "T.C.," as he was known, had been a friend of Phil's since they met during a U.C. Berkeley summer program in 1961. "Phil and I had our first LSD from the same batch in early '63, when it still came on sugar cubes," he told me in a 1984 interview. Both took a class with experimental music composer Luciano Berio at Mills College in Oakland for a semester. T.C. continued studying with Berio and two other modern composers, Karlheinz Stockhausen and Henri Posseur, in Europe, then joined the Air Force as a way to escape the draft (and reduce the risk of being sent to Vietnam). He still managed to visit Phil during furloughs, and he became friendly with the other members of the Dead and kept his finger on the pulse of San Francisco's psychedelic culture. Interestingly, it was Garcia, not Phil, who actually recruited him to work on the electronic collage for the new album.

"It was like a magic carpet that was there for me to step on, and I would have been a fool not to step on it," T.C. recalled. "[Jerry] said something like, 'I think we can use you.' It was at Columbus Recorders in San Francisco." (In a later interview he spoke of first working on the abstract piece at American Studios in L.A. late in 1967, much to the horror of Dave Hassinger.) T.C. employed a number of avant-garde techniques in the piece, including "prepared piano," in which foreign objects are placed on and between the piano's strings to alter the sound in unusual ways; John Cage had pioneered the technique in the 1940s, but it was new to popular music when T.C. tried it with the Dead.

"The most striking [piano preparation] was when I took a gyroscope, gave it a strong pull, and put it against the amplified sounding board. It's kind of a chainsaw sound," he recalled. "One of my other favorites was obtained by using coins. At that time I used dimes…. There's a sound like woodblocks that comes from some stuck on the piano's higher strings. Another I liked was clothespins on the lowest strings, played either with the keys or on a string directly." T.C. also blended in parts of a tape he'd made of a ring modulator while working at Posseur's Brussels studio in 1962.

"The idea was that this chaos would come out of 'The Other One,'" he explained. "The final part was an overlay of several live performances, whence it gets that incredible depth; it's a remarkable effect. So they wanted to take that up and swirl it into an explosion, and out of the ashes of that would stealthily enter the warm, misty waves of 'New Potato Caboose.'"

The band's studio experimentation stretched to other songs, as well. Inspired by the Beatles, there were backward tracks, odd combinations of instruments, and unusual processing and effects. For Garcia's "Cryptical Envelopment" portion of the "That's It for the Other One" suite, Healy put the lead vocal through a whirling Leslie speaker (normally used with Hammond B-3 organ). On "Born Cross-Eyed," there was backward piano and organ, blends of electric and acoustic guitars, timpani, and even a section where acoustic guitar, trumpet (played by Phil), and separate overdubbed snare drum appear in the chaos. And on the jam during "Caution," there's a passage where the tape radically speeds up and slows down, a very unusual effect. "Healy was great," Garcia said. "Man, there were times when he would be there with a thumb on the capstan motor of two machines, slowing down the speed…trying to get them in phase. We had to do two-channel panning with faders, which is in a way more sensitive than [using] pan pots."

When it came time to mix the album at Columbus later that spring, Healy, Garcia, and Lesh found that working with 2-, 4-, and 8-track tapes was a difficult proposition, and the studio wasn't really set up to be able to do what they wanted. The old custom console, for example, "had 12 inputs but only mixed down to three: left, center, and right, as they called it in those days," Healy said. "And so we modified it to have fader-outs, so that we had the 12 front-end mic preamps and then the 12 input faders. Then we stayed up several nights in a row and re-wired the patchbay so you could get individual access to the output of each one of these mic channels, and through that you could record on the 8-track [we had obtained]."

As for the recorders on hand, "Columbus had three 2-tracks, a mono, a 3-track, and an 8-track, which was a brand new thing that was the hot-dog machine. We had to convert all the performances down to whatever tape machine was in the studio. Some of the performances we took down to 3-track, and some we took down to 2-track just so we could have enough machines to simultaneously run it all. Then we transferred it all onto the 8-track machine [during the mix]." Further complicating the process is that some of the tapes had been recorded at 7 ½ IPS, and others at 3 ¼ IPS.

"There are zillions of [edits]," Garcia said. "They're everywhere—all over the fucking place. A lot of them are not in obvious places at all. There are things like three or four splices every two or three bars, and in a couple of transitional places where we would have to piece things together to get it to work."

Speaking more generally about the mix, Garcia observed, "It all ended up on two pieces of continuous sides of 8-track tape. The way we [Garcia, Healy, and Lesh] went at it, we shot at performances of the mix, rather than mixing little bits and tying them together. We ended up mixing almost the whole side in big flows to get smoothness through the transitions. It was the most complicated fucking mixing you could imagine. If one fader wasn't down when it was supposed to be—BAM!—this big, loud noise would come through. It took a long time, but we took lots and lots of passes and then went through the best of them. Maybe we edited a couple of times, but not much, really.

"Each performance of the mix of those 8-tracks is like throwing the I Ching. You know it will all work—any possibility will work; any combination would produce a version of it that you could dig…. There are places of extreme awkwardness, but it wasn't hurting for imagination."

Indeed, *Anthem of the Sun*, which came out in July 1968, is in many ways a revolutionary rock album: the first to blend live and studio tracks, the first to combine all the songs on a side into a continuous, flowing work, and the first to utilize jump cuts and montage techniques usually found in film, not music. It's rough, it's chaotic, it's confusing, but it's also haunting and provocative. Garcia famously noted that the album was "mixed for the hallucinations," and it remains one of the great experiments to come out of the late-'60s psychedelic culture—even though, predictably, not many people bought the album: too dark, too weird. But at least it was *real*.

The band's performances during this era were no less adventurous, if perhaps a tad less chaotic. By mid '68 the Dead had all but abandoned the short, punchy songs that dominated their sets a year earlier, in favor of the sort of open-ended material that was on the album, and a raft of exciting new songs written by Garcia and/or Lesh with lyrics by Robert Hunter—including "Dark Star," which seemed to grow longer and stranger with each performance, "China Cat Sunflower," "St. Stephen," and "The Eleven." This was a period when the band was practicing four to six hours a day at their rehearsal room— the funky, run-down Potrero Theatre in San Francisco—working on mastering different rhythms and time signatures, learning to breathe fire as a single beast.

As usual, there were a number of instrument and technology changes within the band.

NEW GUILDS FOR BOB

During 1968, Bob Weir alternated between several guitars: a Gibson ES-335, a Gibson 345, a Guild Starfire V, and another custom experimental axe from Guild, the latter two passed to him by Guild's Mark Dronge.

In various 1968 photos (including those taken at the famous free concert on Haight Street that March, the band's swan song to their old neighborhood before they gradually shifted their scene to Marin County over the next several months), Weir can be seen playing a beautiful blonde Guild Starfire guitar that was quite similar to the Gibson. The double-Florentine-cutaway Starfire V was identical to the Starfire IV (introduced in 1963 and popularized by Buddy Guy and others) except for the addition of a Guild/Bigsby vibrato tailpiece. It had a multi-laminate maple top, maple sides, a three-piece mahogany neck, rosewood fingerboard, two Guild HB-1 humbucking pickups, Adjust-o-Matic bridge, and two volume and tone controls. Weir's guitar had no pickguard. One feature that confuses me is the headstock: On Weir's guitar it has the Guild "G-shield" logo, more common to Guild acoustic guitars, rather than the "Chesterfield" headstock I've seen in every other photo of Starfire guitars.

Speaking of Guild acoustics, it was during this period, too, that Weir (working with Mark Dronge) helped design a guitar which he would use occasionally with the Dead in the studio and onstage in the late '60s. On the summer '05 afternoon I interviewed Weir for this book, he walked over to one of the two walls in his studio that are covered with various acoustic and electric guitars, and pulled down a lovely Guild acoustic. "This is one of the prized guitars in my collection," he said. "It's the first one I ever designed.

"How this came about is, I was taken by how well [archtop guitars] projected, and though I wasn't about to go with an archtop for the style of music we were playing, the sheer volume was pretty impressive, and I said to Mark, 'Why don't we do a flat-top with an arched back?' This is what they came up with for me. It's loud and it's got beautiful tone. There were three of them made— Ram Rod got one and [future Grateful Dead crew chief] Rex Jackson got one. It's an arched back with an oversize peghead, which improves the sustain: A smaller peghead resonates more, which dissipates some of the energy of the string."

An experimental electric Guild that Weir played onstage a few times was another thin hollowbody model, but with a through-neck design Weir and Dronge had discussed during one of the band's trips east. "I remember we were driving to the

Bobby with his Guild Starfire V, at a free concert at Columbia University in Manhattan, May 1968.

PHOTO: ROSIE McGEE

amplifier factory out in Elizabeth [New Jersey]," Dronge remembered, "and we were talking about how Gibson made the Les Paul sort of as a one-piece unit, gluing it the way they did and having this solid body—getting that whole heavy mass to vibrate together was the source of the wonderful sustain the Les Paul had. And we talked about making a neck-through for an acoustic body, like a jazz guitar. That guitar Bobby had was like a CE-100, modified with different pickups, but it wasn't made quite right. The whole point was the neck should be one block of wood like the neck-throughs have become, but nobody [at Guild] understood that at the time. It was right around then that I left, so I didn't have a chance to oversee it, and it never became what we hoped it would." (Parenthetically we must also note that on a couple of gigs in 1968, such as a free concert in New York's Central Park, Weir played a white Fender Telecaster onstage: "It was probably just once or twice. I couldn't tell you whether it was even my guitar," he laughed. "It obviously wasn't the sound I was looking for.")

Meanwhile, Garcia was playing a couple of different Les Pauls. Besides the black '56 model, he obtained a 1955 gold-top, also equipped with two P-90

Garcia with a Les Paul, Pigpen on the B-3, and various Fender and Sunn amps. Newport (Calif.) Pop Festival, August 4, 1968.

PHOTO: JIM MARSHALL ©

single-coil pickups, but with no Bigsby tailpiece/vibrato. And at one point in '68 he picked up another black Les Paul, this one also without the Bigsby accoutrements. (Some have wondered if this was the '56 Les Paul with the tailpiece removed, but in photos it looks like a different guitar.)

By this time, too, Garcia's amp/loudspeaker setup had grown considerably from the early days. It was still based around Fender Twin Reverb heads, but now he had three 2×12 combos and two 4×12 extension cabinets refitted with JBL D-120 speakers, an Owsley innovation: "I wound up having a sort of production shop at the Carousel hot-rodding these [amps]," Bear told David Gans. "I'd drill an extra hole in the front and put in a middle control so it had treble, middle, and bass. The whole idea was to bring the equipment—which was basically pre-war design—up to date. We'd open up one of those things and it would be full of wax capacitors. We'd pull out all of those things and put in modern mylars…. We'd change the grounding systems; we put shielding in the guitars; we found wire that was foil-shielded…."

Weir was playing through a Fender Dual Showman Reverb, which was introduced that year—a potent two-channel, 85-watt unit with a pair of 15″ JBL D-140 speakers in the cabinet. With separate brightness, treble, midrange, bass, vibrato, and reverb switches, it proved to be an effective means to cut through the Dead's increasingly dense sound. However, within the next year—it's unclear exactly when—Bob would switch to a Twin Reverb setup as well, while Phil would move to a Dual Showman.

Mickey also got into the act, expanding his onstage setup with the addition of a couple of Chinese gongs he obtained from Zildjian. "At that time," Mickey says, "old man Zildjian—Avedis Zildjian—still had the company in this place that was like a little triple-garage, but taller, someplace in Massachusetts. We were on tour, and Ram Rod and I went to the factory to get some cymbals. Zildjian made gongs that were terrible, but while we were there I noticed these really nice Taiwanese gongs sitting up on a high shelf. Ram Rod had brought along some icebag [the infamous pot:"The best we had ever seen," Owsley says. "It was pure buds; no sticks or leaves."], so we closed the door and lit up with one of Avedis's sons, and we got really, really stoned. I looked up and I said, 'I want that!' 'You want a gong?' So they gave me a bunch of gongs, and they even gave me the cymbals. Then, when we were driving back to the gig—maybe it was in Boston—I said to Ram Rod, 'Holy shit, we don't have a stand! How are we going to suspend the giant gong?' So Ram Rod hits the brakes and he backs up into this gas station where there was a Sunoco sign—this rusted old sign advertising motor oil—hanging on a stand. He throws it in the back and he gets in the car, and then

Mickey and his Rogers setup at the May '68 Columbia concert.

Ram Rod, a man of few words, says, '*Now* we've got a gong stand.' And that became the first gong in rock 'n' roll. We ended up using it on 'Dark Star' and some other things."

The grand experiment over at the Carousel Ballroom was idealistic but probably doomed from the start: "hippie business" turned out to be oxymoronic, and by summer Bill Graham had taken over the lease and re-christened the joint the Fillmore West. Healy went to work with Quicksilver Messenger Service (and others) for a period, and Owsley went back to doing sound for the band.

With Hunter and Garcia turning out new songs with increasing rapidity, the band decided to jump back into the studio in the fall of 1968, booking time at a new facility in San Mateo (south of San Francisco) called Pacific Recording, where Bob Matthews and Betty Cantor were working. Although it would become a major player in Bay Area recording for a while after a pair of New Yorkers—producer David Rubinson and engineer Fred Catero—set up shop there, at the time it was being run by Paul Curcio, one-time member of the Mojo Men. "It was fun and funky," Catero would recall of Pacific many years later. "There was no glitz at all, but some great records were made there," including, after the Dead's time there, the first two Santana albums, and discs by Linda Ronstadt and Taj Mahal.

"This was the first opportunity I got to be a recording engineer, which was something I'd wanted to do for a long time," Matthews said. "[Pacific] had an old Altec board from McCune's, with giant rotary faders—a broadcast board with a patchbay that enabled us to hook into an Ampex [440] 8-track—and we started bumbling through these groups they would send down to us. Fortunately, most of the groups were as impressed to be in a studio as we were to be recording them. We did a lot of demos, including one for Santana; that was our claim to fame for a while."

By the time the Dead came down to Pacific Recording, Bob and Betty were starting to feel comfortable, and certainly the camaraderie that existed between them helped immensely in making everyone on both sides of the glass feel comfortable. "*Aoxomoxoa* was the first album they were allowed to do completely on their own," Matthews said. "I think you have to give a little bit of credit to Warner Bros. for letting them pull off *Anthem of the Sun*. But this was their opportunity to be in charge, and this was our opportunity to get better at being recording engineers." Betty: "We experimented *a lot*." Bob: "We learned the wrong way to do everything! We would be given a task—either a specific technical description or an aesthetic goal—and it was our job to do whatever we could to realize that for them. Their ideas were as new to them as our solutions to provide a response were to us; we were both finding our way. But it was very positive."

THE AMPEX CONNECTION

Over the course of many long, stony sessions, the Dead cut their album on the Ampex AG-440, which Matthews complained had a sluggish transport, "resulting in different speeds at the head and tail of the tape"—but before they could finish overdubs or start mixing the record, Matthews said, "The guy who was employed part-time as chief engineer and maintenance man at the studio, whose day job was a design engineer in the videotape-machine department at Ampex, showed up one day with a 16-track recorder." This was Ron Wickersham, and the 16-track was just the second that Ampex had ever made—the first had gone to Columbia Studios in Los Angeles.

Wickersham is another interesting character, an electronics genius who was sucked into the Grateful Dead vortex and made significant contributions to the band's technical side for half a dozen years. Originally from Richmond, Indiana, by his late teens Wickersham had worked in a hi-fi store and was already helping to build FM radio stations from the ground up in Ohio and Indiana; in fact, at the time he was the youngest person ever to get a First Class license for that pursuit. He also built the station at Earlham College when he went there, and during a two-year stint in the Army, he trained amateur radio operators how to operate in military frequencies (as part of a national civil defense scheme) and handle communications. After the Army, he worked as a technical consultant for various radio stations, then jumped to the first UHF TV station in the country, in Muncie, Indiana.

"Then I was reading *Newsweek* or *Time* or some magazine that had a cover story about the music in San Francisco, and inside they had pictures of the light show at the Fillmore," Wickersham says. "Actually I had been more into classical music than rock. At one point I even thought I might be a classical pianist, but I couldn't stand performing in public. But I liked rock, and what was going on in San Francisco looked like a lot of fun, so I came out here for the Summer of Love and fully intended to be a hippie; I was 28.

"Well, I spent about ten days being a hippie," he laughs, "but I got restless and then looked around for a job. Ampex was a place I always respected for their audio tape-recording equipment. So I went down there [to Redwood City, south of San Francisco] and talked to them and immediately got a job."

Ampex was founded in 1944 by Alexander M. Poniatoff, who took his three initials and added an "ex" for "excellence" to form the company moniker. During the last years of World War II Ampex primarily made radar motors and various kinds of generators for the U.S. military; when that dried up after the war, Poniatoff was inspired to develop tape recorders, after seeing a captured German Magnetophone made by AEG. By 1948, the Ampex Model 200 tape recorder had been introduced, and the company had found its direction. Over the next several years Ampex pioneered a number of new recording devices, including a multitrack recorder in 1954, and a videotape recorder in 1956, the VR-1000 (later called the Mark IV). Later innovations included helical-scanning recording, electronic video editing, the first color videotape recorder…the list goes on. In short it was a company full of bright, forward-thinking folks: "You had the guys who knew the most about filters, knew the most about color television, guys who were doing *really* advanced stuff," Wickersham says. His first job at Ampex was making color TV generators—"generating color bars and test tapes; there were 18 different standards at that time."

Even that seemingly straight environment, however, couldn't keep the Call of the '60s out of the building. Wickersham says that a number of people at Ampex used psychedelics, particularly in the days when it was legal (until October 1966) and being tested nearby at Stanford University. "There was one guy who was called Cowboy who sat under the conference table for maybe three months," he notes, "but he'd contributed a lot to the company in the past, and they always had a high tolerance for the way people were."

Wickersham's brother knew one of the original investors in Pacific Recording, and Ron actually started doing some work there when it was still a 2- and 4-track studio. By the time Bob and Betty turned up and the studio's problematic Ampex 8-track needed work, Wickersham was involved in a number of different areas there, including devising the first console with a simultaneous mixdown section, and mentoring Bob and Betty and other engineers who worked at Pacific in the peculiarities of the mammoth new MM-1000 16-track, which had been developed from a video deck that ran 2″ tape (double the width of 8-track tape).

Now, some groups, given the opportunity to expand to 16 tracks, might have transferred the 8-tracks to the MM-1000 and built from there—but the Dead and Bob and Betty didn't want the generation loss the transfer would have represented, and more to the point, they saw the 16-track's arrival as a chance to re-think the arrangements and start over again from scratch. "We all knew we could do it better," Matthews says. Besides, what was the harm? After all, Warner Bros. was footing the bill…or so it must have seemed, for the bills always went to the label, not the band, and the debit sheet that was growing at an alarming rate down in Burbank because of expenses racked up—first during *Anthem*, and now the third album, with only minimal record-sales income to offset the costs—didn't feel like a tangible thing to a band engrossed in the studio wonderland. This head-in-the-sand approach would come back to haunt them shortly. (A couple of August '68 8-track jam sessions from Pacific Recording survived and were released in 2003 on an expanded version of *Aoxomoxoa*.)

In late November 1968, Tom Constanten, fresh out of the Air Force, was invited to join the band, replacing Pigpen as the keyboardist. Pigpen's playing had never been more than rudimentary (though almost always tasteful and,

Garcia (with a Martin D-18) and Ron Wickersham with the Ampex MM-1000 in the control room at Pacific Recording.

once he got the B-3, quite soulful), and it was believed that T.C. could bring a little more color to the keyboard chair. "There was one exquisite gig in Cincinnati where both Pigpen and I played keyboard," T.C. recalls. "He had the B-3 and I had the Continental." Not long after that, however, "The B-3 got repossessed because they didn't pay the guitar bill or something, so I had to play a Vox Super Continental. Our credit was not the very best back then," he says with a chuckle. "But I really felt the unfairness of it all, because the B-3 sounded so good and the Continental was so limited. Mind you, [modern composer] Terry Riley used a Vox Continental for *Rainbow and Curved Air*, and it suited his purposes eminently well. In my eyes he's up there with Jerry Garcia as a major musical light of the 20th century. But I wasn't too pleased about having to play the Continental night after night, because it really had a hard time cutting through all those guitars and drums."

Was it weird for Pigpen to have a new guy in essence taking over one of his roles? Undoubtedly, but as T.C. told me in 2003, "I don't think he felt that threatened [by me coming into the group]. After all, they already had two guitarists and two drummers, and the interpersonal dynamics among the players was already strange enough without worrying about the mitigating effects of instruments. In other words, it's strange enough relating to the guitarists and drummers already—in terms of the music, dynamics, balance. If anything, adding my keyboard stabilized it rather than disrupted it. I never felt any professional jealousy in that situation; it seemed much more like brotherhood and connection."

In live performances during this period, Pigpen was still one of the band's driving forces, with his version of Bobby "Blue" Bland's "Turn On Your Love Light" always a sure-fire show-stopper. But eventually, with T.C. in the group, Pig stopped playing keyboards onstage, and he was not part of the *Aoxomoxoa* sessions, except to lend moral support from time to time. T.C., on the other hand, flowered in the studio setting (more than live), and his contributions to the album-in-progress—including a calliope-like organ sound on "Dupree's Diamond Blues" and harpsichord on "Mountains of the Moon"—were striking and original.

Those songs—and the feathery Hunter-Garcia number called "Rosemary"—were also notable in that their musical foundations were built around acoustic, rather than electric, guitars. Weir played his custom Guild on the sessions, while Garcia picked the same Martin D-18 he'd bought back in 1962. Besides using the D-18 on *Aoxomoxoa*, during the first few months of 1969, Garcia also played it onstage during performances of "Dupree's" and "Mountains of the Moon," which were paired together, accompanied by Weir on either his acoustic Guild or his electric Gibson. Typically, "Mountains" would drift off into a spacey interlude after the song, during which Garcia would switch to his electric axe and steer the jam into "Dark Star."

By the end of 1968 or the very beginning of '69, Garcia switched electric guitars again, moving away from the Les Paul to a slimmer, cherry-red Gibson SG. The SG ("solid guitar") had actually been developed to be a more modern replacement for the Les Paul, and for the first two years after its introduction in late 1960, the SG was known as the Les Paul SG. In truth, Paul had nothing to do with the SG's design, and by the end of 1962, the guitarist's name had been taken off the instrument. Still, with or without Paul's endorsement, the SG evolved into one of the most popular guitars in rock: It's one of the guitars George Harrison played on many of the Beatles' late-'60s albums (from *Revolver* on); Eric Clapton used one in Cream, as did Robbie Kreiger in the Doors; and in San Francisco, Barry Melton of Country Joe & the Fish, Sam Andrew of Big Brother & the Holding Company, and perhaps most recognizable of all, John Cipollina of Quicksilver, all preceded Garcia in adopting the SG.

At live shows, Pigpen (and later, T.C.) usually played a red-topped Vox Continental organ (when the band couldn't afford to carry a B-3). This is another view of the May '68 Columbia free concert.

PHOTO: ROSIE MCGEE

The SG had two distinctive, sharp-pointed cutaway "horns" and a solid mahogany body and neck. Judging from photos, Garcia's was an SG Standard: It had two humbucking pickups and a black pickguard. In clear photos from April and June 1969, the pickguard completely surrounds the pickups, which suggests the guitar was a model made sometime between 1966 and '68. (In mid-to-late 1970 Garcia would obtain a 1961 or '62 Les Paul SG, which had a wider and fatter neck and a custom fixed bridge.)

It's only natural that the Dead would look at the Ampex MM-1000 and fantasize that it could be the vehicle to finally capture the band onstage in a way that would give them maximum control over the live recording. There was a major obstacle, however: They didn't have a machine, and the recorders were cumbersome, to say the least. Toward the end of 1968, they managed to lease a recorder to try their experiment. "Ampex said, 'You're crazy. You can't do that; it's not portable,'" Matthews remembered. "We said, 'Oh, yeah? Then why does it have wheels?' They lost that round, and we put it in the back of the truck and took it over to Winterland for the Dead's New Year's Eve show. Unfortunately, we used some off-brand microphones that needed a bunch of batteries and constantly failed—these Synchrons [most likely Au7a condensers]. We used them because they had enough output level to drive a line-level input, but we had so many problems that the tapes ended up not being useable. But that was the first live 16-track recording anywhere, and even though it didn't work, Ampex was a little impressed. And then, when February came around and we went to do the Avalon, we got ten people with ropes and we carried it like a sedan chair up the stairs into the Avalon." This time, the recordings sounded terrific. Then at the end of February '69, they hauled it upstairs into the Carousel Ballroom and recorded four nights, which some believe were the

Suggested listening: The two-record Live Dead, *released in November 1969, was the greatest album of psychedelic rock released in that trippy decade. Three-and-a-half decades later, the Dead organization put out a magnificent 10-CD set of the four shows that had provided most of the material for* Live Dead.

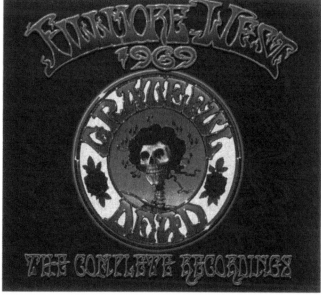

greatest series of shows the Grateful Dead ever played: 2/27–28 and 3/1–2/69. The bulk of the Dead's grand psychedelic opus, *Live/Dead* (released in November '69), would come from that series; 36 years later, all four shows would be released as a ten-CD box set (*Fillmore West 1969: The Complete Recordings*), which sold out its full 10,000-copy run months before it was released. (A three-CD condensation was also released at the same time.)

"The process by which we recorded was a simple one," Matthews told David Gans on the *Grateful Dead Hour* radio program in 2005. Using a method suggested by Bear and Ron Wickersham, "microphones that [were] used for the PA split [Wickersham designed a splitter box] were placed on the stage, and those same microphones went directly to channels on the tape machine, with no signal processing in between. No artistic decisions were made [concerning] the electronic signal." The tracks were allotted as follows: Pigpen vocal, Garcia vocal, Lesh vocal, Weir vocal, Billy kick and snare, Billy overhead, Mickey kick and snare, Mickey overhead, Mickey gong track, T.C.

Garcia made some of his coolest music playing a Gibson SG. This shot is from the Fillmore East, 1969.

organ, Garcia guitar (the SG), two bass tracks (high and low amps for Phil's Guild), and Weir guitar (Gibson 335). There were two tracks that were not used, and, perhaps surprisingly, no audience tracks. (Bob Matthews disputes that the kick and snare for each drummer were on single tracks—he claims he recorded drums on three or four tracks—but the above info comes from engineer Jeffrey Norman, who mixed the 2005 box set from the original multitrack masters. Matthews may be remembering details of either "Skull & Roses" or *Europe '72* instead. Just to muddy the waters further, Owsley claims that he used only 12 mics for the PA and that his MX-10 mixers totaled just 13 inputs plus a spare: "The MX-10 had four inputs selectable 'mic' or 'line.' One mixer had all four inputs set to 'mic,' the others were cascaded and had only three mics and one stereo line in for each. They were not a real mixer, and did not have a global summing amp for all channels—each unit just added in the signal from the one before.")

It would be some time before the live tapes would be mixed for release; in the meantime, *Aoxomoxoa* had to be completed. The band had a falling out with Pacific Recording's Paul Curcio, and so, with the MM-1000 in tow, they relocated to a San Francisco studio called Pacific High Recording for overdub sessions and mixing. (Curcio would later unsuccessfully try to sue the Dead when his studio's credit was intentionally left off the finished album.)

Pacific High has a brief but glorious place in the history of San Francisco recording. It was started by a recording engineer and audio freak named Peter Weston, who took a considerable inheritance and went into the recording business. The first Pacific High was located down by the boat docks in Sausalito, but during 1968 it moved to 60 Brady Street in San Francisco. "It was a big room," remembered Bob Schumaker, who worked as an engineer and tech at PHR (as it was known). "The studio itself had been a one-room warehouse with an upper floor at the front. So it was cut in half, with the studio on one side and the control room on the other. It was not treated well enough [sonically]; it was more 'live' than it should have been. But bands seemed to like the sound of it, and a lot of that came from its sheer size."

"Peter was a real purist when it came to music, and that's probably one of the things that attracted a band like the Grateful Dead," says Phill Sawyer, who was brought up from L.A. to be chief engineer at PHR after a very fruitful career working with a range of acts from the Beach Boys to the Rat Pack. "He loved the idea of being able to use the new technology to get the cleanest possible sound, so you could get stringed instruments to sound the way they are supposed to. It was a wonderful specific goal to record things without a lot of processing; you could always do that later. Peter also got involved with Ray Dolby and was among the first to embrace Dolby A [noise-reduction units], which in those days were these big clunkers that looked like Sony 17″ TVs."

Dolby was another former Ampex employee who had left to follow his own path. And actually, Owsley already owned a Dolby A unit and had previously rented one before the Dead went to PHR, for some sort of event involving the Dead at Grace Cathedral in San Francisco.

The studio's custom console was dominated by Electrodyne modules—"all consoles back then were at least semi-custom," Bob Shumaker notes. "Peter did an interesting thing with that board: He had a mixdown section that was a totally separate set of modules, so you could actually be hearing a real mix while you were multitracking, which was very unusual in those days. It had 20 inputs and originally was set up as a 12-track board, and then it got pushed out to be 16. The failing of the Electrodyne board was the combining networks, so originally mixing was not the greatest through that console. But Carl Countryman built a box—he designed an active combining network that replaced all the combining networks in the console, and he replaced the pan pots, too."

As for the recorders there, "Peter had been a Scully guy, and he had a 280 4-track and a 280 1″ 8-track. And with a 12-track 1″ head stack, you could then tie the 4-track and 8-track electronics together and make a 12-track. He also had automatic switching with Dolby A for all of that. Then the Dead came in with their MM-1000, and that was a great machine. They'd leave it at PHR when they weren't using it [for live recording]. We did a lot of sessions on it. Ampex even sent a guy to watch me use it for Quicksilver."

Phill Sawyer recalls that when he arrived at PHR in the spring of '69, Dan Healy was working there on an album with the Charlatans and was also hanging out around the Dead when they came in to work on *Aoxomoxoa*. "He was a wonderful maniac at that point—lots and lots of energy, kind of overflowing with ideas—a really good guy. He also knew *a lot* about recording and equipment; you'd get him going and he'd just talk for hours. I think Bob Matthews was slightly annoyed by him, because Healy always had ideas about everything. And then you add Owsley to that; he had sort of his own scene and was another guy with really strong opinions about sound. So it was quite a collection of people.

"We had one of the early Moog [synthesizers] in there at that time, and the Dead seemed to enjoy fooling with that for hours at a time. I got to know Jerry and Tom Constanten the best of any of the guys in the band. Tom was very likable and very funny. They seemed to be the ones who, every so often, would actually try to get something done," Sawyer laughs. "I helped some with the mix on 'Mountains of the Moon,' which was a very interesting piece. But a lot of times on that record, it was like a circus in there."

Indeed, it was at PHR that the band brought in tanks of nitrous oxide—equipped with multiple tubes for simultaneous sucking—into the control room, to "aid" in the mixing of Garcia and Hunter's odd tune called "What's Become of the Baby." "I had something in mind that was extremely revolutionary [for that song]," Garcia told me in 1991. "I wanted to use the entire band, but I didn't want to use it in a standard rhythm-section-and-lead-instruments way. I wanted something more like the stuff we did in the bridge section of 'Saint Stephen'—'Lady finger dipped in moonlight'—that weird scratchy shit, but which also included feedback and other stuff, and it would all be gated through the mouth...it would all be somehow enclosed inside the voice. But, well, you know how it goes," he chuckled. "I think, 'Why the fuck did everyone let me do that?'" Because they were high!

Suggested listening: Though it was expensive to make and not very representative of how the 1969 Dead sounded, *Aoxomoxoa* remains a grand studio experiment, filled with magic, wit, invention and plenty of weirdness.

By the time *Aoxomoxoa* was completed, the Dead had racked up hundreds of hours of studio time between the two studios in San Mateo and San Francisco, to the tune of nearly $100,000—an astronomical sum in those days. When it was released in June '69, it fared better than *Anthem of the Sun* had—FM radio gave it some airplay—but it certainly wasn't what anyone could call a "hit." Nearly a quarter-century later, Garcia would dismiss the album this way in one of our interviews: "The live show was what we did; it's who we were. The record was like dicking around. It was like a day job or something; it wasn't that relevant."

So returning to *Live/Dead* later that year was probably more to Garcia's liking. Initially, Bob Matthews says, members of the Dead—presumably Garcia and Lesh—tried mixing the *Live/Dead* tapes themselves, "from their perspective onstage, which is their mindset. It didn't work. It's not that it was 'wrong'; it was just different. It didn't have any dimension to it. I always listened to the band from the hall, so when I got the chance to mix *Live/Dead*, that was the perspective I was looking to recreate: how it felt to be in the hall. We [the listeners] were the 'audience' in some respects."

Recreating that spatial environment wasn't technically difficult, Matthews says, but it required some thought and then a bit of experimentation: "Going in, you figure out the phase plans of all the input sensors—the microphones, where they were, and how they fit together. That's the template. Then, adding to that, what is it that makes things sound locational when you're in a room?

Your brain sums and differs all the different sources that are direct and indirect. So by utilizing time—such as delay and reverberation decay—in a very musically defined and tuned manner, you can add the dimensionality that makes it feel like it's in a real space."

Whatever the technical details, Matthews's methodology *worked*. *Live/Dead* still stands as one of the crowning achievements in the Dead's rich canon.

ALEMBIC

ALEMBIC was Owsley's idea. The word is of somewhat mysterious derivation, borrowing mostly from late Greek, but also filtered through Arabic, medieval Latin, middle English, and French. It's usually defined as a type of vessel used in distillation, or a chamber where liquids can be mixed and observed, as in alchemical processes (another of Bear's interests). The metaphorical alembic, however, is anything that aids in distillation or refinement, whether of things or ideas, and that is probably more to the point here.

Chapter Six

1969

"Shortly after I joined back up with the Dead [in the summer of 1968]," Bear explained to David Gans, "they found a warehouse out near Hamilton Air Force Base in Novato [Marin County] and moved out there [to rehearse]. During that time I had met Ron Wickersham because he was working on the recording scene on *Aoxomoxoa*. So I knew he was an electronics whiz, and a tape-recorder whiz, and an audio expert. And along the way, through connections with the folk-music scene...I'd met this fellow whose name was Rick Turner, who I knew was an absolutely beautiful maker of acoustic instruments. And he knew how to do the wood and all that sort of thing....

"Neither of them really wanted to do it, [but] I sort of stuck them together in the same pot and said, 'We gotta build better instruments, and we gotta get the electronics together.' I thought [the company] should be called Alembic, because the alembic was the vessel in which chemical verification takes place. First everything breaks down, and then it's built back up; it's distilled into the right thing. That's what we were trying to do—we were trying to take all of the

Rarely photographed, Owsley Stanley (a.k.a. Bear) is captured here backstage at the Fillmore East in 1970.

PHOTO: AMALIE ROTHSCHILD

technology and all of the experience and put it in a vessel.
It was also the concept of the vessel, the concept of a place
where it could be done…the warehouse was sort of thought
of as the alembic."

That's a nice telescoping of Alembic's early history,
but the story is actually a little more complicated. The
pink Novato warehouse, which was surrounded on all four
sides by the Air Force base (with just a driveway cutting
through) and behind Pinky's pizza parlor, housed the
Dead's rehearsal space, their business office, and a workshop for Owsley, the inveterate tinkerer.

"Bear probably doesn't get as much credit as he should
for how much he did," says Ron Wickersham, who had
become disillusioned with the increasingly corporate culture at Ampex, more vocal about flaws he saw in some of
their products, and happier working at Pacific Recording…at
least for a while: "Bear was why I left Pacific Recording.
He lured me away from there to work full-time on Grateful
Dead stuff up in Novato. Bear had a big lab that had lots of electronic gear in it.
The first day I showed up to work there was also the first day that Mickey's
father [Lenny] became the manager, and he said I *didn't* have a job there. So
Bear basically said, 'Okay, I don't want you to go back and get another job, so
here—found a company.' Alembic was forced to be founded in a way," he
chuckles. Alembic began as a partnership between Wickersham and his wife,
Susan, whom he'd met at Pacific Recording when she was commissioned to do
a painting for one of its walls.

Alembic's logo was designed
by Bob Thomas, who also
painted the cover of *Live Dead*.

"Bear gave us some money to buy some pieces and set up. But then we lost
this really nice lab, and so we moved into some temporary sheds that were in
the back of the warehouse. Susan was pregnant, and we didn't have any place
to live, but Bear convinced me this was an important thing to do, so we lived
back there for a while. There weren't even any doors, and the door to the outside was thin Visqueen plastic." Bear's friend Bob Thomas, who would create
the cover painting for *Live Dead* and, with Bear, conceive of the Dead's iconic
skull-and-lightning-bolt logo and dancing bears, lived on the building's mezza-
nine. And though Alembic's early history was inextricably linked with the
Grateful Dead, the two were actually always separate entities. Bear said from
the outset that he was not interested in being an actual financial partner in
Alembic—generally speaking, he abhorred business—but his creative influence,
inspiration, and largesse should not be underestimated.

From the outset, Alembic was doing work on several fronts. In the instrument area, "Bear had modded all their guitars, shielding them, because commercial guitars didn't have much of that going on," Wickersham notes. "He
was also interested in getting the signal down the cable better, so you didn't

This shot, possibly from 1971, shows Phil's Alembicized Gibson EB-0 with Hagstrom pickups and the cool paint job by Bob Thomas.

have to use a two-foot cord or something, but it would still sound good. We also put buffers in the instruments, which was my idea. Bear's thing was always that he was trying to solve specific problems, which appealed a lot to me, because that's the way I liked to work, too. And he tended to relate to the player's vision of what needed to happen.

"At that time, too, he was working a lot with the Jefferson Airplane people, and he had done some work on one of Jack's basses. He put in a switch that was like a two-pole lowpass filter with a resonance built into it. That resonant peak gives a character to the tone that's a little like the electronic analog of what you get from an acoustic instrument's body. They liked the results of that, and then Jack wanted one with more switch positions, because he wanted some of the in-between positions."

Not surprisingly, Phil was intrigued by this development, and in late spring 1969 he turned over his own Guild bass for what would turn into some *very* heavy mod work. He switched back to his solidbody SG-style Gibson EB-0, which had been hot-rodded itself, with the addition of Guild/Hagstrom pickups (favored by Bear and Casady), not to mention a spectacular (but wonderfully subtle) psychedelic paint job by Bob Thomas. Phil would play this bass through the spring of 1971, after which he would unleash the "Alembicized" Guild Starfire—more on that later.

DRAFTING RICK TURNER

At some point in late 1969, too, Bear recruited Rick Turner to help modify some of the band's instruments, and to start developing a new generation of electric guitars and basses that would carry the Alembic name.

Raised mostly in Marblehead, Massachusetts, Turner grew up listening to and playing folk music—he and Garcia shared many of the same influences. Besides playing what he jokingly called "punk bluegrass—old-timey music with a really bad attitude" in Boston coffee houses, he also learned about guitar repair and worked in a shop in Cambridge. For eight months in '64–'65 he toured with the popular Canadian folk act Ian & Sylvia, and when that gig ended, he moved to the heart of New York's Greenwich Village. In 1966 he formed a rock band called Autosalvage: "I was an acoustic musician used to playing nice Martins," he told Jonathon Peterson in *American Lutherie*, "and to suddenly start playing a Stratocaster or a Telecaster—these things seemed incredibly crude."

Autosalvage was "a psychedelic rock band on the wrong coast, but we got signed to RCA." The band did some recording but split up soon after, and Turner, at the urging of friends who had migrated to Northern California to form the Youngbloods, moved to rustic Inverness in western Marin County in the spring of 1968. He managed to land some studio work, and he also went on the road mixing sound and handling equipment for the Youngbloods. On the side, Turner was starting to build instruments and do some minor electronics work—winding pickups and such.

A confluence of events brought Turner to Alembic. Phil Lesh's girlfriend at the time, Florence Nathan (a.k.a. Rosie McGee), was working as a secretary for the Youngbloods, and she introduced Turner to Phil and the Dead. That led to him going over to the Novato warehouse/rehearsal space, where he struck up a friendship with Owsley and Wickersham. The former was intrigued by Turner's exquisite woodworking and inlay artistry, the latter by his work in making pickups, which fit in with Wickersham's and Bear's ideas about adding active electronics to existing instruments.

"Basically, magnetic pickups make lousy line drivers; they do not drive cable well," Turner explains. "They lose signal—they lose frequency response—and in some cases they lose actual level." The other piece of the equation, Turner explains, is that guitar pickups, generally speaking, are not wide-frequency-response devices. Their frequency response is inversely related to their impedance: The lower the impedance, the wider the frequency response. However, to reduce a pickup's impedance you need to either wind fewer turns of wire on the pickup, or use heavier-gauge wire, or both—and that can reduce the pickup's output level. So it's a tradeoff. "It's all this numbers game: how many turns, what size wire, what's your frequency response," he says.

"Up to that point, the Guild/Hagstrom pickups had shown the best frequency response of anything Ron had measured. They're wonderful—and Fred Hammon [of Hammon Engineering] has done a fabulous job of reissuing them [as Dark Star pickups]; I've sort of been an advisor on that whole project. Anyway, I started this series of experiments: I would go home and keep the magnet structure the same, but I'd wind different numbers of turns with the same-gauge wire, and I'd bring them out to Ron and he'd measure them, and we'd plot it out, and eventually we figured out what made what happen. This kind of stuff is common knowledge now, but in those days, there was no information out there; zero. And the people who did know anything—whether it was Leo Fender or Ted McCarty [of Gibson]—didn't tell anybody. In those days you couldn't even really buy pickups. You could get DeArmonds, but you couldn't buy a Gibson pickup from Gibson, or whatever, and it's before Seymour [Duncan] and everyone else came into it. So I had to make pickups because I didn't know where to buy them. I did know Dan Armstrong, and I figured, well, if Dan can do it, I can do it. You get a magnet and wrap some wire around it. So bit by bit we figured it all out, and eventually the pickups [we were making] had a better frequency response than any of the ones Ron had come across."

Some of the first work Turner did for the Dead was on one of Phil Lesh's basses: "Phil had picked up this fretless Guild bass—an M-85 custom," Turner says. "Guild made Bobby a guitar, and they made a bass for Phil, a hollowbody bass which is now owned by Dan Schwartz. So Phil heard that I did inlay work, and he asked me to do an inlay job on the fretboard of that instrument. I was one of not very many people who were doing custom inlay work at that time; we were all sort of inventing modern inlay work back then. I mostly used a lot of mother of pearl and abalone for inlays, and on that bass I think I stuffed the eyes of the skull with hash," he laughs. "I had a sort of 'One pill makes you larger' design on there, too: I inlaid a gel-cap design that's half abalone and half mother of pearl."

Wickersham adds, "That bass also had the first active electronics in it, which were a Darlington emitter-follower built right onto the pickup." (It's doubtful Lesh ever played that Guild fretless onstage with the Dead; no photo has ever surfaced, and today Lesh says he has no memory of the instrument.)

LIVE SOUND CHAIN

In the early days of Alembic, Wickersham and company also devoted much time and energy to the Dead's live sound chain. "Bear was also very interested in developing a much better live sound system for the Dead," Wickersham says. "At that point they had a whole bunch of little pieces of gear from different companies—like they had some Sunn and Acoustic [cabinets]—and he wanted to get a little more consistency and reliability, so he was the one pushing the JBL [loudspeakers for the PA], which is the direction it eventually went."

The power amps of the day were a combination of Crown DC300s, which Wickersham describes as "an interesting quirk of history—they had the minimum amount of silicon you could possibly put in a device to make 300 watts," and modified McIntosh 75s: "We used to carry around crates of tubes," Wickersham says. "The McIntosh circuit gets more power out of these certain tubes than you can get out of any circuit…one thing we did with those is dramatically reduce the feedback, maybe to 6dB or so, so they recovered from clipping faster and sounded dramatically better."

Wickersham also tinkered with Phil's Fender Dual Showman amps. According to Rick Turner, "Ron took the front-end preamp stage of the Dual Showman, which is a two-channel thing, and put it on a modern printed circuit card and loaded it with military-grade parts, put it in a single-rackspace box, and that is [what became] the Alembic F-2B [preamp]. That preamp has a mono out and individual channel outs. One of the things we were able to do is take a two-channel output from the bass, with the neck-position pickup and the bridge-position pickup, send it on down the cable to the two channels of the F-2B, where you had separate EQ on each channel, then blend the pickups electronically rather than passively in the instrument. That was one of the tricks."

It wasn't long, too, before Alembic started constructing its own PA speakers, using JBL components mostly—four dual cabinets, with two 15″ JBL 130s in each, stacked in columns, and a couple of JBL horns, "which were always difficult getting enough level out of," according to Bob Matthews. Monitors "were constantly changing," Turner says, but leaned more often than not to JBLs as well. The Alembic crew also got into building other pieces of touring gear, and all this activity demanded more manpower: It was through Alembic that a number of future Dead crew members, including Bill "Kidd" Candelario (Alembic's first official employee), Sparky Raizene, and Joe Winslow came into the scene initially.

For sound-reinforcement microphones, "we had a shitload of Sennheiser small-diaphragm condenser mics and [Electro-Voice] RE-15 and RE-20 [dynamics]—which were also what Matthews liked for the recording system, which became integral to the entire PA system," Turner remembers. (Bear: "The only E-Vs I ever used in the PA were the 15s.")

"We weren't that attracted to the large-diaphragm mics," adds Wickersham. "They would use them sometimes in the studio, but for being documentary, with all the proximity effects and all that, they weren't as good. So we ended up being steered to small-diaphragm omnidirectional mics. Bear collected a zillion different ones. E-V had a collection of fairly flat little-diaphragm mics, which Bob and Betty chose because they thought they were good for enhancing some particular aspect of an instrument. I think we also used E-V 635s, which don't have much of a particular character, but if you were using them in a live recording, it didn't matter if they weren't lined up exactly right or if they got knocked a bit out of place. They were perfect for the road." (The 635 was also one of the most popular mics for television and radio remote broadcasts and recordings.)

"We made our own stage boxes and snakes and all that kind of stuff, and the stage boxes had transformer splitters on each channel, so we could send one snake to the [Ampex] 16-track and the other to the house [front-of-house mixer]," notes Turner. "That was just part and parcel of the whole thing, whether we used it or not.

"The other thing is the 16-track—the MM-1000, with the AG440 electronics—has a transformer-coupled input stage. Normally, you've got an isolation transformer, which is 1 to 1, but when you replace it with a step-up transformer, suddenly from a normal dynamic mic you've got enough juice stepped up with the transformer to drive the 'record' electronics without a mic preamp in between. So rather than running through a record board, you would actually set the levels on the MM-1000 itself, and that eliminated a whole slew of electronics, which cleaned up the sound that extra little bit and gave [the recordings] more dynamics."

For a live-sound mixing system in this era before there were widely available multichannel models, the Dead would stack three Ampex MX-10 two-channel tube mixers, which gave Bear the 12 inputs he needed for the stereo PA. "Jerry's guitar and Phil's bass were killer loud on stage," he says, "and did not need any PA boost. I did, however, mic both of their amps—one each—and added them separately into the tape feed at a low level by means of two built-in mic preamps in my tape machine." (Later, a fourth MX-10 was added to accommodate more mics.)

By mid 1969, the Dead's music was changing in both subtle and obvious ways. Hunter and Garcia, who were living together in a house in the Marin County town of Larkspur (along with Garcia's paramour Mountain Girl and, occasionally, Merry Prankster Ken Babbs), began to move away from the dense psychedelic constructions of *Aoxomoxoa* in favor of simpler songs that clearly had roots in traditional American folk and country styles. Hunter has said he was influenced by the first two albums by The Band during this period, and Garcia was listening more and more to country pickers like Don Rich (of Buck Owens's band) and Roy Nichols (of Merle Haggard's group). For his part, Weir started to incorporate various country cover tunes into the Dead's repertoire around the same time.

In March '69, on his way back to California after a Dead tour, Garcia stopped in Boulder, Colorado, and made a purchase that would have a huge impact on his music for the next several years: a Zane Beck (ZB) steel guitar. Though he had owned another pedal steel as early as '66, he found the instrument difficult and forbidding at that time—but now he was ready to dive in with his characteristic zeal. It helped that one of his close friends, a musician named Peter Grant, already owned a pedal steel; indeed, he appears on "Doin' That Rag" on *Aoxomoxoa*.

The Arkansas-born Zane Beck had been involved with steel-guitar manufacture since the late '50s, when he hooked up with a young company run by steel players Buddy Emmons and Shot Jackson, developers of the Sho-Bud line. By the early '60s, however, Emmons had broken off to sell his own line of pedal steels, and Zane Beck emerged as an important and respected maker himself. Garcia's ZB was a custom-model D-10 (double-neck) with ten strings per neck, C6 and E9 tunings, and eight pedals and two knee levers. According to Peter Grant, Garcia played that instrument for about a year before giving it to Grant and buying himself another. Then, for the new one, he had the C6 neck dismantled "because I'm just not into the C6 tuning," he explained to *Guitar Player* in 1971. "There is nothing in any of the kinds of music that I play that requires that sort of tonality.... The E9 tuning is that open-er, more country sound, and that's the one I dug. That's the whole reason I wanted to get into pedal steel. So now I just use the E9 neck and the three pedals to raise the tone and two levers to lower it."

Garcia started playing his ZB immediately after buying it. After woodshedding briefly at the Dead's Novato practice hall, he got together with his old friend John Dawson (better known as Marmaduke), who was writing his own country songs as well as covering hip Bakersfield and Nashville tunes. They

The Dead onstage at the Fillmore West, Feb. 27, 1969, one of the shows recorded for *Live/Dead*. Jerry's playing a Gibson SG.

PHOTO: MICHAEL MERRITT/GRATEFUL DEAD

Suggested listening: Recorded at the Fillmore Auditorium 11/8/69, *Dick's Picks Vol. 16* features early versions of some of the songs that would turn up on *Workingman's Dead* in the spring of '70, as well as mesmerizing psychedelic jams galore.

played Wednesday nights as a duo in a small coffee house in Menlo Park called The Underground. Eventually the pair formed the fine country-rock band the New Riders of the Purple Sage. By June '69, too, Garcia had started to play pedal steel onstage with the Dead occasionally, and by that fall he was confident enough to branch out and play steel on other musicians' sessions—first on the Jefferson Airplane song "The Farm" (on *Volunteers*), but more famously on Crosby, Stills, Nash & Young's "Teach Your Children."

"With the steel," he said in that *Guitar Player* interview, "I'm going after a sound I hear in my head that the steel has come the closest to. But I have no technique on the steel. I've got a little right-hand technique from playing the banjo, and I've listened to records, but my intonation with the bar is still really screwed up. I still have to do it by ear." That may be true on a technical level, but the fact is, Garcia became as unique a stylist on the pedal steel as he was on electric guitar, and there's a raft of albums from the early '70s that show the depth of his imagination on the instrument.

SWITCH TO STRAT

By the fall of 1969, Garcia had also switched his main axe, as well, dropping the Gibson SG in favor of a sunburst Fender Stratocaster. This was in keeping with the turn toward a country sound, too, for though the Strat was already a famous rock 'n' roll guitar (having been championed by everyone from Buddy Holly to Jimi Hendrix to Jeff Beck since Leo Fender introduced it back in 1954 as the first double-cutaway solidbody electric), it was also used by a fair number of country guitarists, admired for its distinctive twang.

When David Gans and I interviewed Garcia in 1981, he explained his reason for the switch: "It was more of a challenge. It wasn't that I wanted to lose the SG part of my playing. My reasoning was something along the lines of, 'I think that no matter what guitar I play, I won't have any trouble getting a sweet sound'—even though the most difficult thing to produce on a Strat is a sweet sound. What I really wanted was to be able to get some of the metallic clang that Strats have…. I was [also] looking for that crispness that you associate with country & western guitar players."

Bob Weir noted, when I asked him about the switch, "Obviously we were never going to be playing the same guitar onstage at the same time, but I didn't really have a problem with him playing an SG or a Les Paul while I was playing a Gibson. At some point, though, it occurred to me that if he was playing double-coil pickups, maybe I should be looking elsewhere. The deal is, if we're both playing lines through Twin Reverbs and we were in the same neighborhood and we were somewhat in the same register, sometimes it got pretty difficult to tell what I was playing and what he was playing. That happened a few times, and I was immediately going to go to some other kind of pickup, but Jerry did instead. I think it was about the time I was on a 335 or 345. From that point on, we made an attempt to stay out of each other's neighborhoods, pickup-wise. That said, the choices are so many and varied. I did stay with double-coils for a while, and then I went to single-coils in the '70s and stayed there for a while."

Of course, no discussion of the Grateful Dead in 1969 is complete without mentioning Woodstock and Altamont. The former is interesting from a technical perspective because it was such a famous disaster for the Dead. As Rock Scully explained to me in 1989, "In order to facilitate the switching of bands, all the different groups' gear was sitting on large, movable pallets with wheels under them. Those pallets then slid together to form a riser, which the band played on. Well, even then our equipment was way heavier than most bands', and the wheels on one of the pallets broke, and that slowed us up a lot. So there we are at sundown, when we're supposed to be playing, scrambling to move all the equipment off one pallet and onto a new one, which already had gear from the next band on it. So that took about an hour or even more. It was just one of those bummers."

At Woodstock, the Dead's equipment was so heavy that it broke the wheels on the revolving stage pallete, causing one of many delays before the Dead hit the stage later that night for what all agree was a weak performance.

PHOTO: JIM MARSHALL/C. 2006

But the bummer was just beginning. During the Dead's set the winds and rain picked up, and the giant light-show screen (which had been lowered into place behind the band just before they went on) began to act as a sail, and the entire stage started to inch backward into the mud surrounding it. "So all the crew and myself and a few others whipped out our buck knives and started rending huge holes in this monstrously expensive screen to let the wind through," Scully remembered.

Meanwhile, onstage, the band was experiencing a grounding nightmare. Garcia spoke of seeing blue balls of electricity bouncing around, and according to Weir, some 35 years after the fact, "Bear [who was doing the front-of-house mixing] almost killed me on that show. He changed the ground, and every time I touched my instrument, which I had to do to play, I got a very irritating shock, and everybody else was, too. It was low-amperage and I had to just grit my teeth, but one time I got close to the microphone and this bolt arced, lifted me off my feet, and sent me through the air back against my amplifiers. I came to with a fat lip and played the rest of the set that way. It was not fun." Is it any surprise, then, that the band played badly at Woodstock?

But at least they played there. At Altamont in December '69, the Dead were set to join a bill of top California bands including Jefferson Airplane, the Flying Burrito Brothers, Santana, and Crosby Stills & Nash. All of them were in support of the Rolling Stones, who wanted to end their fall '69 U.S. tour, which was being filmed for a documentary, with a triumphant free concert in the cradle of free music—the Bay Area. But the concert was fraught with problems from the beginning. For one thing, the promoters didn't have a site for the event until less than 24 hours before it was set to begin. Choosing the Altamont Speedway, 45 minutes east of San Francisco, was a desperate last-minute move—after all, many thousands of people were streaming toward the Bay Area for the show. The entire Dead and Alembic crews, along with nearly every other sound professional in the Bay Area, descended on the site to erect the huge sound system, which was a pastiche of many different brands culled from all the Bay Area's major rental companies (and several of the bands). Bob and Betty, Owsley, Healy (who was working mostly with Quicksilver during this period), Turner, and Wickersham were all there in one capacity or another (Alembic's 16-track was used for recording, for instance). However, when violence by the Hell's Angels security force continued to escalate during the concert, the Dead eventually decided not to play at all. They spent much of the evening cowering backstage and even in the Dead's equipment truck, trying to turn a blind eye to the bummer going down around them. How was the sound? Considering it was Frankenstein cluge, not bad in general.

One final note about the Stones, though: When they came through the Bay Area earlier on that tour for regular concerts at the Oakland Coliseum Arena, "They blew up all their equipment at the first show," Betty Cantor-Jackson relates. "They had all this Ampeg equipment, and it just went *Fffffttt!* They were in a panic, so Ram Rod and Jackson raced to our warehouse and brought down a bunch of our Fender amps for them, and the next show we sat up onstage while they played, and it sounded amazing. That was one of the times Bill Graham was nice to us," she laughs. "Anyway, I remember the first note Keith [Richards] played through Jerry's amp—he turned around and looked at the amp, and his mouth just dropped open. 'Whoa!' He couldn't believe the power and the clarity." "Still," Owsley adds, "the next day Ampeg rushed more amps and speakers to them and they went on as if nothing had happened, but the fact is the Stones's gear was woefully inadequate for professional use."

STRIPPED DOWN AND SIMPLIFIED

ALTAMONT was a pretty bad scene all the way around, and it has come to be associated with the dark side of the 1960s—the anti-Woodstock—but the fact is, most things in the Dead's universe were moving in a positive direction at the turn of the new decade. Everyone agreed that Hunter and Garcia were producing some of the best songs of their partnership. Each week, it seemed, brought another future classic: "Dire Wolf," "Casey Jones," "Uncle John's Band," "Black Peter," "Cumberland Blues" (co-written with Phil), "High Time"—strong, simple tunes with folk and country leanings. Add the rumbling and ominous "New Speedway Boogie"—obliquely about the hard lessons of Altamont—and the gritty Pigpen-sung Hunter song "Easy Wind," and you had the makings of a fine follow-up to the dense and opaque *Aoxomoxoa* of just half a year earlier. Same band, but very different vibe. There was one personnel change that went down in the first month of 1970, too, which changed the group's sound: Tom Constanten left the band to pursue other avenues, so Pigpen went back to playing B-3 onstage.

Chapter Seven
1970-1971

Aoxomoxoa had been a financial disaster for the Dead—by mid '69, the six months of experimentation and revision had left them nearly $200,000 in debt to Warner Bros.—so it's no surprise that the band was interested in taking a simpler approach to making their next record, *Workingman's Dead*. (In the meantime, they released the very inexpensive-to-produce *Live Dead*, immediately cutting into some of that debt.)

"*Workingman's Dead* was done very quickly," said Bob Matthews, who co-produced the record with Betty Cantor and the band. "After the experience of *Aoxomoxoa*—so much time, so much loss of direction, so many hands involved—on *Workingman's Dead* we went into the studio first and spent a couple of days basically rehearsing—performing—all the tunes, recording them on 2-track. When that was done I sat down and spliced together the tunes—beginning of Side One to end of Side One; beginning of Side Two to end of Side Two. I got that idea from listening to *Sgt. Pepper*: Before we even start, let's have a concept of what the end product is going to feel like, sequencing-wise. We made a bunch of cassette copies and gave them to the band. They rehearsed some more in their rehearsal studio, and then they came in and recorded. But at all times there was the perspective of where we were in the album."

The Dead perform at San Francisco's Family Dog on the Great Highway, 2/4/70, for a public television program called *Night at the Family Dog*, which also featured Jefferson Airplane and Santana. Garcia is playing a Strat, Phil his EB-0, Bob a Gibson 345.

Jim Furman (rear), Betty Cantor, and Bob Matthews backstage at Winterland.

By the winter of 1970, the band had moved out of their Novato practice facility and had set up a space out near Pt. Reyes in rural West Marin. In February '70 Ron and Susan Wickersham found a new spot for their expanding and increasingly autonomous business, at 320 Judah Street in San Francisco's Sunset district. The former warehouse was divided into a studio room (containing the MM-1000, when it wasn't on the road with the Dead, and a Spectrasonics mixing console), a workshop/repair area where Rick Turner and others plied their trade, and a lair in the basement for building speakers. "It was definitely time to move," Ron Wickersham says. "There was no woodworking shop in Novato, and we wanted space to be able to build the speaker cabinets. Also, my shop was this tin shack with a leaky roof and no heat, and we didn't have any place secure to store stuff in Novato. It was all open and unlocked. Being in San Francisco also made us more accessible to other musicians besides the Dead," and indeed a steady parade of Bay Area musicians availed themselves of Alembic's services once the business opened on Judah Street.

The *Workingman's Dead* sessions took place at Pacific High Recording in San Francisco during a couple of weeks in February, using Alembic's MM-1000. (The studio's regular recorder was a Scully 1″ 12-track.) As Matthews noted, the recording was relatively quick and painless, which isn't to suggest it was in any way rushed or careless. On the contrary, Garcia and Weir put great thought into the guitar textures they wanted for each song, and for the course of the sessions the big studio room at PHR was littered with virtually every axe each of them owned. So, rather than relying exclusively on the Strat he was playing onstage at that point, for the album Garcia also used some Les Paul and SG (as well as his Martin D-18 acoustic). Weir similarly looked for different colorings from a variety of instruments and amps: For instance, on "Casey Jones" he double-tracked his part using both a Twin Reverb and a Leslie. Tracking was largely "live," with everyone playing together and the singers laying down scratch vocals, with overdubs (ranging from acoustic guitars to pedal steel to harmonica) added later as needed.

The LP was mixed by Bob and Betty on Pacific High's custom board, and by June it was in the stores and all over FM radio: "Uncle John's Band" and "Casey Jones" became mainstream favorites, and for the first time in their

Suggested listening: After the baroque experimentation of *Aoxomoxoa*, the stripped down and simplified sound of *Workingman's Dead* was like a breath of clean country air. The record also made the Dead bona fide stars. Meanwhile, *Dick's Picks Vol. 4*, recorded around the same time (2/13–14/70), shows what a potent force the band was live in that period. The "Dark Star" on the three-disc set is among many Deadheads' favorites.

career, the group was actually selling a lot of records, wiping out most of their debt to Warner Bros. in the process. (A good thing, too, since it was revealed during this period that manager Lenny Hart, Mickey's dad, had ripped them off royally during his tenure with the group.) As a live act, too, the Dead was clearly on the ascension, regularly selling out most concerts—which, during 1970, became marathons. Many shows would open with a set from the New Riders (with Garcia on pedal steel) and then feature a short acoustic set by Garcia and Weir (with other members periodically joining in), followed by full-blown electric sets which, even with the addition of the new shorter tunes, still featured many long and intense jams.

THE POWER OF WAH

One wonders if perhaps Garcia's experience using an SG on some *Workingman's Dead* sessions influenced his decision to return to that axe in May '70; he appears to have stuck with the '61 or '62 LP-SG for most of the rest of that year. It was also during this period, as far as I can tell, that Garcia picked up his first guitar pedal: a wah-wah that would become an important part of Garcia's sound in the coming years, particularly from 1971–74, when he regularly incorporated the effect into jams on "Dark Star," "Playing in the Band," and other tunes.

Though some of Leo Fender's lap steels from the mid '40s were apparently capable of an effect similar to wah-wah, and country guitarists in the late '50s and early '60s could approximate the sound by working their tone controls, the modern foot pedal we know and love dates back to 1966. It was invented by Brad Plunkett of the Thomas Organ Company and marketed originally through the British manufacturer Vox. Within a year, many other companies were selling the pedals, too (Thomas/Vox had not patented it), and by 1967 it started turning up on rock records—who can forget the ethereal wah-ness of Cream's "Tales of Brave Ulysses" from *Disraeli Gears*, or the supreme wah flavorings sprinkled throughout Hendrix's epic 1968 *Electric Ladyland* LP? The legendary Vox Crybaby was introduced in 1968, and though some have suggested that was the pedal Garcia used, the photographic record is unclear. Steve Parish (who came to work for Alembic near the end of '69, and by 1970 was working as a roadie for both the Dead and for Garcia's solo ventures, along with Ram Rod) insists that Garcia did play some sort of Vox wah. By 1972, though, Garcia was definitely using a wah + volume pedal made by an English company called Colorsound. That was one of a number of cool effect pedals devised by brothers Larry and Joe Macari, whose greatest claim to fame was devising the much-used Tonebender fuzzbox in 1965.

That spring and summer was dotted with interesting and unusual Dead gigs. There was a one-off show at the Hollywood Festival in Newcastle-Under-Lyme, England—their first overseas jaunt—and also the famous trans-Canadian trip in which the Dead, The Band, Janis Joplin, and various others hopped on a train for gigs in different venues across Canada—a journey immortalized in the wonderful 2004 documentary *Festival Express*, and in the 1975 Hunter-Garcia tune "Might As Well."

In June 1970, Alembic officially incorporated, with the Wickershams giving shares of the company to Rick Turner and Bob Matthews (who was named president). "It was designed to be a triumvirate," Matthews says. "I was recording, Rick was instruments, and Ron was electronics; that was how it came together, based on our individual passions. Of course in truth everyone did a lot of things, and there were more and more people involved at different levels, designing and building stuff."

One of the new hires was an electronics expert named John Curl who, like Wickersham, had worked at Ampex in a number of capacities—in its instrumentation group, audio department, and research departments, toiling on everything from high-speed tape recorders developed for NASA to motor controllers. He had also worked on perfecting the MM-1000 ("supplementing the electronics to make it RFI-proof," he says) and had briefly helped Wickersham tame the new recorder at Pacific Recording. Curl had also spent time working at Berkeley Custom Electronics, doing repair work and designing *very* high-end home audio systems, but he was out of a job when Wickersham offered to bring him on board at Alembic.

"The Grateful Dead wanted a new [mixing console] made, but they wanted it to be solid-state because the tube stuff wasn't that road-worthy," Curl says. "They wanted something that would hold up better. So Ron [Wickersham] and I built a board together. We were pretty proud of it, and I thought we'd done a good job—the measurements looked good. It was quite sophisticated in some ways. But the truth is, it didn't sound that good, and one reason was we didn't have the best parts in some areas." In the end, the console, which was quite expensive to develop, was deemed impractical, and it never even got a full road workout. Instead the Dead stuck with their stacked MX-10s for the next few years. And though Curl would be laid off by Alembic several months later (he went on to be the primary recording engineer and mixer on the movie *Fillmore*, about the closing of the Fillmore West, featuring the Dead, Santana, Quicksilver, and others), he comes back into the story a little later as a key player in the development of the Wall of Sound.

Another techie who came into the Alembic scene in 1970 was Jim Furman, who was just a year out of Columbia University, where he'd gotten a degree in electrical engineering. "Unlike a lot of my classmates there, I was not going to get a job in the defense industry—I was strenuously opposed to the Vietnam War," says Furman, who underwent a gender transition in 1998 and now goes by the name Janet Furman Bowman. "I wanted to get a job in rock 'n' roll, so I moved to San Francisco, got out the Yellow Pages, and started calling up recording studios. Right off I found Alembic, and believe it or not they were interested in me. Maybe they wanted somebody with an Ivy League engineering background—not that it qualified me to do much.

"Ron Wickersham was my mentor for the first year or so; he helped me understand what the issues were and what I needed to know, and I was a quick learner, so I caught on. The first thing they had me do was tear apart the Dead's Fender guitar amps and 'ruggedize' them. We did it for other bands, too, like the Airplane. What we were doing was replacing some of the components that were known to fail on the road with things that were more vibration-resistant, like tube sockets, for example. We put in heavier-duty connectors that had springier steel and were less likely to cause trouble. We were also replacing some of the pots. We turned it into a package deal, 'Alembicizing' Fender amps." (The practice was actually initiated by Owsley during his days as soundman at the Carousel Ballroom, when he modded one of Elvin Bishop's Fender Princeton amps to make it more akin to a Twin Reverb.)

"That idea got extended to some of the other equipment, too. The Grateful Dead had a bunch of McIntosh power amps, and we had a program to upgrade those, also. It wasn't to make their performance better, because they were really great amps, but to make them more reliable and easier to use from a rock 'n' roll perspective. One of the things we did was replace the screw terminals that were used to connect [to] speakers, which were fine for a permanent installation but were a real pain if you were attaching and disconnecting them at every gig. So we replaced the screw terminals with banana jacks, which were very easy and reliable connectors that could also handle a lot of power. A lot of our business at that time was doing that sort of work, as well as general maintenance [on sound systems] and whatever Rick [Turner] was up to with instruments."

And then there was another New York refugee, John Cutler, who moved to the West Coast in 1970 in part because it seemed to be on the cutting edge of electronics exploration. "I've been a radio amateur all my life, basically," he told me in 1987, "and I got my taste for custom electronics working as an apprentice for Ron Wickersham and Alembic." Although he studied electrical engineering, calculus, and physics at City College of San Francisco and seemed to be on track to transfer to U.C. Berkeley, Cutler ended up quitting school to work for his brother Bill's Bay Area band, Heroes, which enjoyed a good local following in the early and mid '70s. "I tried to build custom stuff for them, but our budget was zero." Cutler would become an important player in the story just a few years down the road.

One gig looked like it was going to be a real plum for Alembic that summer of 1970: The Great Medicine Ball, which was supposed to take the Dead (and a few other bands) across the country in a bus caravan, with shows in various odd and scenic stops along the way. The bands and crews would live in teepees, and the whole thing would be filmed by French director François Reichenbach, with Warner Bros. (then living large because of the success of the film *Woodstock*) reserving the right to distribute the film in the U.S. But at the eleventh hour, the Dead decided they didn't like the way the tour had been planned, were nervous about possibly getting busted (as had happened after a January gig in New Orleans), and withdrew from the tour. However, the Alembic sound system and all the Dead's tour personnel, including Bob and Betty, were already committed to the expedition, so they went on the road as planned, while the Dead stayed home. (In the end, The Great Medicine Ball zig-zagged its way down assorted scenic highways and back roads, stopping for just a few choice, smallish gigs here and there. B.B. King flew in for one. Jethro Tull played another. So did Alice Cooper, of all people. Joni Mitchell was there for the Nebraska leg. Though hardly the high-profile success its organizers hoped for, the GMB was fun and enriching for most of the participants, who closed the tour by putting on a show in England. The film *Medicine Ball Caravan*, edited by Martin Scorsese, was released in 1971 but was a financial bust.)

AMERICAN BEAUTY

With Alembic and the Dead road crew tied up for almost a full month, the band made a fateful decision on their own back home: They began recording their next album, even though *Workingman's Dead* had been out only a couple of months and was still a "new" record. But Garcia, Weir, and Lesh all had new songs they were excited about and eager to record. However, with the trusty MM-1000 on the road and other bands booked into Pacific High, the Dead turned

Engineer Stephen Barncard at the DiMedeo console in Wally Heider Studios.

to the *other* great rock studio in San Francisco: Wally Heider Recording on Hyde Street, a few blocks away from City Hall.

In truth, Heider's had been the top dog among San Francisco studios ever since it opened in mid 1969, as the northern branch of one of the most revered L.A. studios. (Heider himself was a famed engineer and known for being extremely quality-conscious.) Crosby, Stills, Nash & Young, Jefferson Airplane, and Creedence Clearwater Revival were just a few of the bands that kept the facility's two studios (later increased to four) buzzing night and day during its first year of operation. Garcia, in particular, was fond of the place from having played various sessions there with CSNY, Paul Kantner (on his superb *Blows Against the Empire* album), Brewer & Shipley, and others. When the Dead came knocking that August, Heider's offered up one of its young engineers, Stephen Barncard, who, as fate would have it, had recorded Garcia's pedal-steel overdub on Graham Nash's "Teach Your Children." His "audition" for the job, it turned out, was a trial by fire:

"Phil wanted a good bass sound, and that was going to make the difference," Barncard told me in the mid '90s. "My boss said, 'Get a good bass sound, Steve, and we've got the Grateful Dead.' Well, Phil was using the exact same rig as Jack Casady, and I was familiar with Jack's rig. He had a big amp for the low end and thud, and then a little amp for the buzz in the middle. So between those three inputs [two amps and a DI], I was able to make a bass track that worked for him. We did it in Studio A," which was equipped with a Quad 8 console and a 3M 16-track. The song was "Till the Morning Comes." "A wonderful thing that happened on that track, at least from my perspective," Barncard said, "was they didn't insist on using two drummers, so it was Jerry, Phil, Bill, and Bobby—the quartet. Nice, clean tracking session. We did it live and then added the vocals later." This was the beginning of what is arguably the Dead's greatest studio record, *American Beauty*.

The bulk of the album was cut in Heider Studio C, which had a Frank DeMedeo custom console. "He needs to be remembered because he brought a lot of quality to Wally's studios," Barncard noted. "He used these massive Switchcraft pushbuttons and telephone-type lever switches and big relays and UREI plug-in amplifiers. It was an incredibly well-built and simple thing: 24 channels, 8-bus…. Everything was transformer-balanced. No op amps. And the EQ modules were just UREI EQs on the way to the line amplifier…. It had Gotham faders, which at the time were 2dB per step, so they were a little clunky to work with…but it was a step above rotary pots. At the time it was very high-tech." Studio C's small control room was equipped with Altec 604 speakers, and Barncard had a nice complement of foreign and American microphones to choose from for the sessions: Neumann 67s and 87s, Sony C-37s, AKG C-60s (which he liked for acoustic guitars) and 451s, Shure 56s, 57s, and 547s.

"It's a very live record, and it was fun all the way through," Barncard said.

Garcia spent a lot of time at Wally Heider's during 1970 and '71, working with the Dead, on his first solo album, and on numerous records for other artists, ranging from the New Riders to David Crosby. Here, he lays down a track on his ZB pedal steel.

PHOTO COURTESY OF STEPHEN BARNCARD

"I had heard bad stories about engineers' interactions with the Dead and about how they always had a thousand people in the control room and hippies camping out in the studio and massive acid parties. What I found were a bunch of hard-working guys—a great, tight band who had woodshedded everything and who knew exactly what they wanted to lay down and where they wanted to go with it.... There was not a whole lot of experimentation. They had sat around in a circle and rehearsed this record, so they were ready to go when I got them. Some records sort of assemble themselves. You do a take and everybody says, 'Yeah, that's it. Let's move on.' And everything falls into place."

Even vocals, which had always been the Dead's weak spot, came easily on *American Beauty*. Garcia, Lesh, and Weir had definitely been influenced to work on their harmonies after listening to their friends Crosby, Stills & Nash, but even so, Barncard admitted, "I was skeptical going in. But they were brilliant. They walked in and just did it. People don't believe me when I say this!" For the harmonies on songs such as "Attics of My Life," "Brokedown Palace," and "Till the Morning Comes," "I used three 67s [for Garcia, Lesh, and Weir], ran each one through a separate limiter, and then doubled it," to make it sound fuller. Other classic songs to come from these sessions included "Ripple," "Candyman," "Truckin'" "Sugar Magnolia," "Friend of the Devil," and Phil and Hunter's moving "Box of Rain."

The layering of instruments was even more complex than on *Workingman's Dead*, so there were quite a few overdubs: acoustic and electric guitars, pedal steel, organ by Howard Wales (who played in an unassuming jazz-rock club band with Garcia at the time), and piano by Commander Cody. Still, it felt seamless and timeless. And when it was released in November it was an instant sensation; coupled with *Workingman's Dead*, it represented a huge push into the mainstream, and it's fair to say that the momentum those two albums created helped sustain the band for the next quarter-century.

Not surprisingly, Bob and Betty were disappointed that they were not involved with the recording of what turned out to be a landmark album, but they were plenty busy dealing with the Dead as a road band during this period. With Owsley in jail beginning in the summer of '70 because of an old (and one more recent) drug charge, Matthews stepped into the FOH role most tours, and Betty

Suggested listening: *American Beauty* continued the move in a folk and country direction that began with *Workingman's Dead* several months earlier.

handled recording and other sound tasks. As it turned out, Barncard would never record the Dead again; however, he engineered the first New Riders album at Heider's, which had Garcia on pedal steel, and he also worked with Jerry on various outside projects there, including David Crosby's magnificently evocative first solo album (recorded that fall of 1970 and winter of '71), *If I Could Only Remember My Name*.

The beginning of 1971 brought another personnel change in the Dead: Stung by his father Lenny Hart's embezzlement of thousands of dollars and subsequent disappearance, Mickey left the group for what turned out to be about five years (though he remained on good terms with the band members during that period). With Mickey suddenly out and Pigpen in precarious health because of what turned out to be advanced liver disease, Jerry, Bobby, Phil, and Billy often played as a quartet during much of 1971, giving them a stripped-down but no less exciting sound. (Pig would sometimes play organ or congas, but only sporadically.) The flood of fantastic new songs continued unabated: The winter tour saw the introduction of "Bertha," "Wharf Rat," "Playing in the Band," "Loser," "Greatest Story Ever Told," "Deal," and "Bird Song"—all cornerstones of the live repertoire for the rest of the band's history.

AN ALEMBICIZED STARFIRE BASS

The biggest news on the musical-instrument front that winter was the introduction of Phil's Alembicized Guild Starfire bass, all but unrecognizable after the major cosmetic and electronics overhaul by Rick Turner and Ron Wickersham. "The Godfather," as the bass became known for reasons Rick Turner can't remember, was a magnificent piece of work. (In recent years the bass has usually been called Big Brown.) Very little of the original Starfire remained: the neck and the overall body design, although even that was heavily modified, with the *f*-hole filled with foam rubber to cut down on feedback, and the entire bottom half of the guitar devoted to an easily accessible electronics compartment and *14* knobs. It had a new headstock with the Alembic logo, which had been designed by Bob Thomas. There were three Alembic pickups: two low-impedance trapezoid pickups with external hum-canceling coils, and one that was quad (an output for each string). The extensive network of electronic modules allowed for control of bandwidth, frequency response, resonance, and various filtering (highpass, lowpass, bandpass, and notch—a control layout that later became known as the Alembic Superfilter). "My goal [with that bass] was a kind of infinitely flexible tone control," Phil comments today, "but it took too many knobs to do it."

"Rick did a lot of work to make the Guild better adaptable so the electronics could be installed in a maintainable way," Wickersham says. "That was an important thing. Coming from broadcasting and then getting the coaching of Bear, I believed everything had to be absolutely reliable. You had to make

things that could be repaired, and
you had to make sure that any
attempt to repair it wouldn't turn
it into something less reliable,
which is a problem a lot of people
had trouble with."

Garcia also briefly played a
Turner creation on the spring '71
tour, though the origins of that
axe date back to Turner's late-
'60s Autosalvage days. Or in this
case, "guitarsalvage": As Turner
explained to Steven Ross on
dead.net in 2005, "A friend of
mine was managing an apartment
building on the Lower East Side,
and one of the units was vacated
by a junkie. Left behind in the
rubble was a 1961 or '62 Les Paul
Custom—one of the ones that pre-
dated the Gibson SG, which was
the later model designation. It had
three gold humbuckers, the side-
ways vibrato bar, and the block-
inlay ebony fingerboard. My pal
sold me the remains for a nominal
fee, and I designed a new body
based on an antique guitar—
probably a Stauffer made in Vienna
by the man who taught Christian
Frederick Martin how to build
guitars. A local cabinet shop on
Broadway near Bleeker cut the
body shape in Honduras mahogany, and I then took it home and

The first version of Phil's
Alembicized Guild Starfire
bass, inside and out.
(Later, two more knobs
were added.)

veneered the back and sides with walnut, inlaid a fancy back stripe, and bound
it in maple. I then wired it in stereo, with the neck and bridge pickups in a kind
of normal two-pickup Les Paul arrangement, and took the middle pickup out
on a separate channel. The two-channel signal then went out to what was probably one of the earliest pedalboards…. This became my main guitar for lead
work in the band…."

Once Turner had moved to the West Coast and, after a time, hooked up
with Alembic, "Jerry saw the guitar one day at our shop, and he liked it, so I

sold it to him. I have no idea what happened to that guitar, though I'd like to track it down…. It could be in a roadie's closet, for all I know. It does represent an evolutionary step both toward Alembic and then the later Turner Model 1 [from his early post-Alembic period], which shares the body shape, except for the addition of the cutaway."

For whatever reason, Garcia played the guitar only a few times onstage, but it happened to coincide with a period when Bob and Betty were recording the Dead's shows for another live album (Turner did the front-of-house mix on that tour), so it was immortalized that way. (There are scant photos of Garcia playing it onstage.) Garcia also got another Turner-built guitar during the Alembic era, but he never played it live, to Turner's eternal puzzlement and disappointment. Garcia would change guitars more in 1971 than in any other year, but his apparent restlessness did not appear to translate to his playing.

(Steve Parish notes that Garcia was always game to try a new guitar. "Back in 1970," he relates, "some guy gave him one that was made out of a tombstone. It was marble or granite or some heavy fucking thing. It had a really weird neck, too. But Jerry played it a couple of times. The guy who made it flipped out and became a street person. The point is, Jerry would experiment, but no matter what he played, he'd still try to say it within that signature Fender Twin sound; that's what he craved.)

In June, Garcia moved back, at least briefly, to a Strat. This one, popularly known in guitar circles as the "Alligator Strat"—after the prominent green alligator sticker that was put on it early in 1973—had been given to him by Graham Nash. "I gave that guitar to Jerry for the wonderful job he did on my music," Nash told me in the winter of 2006. "Not only 'Teach Your Children' but 'I Used to Be a King' and 'Southbound Train' [both on Nash's solo debut, *Songs for Beginners*]. I think he later played that guitar on 'The Wall Song' [from *Graham Nash, David Crosby*]. I believe I bought that guitar in a pawnshop in Phoenix in late 1970. It was $250—a bargain. I wonder where it is now."

This sweet Strat has been pegged by at least one fan-expert as having the swamp-ash body of a '63 Strat and the maple neck of a '57. After Garcia had played it for a while, it was fitted with a custom bridge and, some Garcia gear-heads believe, an Alembic StratoBlaster adjustable-gain onboard preamp, which increased its volume potential considerably.

Then in July, Garcia shows up onstage with a bright whitish-yellow 1959 or '60 Gibson Les Paul TV (with a pair of single-coil P-90 pickups) for a few shows. (Weir also played the instrument briefly during this period, along with a black Les Paul—perhaps one of Garcia's.) In fact, the year is a jumble of different guitars for Garcia and includes a flame Les Paul of unknown vintage in the spring; by the time fall rolls around, he's settled on the Nash Strat, which would carry him through the epic Europe '72 tour and beyond.

In July, too, Garcia started work on his first solo album at Wally Heider's, this time working with Bob and Betty in the smaller Studio D, which was equipped with a Quad 8 console. This was the rare "solo" album that lived up to its name—except for drums, handled by Bill Kreutzmann, Garcia played all the instruments on the album: acoustic, electric and pedal guitars, bass, piano, organ, and all vocals. About half the album consisted of regular Hunter-Garcia songs, some of which had already been road-tested by the Dead: "Bird Song," "Sugaree," "Deal," "Loser," and "To Lay Me Down." Most of the rest of the record, however, evolved out of acoustic guitar-and-drums or piano-and-drums improvisations in the studio. Over the course of several days, pieces solidified into fixed structures, and then Garcia overdubbed other parts on top of those frames. One full-blown masterpiece came out of that process: "The Wheel," which formed slowly but steadily over a number of takes and culminated with Hunter writing the lyrics in the studio during the sessions.

Garcia was the first to admit that working this way was a lark more than a serious attempt to make a commercial solo album. "It's really me goofing around," he told *Rolling Stone* with typical understatement at the time. "Jerry wanted to be very low-key about it," Bob Matthews agreed in 1997. "It was Jerry on his own with a couple of people he liked to be creative with—Billy and Hunter and Betty and me. I felt blessed to be one of those people, and it was a real special record for all of us." (The other person worth noting for his contribution to the sessions is Ram Rod, who was given a co-production credit on the album, though he was mainly an instrument tech.)

"It was no rules; we had an awful lot of fun working on that album," Kreutzmann told me in 2004. "It was totally loose; that's what was wonderful about it. Bob and Betty would start the tape machine, and we'd just go. And it all flowed so nicely. Jerry and I never actually sat down and talked about what he wanted to do for Side Two. We just went in and did it. I'd follow him, add what I needed to—sort of feel my way through. We were all doing that, and it turned out so well."

Pigpen's health had been declining all year, and by the end of August he'd been forced off the road to recuperate. So it was perfect timing when Dead fans Keith and Donna Godchaux approached Garcia at a gig by his club band (with

Suggested listening: Garcia's eponymous first solo album was a close collaboration with Bill Kreutzmann along with engineers Bob and Betty. The cover collage was by photographer Bob Seidemann.

keyboardist Merl Saunders) at the Keystone Berkeley and Donna announced, "Keith is going to be your piano player." Keith was a local boy, raised in the hot suburbs east of the Oakland Hills. He had played primarily jazz and some rock 'n' roll, but never in a high-profile situation, and he was painfully shy, so on the surface he didn't seem a likely candidate for the Dead keyboard chair. But it turned out he was conversant in many styles, and he immediately impressed Garcia and Kreutzmann when he came by to audition. Garcia was psyched to get a piano player into the mix—it seemed perfect for a lot of the band's newer material—so come the October 1971 tour, the Dead's stage was now graced by a nine-foot Steinway grand piano from city to city. Keith was a very quick study; musically he fit instantly and helped take the repertoire to some exciting places. New tunes introduced on that tour included the Hunter-Garcia songs "Ramble On Rose," "Tennessee Jed," the gorgeous but heavy ballad "Comes a Time," and a trio of tunes by Weir: "Jack Straw," "Mexicali Blues" (written with his old friend John Barlow, who would become his primary lyricist), and "One More Saturday Night."

Because Keith was such a quiet and unassuming guy, his role in the band's music has probably been under-appreciated through the years. But if you go back and really listen to the Dead's music the first couple of years Keith was in the band, you'll discover that his piano work was a critical element in the group's sound, both on their regular songs and in the spaciest jams, where the piano added so much to the overall sound.

Steinway deserves a shout-out here; it should not be taken for granted. The company is yet another 19th-century creation by a German immigrant who moved to America to find his fortune: Heinrich Steinweg, who started making pianos in Germany in 1836, moved to Manhattan in 1851, and changed his name to Henry Steinway. He started his American piano-building company in 1853, by which time he'd already made 482 pianos. It was Steinway who introduced both the cast-iron frame that eventually became standard with most piano makers and the concept of over-stringing (for which he received a patent in 1859). It didn't take long for Steinway to become the best-loved piano of concert pianists in the U.S. and around the world (it has long had a factory in Hamburg to make models for the European market), and more than 150 years after its founding, the company is still among the top brands, making some 5,000 new instruments a year. (However, today Yamaha is the best-selling manufacturer of pianos.) Each handcrafted Steinway can take up to a year to build; nobody's churning them out on an assembly line.

Rather than buy a piano outright and lug it around, the Dead usually rented instruments: "We had it on our rider [contract stipulations] that Keith had to have a nine-foot Steinway," says Donna Godchaux-MacKay. "He usually got it, but not always." Rather than capturing the piano sound with conventional microphones in the live setting, they used special pickups designed by Carl Countryman. "The Countryman pickup worked by an electrostatic principle similar to the way a condenser mic works," Bear notes. "It was charged with a very high voltage, and thus was very cantankerous to set up and use. It had a way of crackling in humid conditions and making other rather unmusical sounds if not set up just right, but when it worked it was truly brilliant." Countryman's pickup control box also allowed Keith to attach a wah-wah pedal, which he used sparingly (and always tastefully) during spacey segments from time to time.

Right as Keith was hitting the road for the first time with the Dead, another live double-album was landing in record stores. Titled simply *Grateful Dead*, but popularly known as "Skull & Roses" (after the cover painting; Warner Bros. had rejected the Dead's proposed title, "Skullfuck"), it was the band's third release in just 15 months. A wonderfully *present* recording (by Bob and Betty) that accurately reflected the band's post-Mickey sound from earlier in the year (but was actually out of date by the time of its release), it once again was an enormous popular success.

Another new face at Alembic that fall was Dennis "Wizard" Leonard. A New Yorker, Wizard had "worked the freak-out tent at Woodstock," lived with members of the Hog Farm collective in New Mexico, and moved to the Bay Area around Halloween in 1971, where he was immediately hired by Ron Wickersham at Alembic. Like Jim Furman, he was put to work Alembicizing Fender amplifiers and generally doing whatever needed to be done. He clearly recalls the Dead's sound system at that time:

Suggested listening: *Ladies and Gentlemen...The Grateful Dead* beautifully showcases the Dead in early 1971, after Mickey had left the band, whereas *Dick's Picks Vol. 35* features some stunning performances from Keith's first tour.

"Sometime before I got there, in early 1971 I believe, the Dead had bought the PA from Alembic. That's when they put those great tie-dyes on [made by Courtenay Pollack]. They'd set up the amps and the tie-dyes would make this continuous pattern. Back then the PA consisted of eight Alembic cabinets per side, each with two 15″ [JBL] speakers. They were exactly the shape and size of a Dual Showman cabinet. There were also four JBL 90-degree horns per side with 2440s [midrange compression drivers] on them, and four 2410 drivers for the highs. The monitor wedges were [JBL] D110s on these little stands—that was usually a guitar speaker. The front-of-house mixer was still a stack of [chained] Ampex MX10s. It was really simple, actually, but very hi-fi."

In the Dead's ongoing progression through bigger and more powerful McIntosh tube amps, they had reached the MC-275 by then (designed in part by McIntosh co-founder Sidney Corderman), which delivered about 75 watts

Ron Wickersham doesn't appear to be intimidated by the tangle of wires before him on the Great Medicine Ball Tour, 1970.

PHOTO: ROSE McGEE

per channel in stereo, 150 in mono. (Made between 1961 and '73, it's widely regarded as one of the best tube amps ever made; "new" versions cost up to $5,000.) The live beast needed more, however, and so next the Dead brought in MC-3500s, 125-pound mono low-distortion tube amps that were capable of putting out 350 watts (or more!). At a thousand bucks a pop, they were not cheap…but neither were the Dead (or Alembic). Then the next stage was to buy MC-2300s, which were potent 300-watt transistor amps that soon became the backbone of the Dead's system. Each tour, it seemed, their commitment to better, cleaner (*and* louder) sound became more apparent.

"The funny thing is, the Dead thought they were going to save money owning the PA," says Rick Turner. "Ha-ha-ha-HA! They thought we were getting rich at Alembic renting it to them. So once they owned, then they had to pay for all the upgrades, and over the next couple of years the spending increased geometrically. So it might not have been the best move for them."

EUROPE AND BIG PLANS

GARCIA'S eponymous solo debut was released by Warner Bros. in January 1972, and right around that time—during the Dead's traditional fallow winter break—Bob Weir started work on his own album, *Ace*. He'd written a bunch of songs with John Barlow and was anxious to go into Wally Heider's to record. He hadn't exactly thought through who would play on the album with him, however, and it quickly evolved to become a full Grateful Dead project, with Bob and Betty engineering and co-producing. There were a few guests, including a small horn group on a couple of songs, a string section on another (both firsts for any Dead-related project), and New Riders bassist David Torbert helped out on a tune, as well. The seven-and-a-half-minute version of "Playing in the Band" remains one of the group's finest in-studio performances; it easily eclipsed the more rudimentary live reading on "Skull & Roses" from the previous year.

Chapter Eight
1972-1973

Garcia, Weir, and Bob and Betty supervised the mixing of the album at Pacific High, which was actually in the process of closing down due to bankruptcy, with Alembic assuming ownership of the facility at 60 Brady Street in late 1971. Alembic hoped this would give them the top-flight recording facility they had always wanted, plus more office, retail, and repair space for the growing concern. Rick Turner had a workshop there, of course, but it was also around this time that he moved much of his instrument-building operation up to a one-time chicken ranch in Cotati, in (what was then) rural southern Sonoma County. Pacific High's old console went up to Mickey Hart's ranch in Novato and became the basis for what was one of the first good artist-owned home studios in the Bay Area. Alembic then brought in its own board from the Judah Street operation.

The Dead first talked about touring Europe as early as 1968, but with the exception of two one-offs in 1970 and '71 (in England and France), they stuck to the United States. By 1972, though, they were determined to make the big trip across the pond. With a string of successful albums now behind them, they were in the good graces of Warner Bros. for the first time in memory, so the label was willing to splurge for a large contingent of Dead-related folks to hit

The band is a colorful sight as they play for German TV at the Beat Club in Bremen on 4/21/1972. Jerry's playing the Nash Strat, Bobby an ES-345.

PHOTO: MARY ANN MAYER/GRATEFUL DEAD

the Continent for a nearly two-month tour, which also had ample vacation time built in. As a *Rolling Stone* story at the time noted, "There were seven musicians and singers [Donna Godchaux being the latest addition, on backup vocals], five managers, five office staff, ten equipment handlers (handling 15,000 pounds of equipment, not counting the 16-track recording system), four drivers, and 17 assorted wives, old ladies, babies, and friends." To defray some of the costs, the Dead brought along the MM-1000 to record the entire tour; indeed, the triple-album *Europe '72*, released that fall, turned out to be another commercial triumph for the band and label. Before the tour, too, Ron Wickersham modified the recorder to accept 14-inch reels, which helped minimize reel flips during long, continuous passages of music. He achieved this by taking the machine out of the MM-1000 frame and putting it into a VR-1200 frame.

All the equipment, except for the recording gear, was shipped over to Europe by boat, "and there was quite a lot of it by then," says Betty Cantor-Jackson. "It had gotten to the point in the U.S. where the airlines basically didn't want to deal with us. If we were flying our equipment, we'd have like a hundred pieces checked as 'excess baggage.' After a while they didn't even want to look at our luggage tags; they'd just say, 'Oh, get outta here!'" she laughs.

TOP: Keith relaxes at the Beat Club in Bremen.

BOTTOM: Pigpen at the B-3 in Copenhagen, 4/17/72. The European tour would be his last.

Once the recording equipment landed in Europe, the Dead rented a truck and devised a sort of mobile control room with velour drapes for better monitoring. As for the onstage monitoring, Ron Wickersham built a box he called the AX-10, which was about the same size as an Ampex MX-10 and allowed him to split off a monitor feed and highlight the four vocal mics. Betty supervised the recording in Europe, aided by Dennis Leonard, who would set up the mics at each gig and then help in the truck, and Jim Furman, who worked as a tech for the truck. (Bob Matthews was the front-of-house mixer on the tour; Dan Healy was in charge of the power distribution, etc.) At the end of each gig, various other racks of equipment (and even lighting designer Candace Brightman's small rig) would be packed into the recording truck to move on to the next venue. The tour took the Dead to England (twice), Denmark, Germany, Holland, Luxembourg, and France, and though they were not well known most places they went, they were almost universally well received. Today, the 1972 Europe tour is widely regarded as one of the best of the band's entire history.

Once the group returned to the States, they spent quite a bit of time at Alembic's new studio working on the *Europe '72* album, which contained the

Phil playing "Big Brown" at a free concert in Lille, France, 5/13/72.

PHOTO: MARY ANN MAYER/GRATEFUL DEAD

first sanctioned recordings of such Hunter-Garcia tunes as "Brown-Eyed Women," "Tennessee Jed," "He's Gone," and "Ramble On Rose," as well as the Hunter-Pigpen song "Mr. Charlie" and various GD "hits" (ranging from "China Cat Sunflower," "I Know You Rider" to "Truckin'" and "Sugar Magnolia"). "The band was almost never happy with their vocals on live recordings," Matthews offers. "We had overdubbed vocals on 'Skull & Roses,' too [as well as a few Merl Saunders keyboard parts], but the band was very unhappy about the fact that it *sounded* like it had been over-

A tape box reveals that original title of *Europe '72* was *Steppin' Out*—a title used later on a live CD culled from the tour.

dubbed. Actually there were some discussions about whether we were even going to do *Europe '72*, because of vocal issues, so that's when I came up with the idea of trying to make [the overdubbed vocals] sound more live. The nice thing about the simplicity of our [live recording] system is that every input had been a microphone [picking up a] cabinet [or drums], and each had its place in the huge template." They then re-created the positions of those cabinets with loudspeakers in the big room at Alembic, set up the singers and their monitors in the same positions they had been onstage, and then played back the instrumental tracks to approximate the actual live performance, as the singers laid down new vocals. "It worked really well," Matthews says. "Everybody seemed to like that fine," and Deadheads had no idea most of the harmony vocals were not from the original live tapes. "The band wanted the albums to sound as good as they could make them," Matthews says. "They weren't purists at all."

The conclusion of Alembic's big move to Brady Street took place while the Dead were in Europe, and it was clear from the outset that a serious infusion of capital would be needed to accomplish both the physical remodeling and equipment upgrades that Wickersham and Matthews, in particular, felt were necessary to run the studio successfully. For a while, it looked like they might have found a financial angel in former Creedence Clearwater Revival member Tom Fogerty, who had been playing on and off in the Garcia-Saunders club band, but they were unable to finalize negotiations, and eventually he withdrew his offer of support. At that point, Susan Wickersham called in her friend

Reel no.
Date
City

1. Bass Drum
2. Floor Tom
3. Snare
4. Overhead
5. Hi hat
6. Bass
7. Bass
8. Lead guitar
9. Rhythm n guita
10. Jerry vocal
11. Bob vocal ~
12. Phil vocal
13. Pig Pen vocal
14. Organ
15. Piano
16. Aud/Sync

Warner Bros. Rec,
P.O. no. 20016

Tape - 3M-207
15 ips EQ 35 µSec.

Ampex MM-1000
(modified)

This custom tape label shows the track assignments for the instruments and voices on the Europe '72 tapes.

COURTESY OF ALEMBIC

Sam Field, whose greatest claim to fame in Dead circles is that he financed the legendary 1972 concert film *Sunshine Daydream* (still officially unreleased, but widely bootlegged), and he came on board as a minority stockholder. "Sam saved the day and allowed us to continue," Susan says. "He retains his stock in Alembic to this day."

Later that year, Bob and Betty's personal relationship, troubled for some time, finally unraveled, which effectively ended their engineering partnership with the Dead. Betty stayed on with the band, making stereo recordings at every show and also doing the sound (and recordings) for Garcia gigs. Matthews continued on with Alembic for a while and worked a few more Dead tours, but eventually he traded his Alembic stock back to the Wickershams in exchange for equipment.

On the live sound front, the biggest change occurred toward the end of 1972: "Jerry and Bobby started to use Mac [McIntosh 3500] power amps to drive their [guitar] speakers, where previously they'd been used for the PA only," Dennis Leonard says. "Phil was already using [four] Mac [2300] power amps, but he went back and forth. He had a stack of six Dual Showmen for a while, and then he went to a preamp out, and then custom preamps, all Mac power. He was always into trying new things. Bobby was, too. He was always futzing around, using the latest and greatest—whereas with Jerry, I always got the impression he was very happy just using his Twin."

Then there's this story from that era, recalled by Leonard: "Sometime before New Year's Eve '72 or just thereafter, Rosie McGee, who worked as a secretary at Alembic, was laughing: She had just gotten a call from the Department of Defense, who saw that we had dibs on I don't know how many back-ordered Mac 3500s, the 350-watt amplifier that we were using for almost everything. [McIntosh formally stopped production on the 3500 toward the end of 1971.] The Department of Defense said, 'We'd really like to be able to get a couple of those—can we defer a couple of your back orders?' And we said, 'No, sorry. We need 'em!' Of course there was all this conjecture about what they were using them for. Later, after it was declassified, a McIntosh engineer told me that they would tow this giant remote-controlled transducer miles behind a destroyer and play the signature of various Russian submarines [through underwater speakers]. So they were using the amplifier to do sonar. I think what we were using them for was more important," Leonard laughs.

MEET JOHN MEYER

This seems as good a place as any to introduce an important player in this saga, even though his most significant direct contributions to the Dead would come later: John Meyer, whose name would become synonymous

Suggested listening: Besides the *Europe '72* album—a triple-LP when it was released—the Europe tour has yielded several excellent CDs in more recent times, including *Hundred Year Hall* (recorded In Munich), *Rockin' the Rhein* (Dusseldorf) and *Steppin' Out* (various locales In England).

with state-of-the-art loudspeakers. Meyer was an Oakland kid who, like so many people in the story, gravitated to the world of sound at a very young age. He had an uncle who was a sound designer and tech for Disneyland in its early days (and an aunt who wanted John to become a Mousketeer!), and by age 12 he'd already gotten an FCC radio license on his way to becoming a broadcast engineer for KPFA in Berkeley. At Oakland High, Meyer was part of the student sound crew that helped build equipment for the PTA and various events. By 1966 he was selling high-end Klipsch hi-fi gear at Berkeley Custom Electronics, which led to an association and friendship with musician Steve Miller, a Texan who'd recently settled in San Francisco after playing in bands in Madison and Chicago. Like the Dead during this era, Miller was interested in developing a more hi-fi sound, so Meyer became his house soundman. He worked in that capacity for Miller at the Monterey Pop Festival (where the main sound system was provided by Harry McCune Sound Services, the Bay Area's top sound company for many years), and also became roommates with him in the Haight-Ashbury. Because the Klipsch horns Meyer was using for low end kept blowing up during Miller's shows, Meyer started doing his own speaker-test measurements; this led to the development of his own huge loudspeaker system, called Glyph, which had an eight-foot exponential horn for low frequencies and a four-foot horn for midrange, both constructed out of fiberglass with wood struts. Though actually designed for reproduction of classical music—Meyer's great love—this became the house system at a short-lived club in San Rafael (Marin County) called Pepperland. A number of top bands played there, including Miller, Frank Zappa, Pink Floyd, and Joan Baez, and Glyph sounded good enough that in 1971 Meyer was recruited by McCune to develop sound systems for them.

"They wanted me to build something that might be more practical [than the enormous Glyph] to ship in airplanes and all that," Meyer says with a smile in the conference room of the Berkeley headquarters of his current company, Meyer Sound. Heading a McCune team of nine, he developed the JM-3 loud-

John Meyer In the anechoic chamber at Meyer Sound in Berkeley. Courtesy of Meyer Sound

speaker, "a three-way tri-amped system which became very popular," he says. Indeed, it became the building block of McCune's best PA systems for years to come, going out on the road with untold numbers of bands. The JM-3 consisted of two 15″ woofers, a custom midrange horn, and two tweeters in a single cabinet. A self-admitted quality freak, Meyer was interested in building gear that would be durable and relatively easy to use; part of his philosophy was that functionality should be transparent to the user and not require arcane knowledge for setup and use. He didn't limit his work to loudspeakers, either: He also built mixing consoles "with lines of EQ in every channel so they'd have the control they wanted without having to mess with the sound system. There wasn't anything like that [out there]," he says.

Not surprisingly, Meyer encountered the sound wizards of the Grateful Dead at some point along the road. Healy, too, had done work with McCune (before Meyer) and had great respect for the company—a number of years down the road, as we'll see, the Dead would even employ McCune systems dominated by Meyer components. Meyer also turns up briefly in our discussion of the Wall of Sound in the next chapter.

The year 1973 would turn out to be pivotal for the Dead in almost every area. The biggest event was the death of Pigpen in March. Though he'd been sick for some time and hadn't played with the group for nearly a year, it was still a kick in the solar plexus, a tragedy beyond words. Garcia and Lesh both started playing new custom-built instruments. And the Dead's sound team spent the year refining their gear in the inexorable march toward the Wall of Sound.

CHAPTER 8: EUROPE AND BIG PLANS • **123**

THE PA COMMITTEE

It was near the end of 1972 that Ron Wickersham decided to form a loose PA Consulting Committee to help develop a new sound system for the Dead, who were, increasingly, playing for larger audiences to satisfy the intense demand for tickets, especially on the East Coast. The Committee consisted of Wickersham, Owsley (out of jail since August '72), Rick Turner, Dan Healy, Sparky Raizene, John Cutler, and John Curl (who was working as a sound consultant and had an office at 60 Brady Street).

"The Dead kept playing bigger and bigger venues, and the house or rented sound systems kept sounding worse and worse," comments Wickersham. "So we tried to break it all down and address every area we could, because it wasn't like there was a single thing wrong with the instruments, microphones or recording gear, the live PA, and all that. It was a constant fight to try to get *every* detail better. There were times we'd make little gains in a particular area, and it might not have seemed like it would make that much difference overall, but it *did* make a difference. We eliminated some bottlenecks forever."

Wickersham stresses that everyone involved made valuable contributions to the sound. "You can look at a guy like John Curl, who contributed a lot of design ideas to Alembic. He and I worked on a lot of things together, and I couldn't tell you what he did and what I did. The collaboration was more powerful than either of us individually.

"And that was true of all of us: Rick and Frank Fuller [another luthier who had worked with Turner in San Francisco pre-Alembic] and Bear and the others. It's the fact that we were working together, dedicated on stuff. We were fiercely critical of what was there, and we drove to improve it, together. There may have been some 'eureka' moments, but you didn't have them individually; you kind of had them because you were contributing to the group. It may have been something so radical that you needed somebody else to give you some positive reinforcement. You might have said, 'That's nice, but it's too hard, so I'll put that off,' and somebody else would say, 'No, that's *really* good; let's do it!' You'd get that kind of encouragement.

"One of the things we faced with the sound stuff," Wickersham continues, "was that live music's dynamic range is so much greater than what you get from recorded music, because [recorded music] is already disciplined through boards and limiters and the capability of either broadcast or recording gear. But if you want the dynamics of a live symphony orchestra or the dynamics of a live rock 'n' roll band, you have to approach it differently than the way it was being done at the time. We had the goal to make it better than anything out there, and we were so fortunate that we had the Dead—it wouldn't have happened without them. They were always willing to spend the money."

Jerry Garcia was a very busy guy in 1973. Besides playing 73 shows with the Dead in venues ranging from civic centers to basketball arenas to stadiums—not to mention before 650,000 people at the Grand Prix race course at Watkins Glen (in upstate New York), along with The Band and the Allman Brothers in what is still the largest concert in U.S. history—he also notched 26 shows with his electric club band, and he added a new wrinkle: nearly two dozen shows with Old & In the Way, a bluegrass group that he formed with mandolinist David Grisman, bassist John Kahn, singer/guitarist Peter Rowan, and Richard Greene (later replaced by Vassar Clements) on fiddle. Garcia played banjo (a beautiful Weymann that David Crosby got for him, according to David Nelson, plus a Gibson Mastertone reissue) and sang in the group, which moved easily between classic bluegrass tunes and more modern pieces by Rowan, Grisman, and others. With the exception of two East Coast gigs, their appearances were limited to the Bay Area. (Three exceptional live recordings made by Owsley and Victoria Babcock have come out over the years. The

Phil onstage at Winterland with the modded Starfire, New Year's Eve '72-'73; his stack of McIntosh amps at the same gig.

PHOTOS: STEPHEN BARNCARD

original eponymous album, released in 1975, remains one of the top-selling bluegrass recordings of all time. A studio album was recorded at Mickey Hart's barn studio but never released. "Nothing clicked," Garcia said in a 1991 interview with *Guitar* magazine, to which Grisman added, "It was kind of rushed. It didn't seem to equal what we were doing live.")

That May, Keith added a Fender Rhodes to his setup, giving him a nice alternative to the straight acoustic piano sound he generally favored. Though commonly referred to as an "electric piano," which it technically is, the Rhodes is really its own instrument, nearly as distinctive and different from a piano sonically as an electric organ is. It takes its name from Harold Rhodes (1910–2000), a piano teacher who invented the instrument for the U.S. Army in the '40s as a lightweight and portable keyboard that could be played on a lap in bed by wounded soldiers. His first instrument, which he made from spare airplane parts, was called a Xylette. The Army liked Rhodes's design so much that for a brief period they made the instruments themselves and shipped them around the world to troops. After the war, Rhodes started his own company, but it wasn't until the late '50s, when he hooked up with Leo Fender and the "Fender Rhodes" was born (Rhodes insisted that Leo did make some valuable suggestions), that it started to be noticed. Fender's first keyboard was a bass piano, but later models added more keys and higher registers. In the Rhodes, rubber-tipped hammers struck metal rods called "tines" and activated tuned resonators that vibrated near magnetic pickups, the output of which went to an amplifier. Various controls—the most popular being a stereo tremolo or vibrato—colored the sound in different ways.

The Rhodes was actually only a so-so success for Fender; it didn't really take off until CBS acquired Fender in 1965 and released a 73-note version shortly afterward. By the late '60s, the Rhodes started to turn up on all sorts of rock and jazz records: Herbie Hancock played it on Miles Davis's *Miles in the Sky* in 1968, and then Chick Corea and Hancock both used it on Miles's influential *In a Silent Way* and *Bitches Brew* albums, assuring a foothold for the instrument in the jazz and fusion worlds. Billy Preston used a Rhodes on the Beatles' *Let It Be* sessions, in 1971 it was the centerpiece of the Doors' sound on "Riders on the Storm," and Stevie Wonder championed it on a number of songs, which led to its widespread adoption by funk and soul bands.

Weir played a Gibson SG for much of 1973. "I can't remember what year it was," Weir says, "but I think it was older than Jerry's." Weir's also had a whammy bar, whereas Garcia's didn't, "but I didn't use it that much because it would throw the guitar out of tune more than on some of the guitars I'd owned. In fact, keeping that guitar in tune in general was a problem. The trouble with these guitars is they've got wonderful, fast necks and good tone, but you can't play 'em in tune. The heel-block assembly is such that the neck bends with the slightest urging, and if you're a physical player like me, even just by singing and playing chords the whole guitar would go substantially sharp. I couldn't understand why everything sounded a little out of tune, and then I realized it was me." By the fall he'd moved on to a lovely sunburst 335, which had a maple top, back, and sides, mahogany neck, rosewood fingerboard, and was appropriately Alembicized inside.

WAKE OF THE FLOOD

Also in '73 the Dead left Warner Bros. and founded their own labels: Grateful Dead Records and Round Records (the latter for solo/offshoot projects). In August they made their first studio album in more than three years, *Wake of the Flood*, their debut disc for Grateful Dead Records. The band had a solid selection of tunes they'd been road-testing that year, including an extremely diverse batch from Hunter-Garcia: "Mississippi Half-Step (Uptown Toodeloo)," "Row Jimmy," "Eyes of the World," "Stella Blue," and "Here Comes Sunshine." Bob Weir brought in his most ambitious composition to date, "Weather Report Suite," and even Keith Godchaux got into the act with his first (and only) composition and lead vocal for the Dead, "Let Me Sing Your Blues Away." There were jazz influences, a touch of both reggae and samba, some Richard Greene country fiddle snaking through "Half-Step," and horns on Keith's tune and the "Let It Grow" section of "Weather Report"—plenty of new directions, but still unmistakably Good Ol' Grateful Dead. For these sessions, the band, with Healy taking over as engineer, migrated to one of the area's newest studios, the Record Plant in picturesque Sausalito, just on the Marin side of the Golden Gate Bridge.

The Record Plant had opened with a bang around Halloween 1972, with a grand party that attracted scads of stars—including John and Yoko, who came dressed as trees—and music-industry bigwigs. The studio had a good pedigree: Owners Chris Stone and Gary Kellgren (the license on his purple Rolls Royce read GREED) already had successful Record Plant studios in New York (where Jimi Hendrix cut *Electric Ladyland*) and Los Angeles. In the early '70s, the Bay Area looked to be an unending font of hot talent, so it was natural to expand there. And rather than creating another utilitarian room in San Francisco to compete with Heider's (who, truth be told, had sought to expand to Marin, but couldn't get together the necessary permits for the space they were interested in), Stone and Kellgren created a "destination" studio: It was luxuriously appointed in rich woods and deep carpeting; has two nearby guest houses that could accommodate bands, their crews, and friends; on-call organic chefs; a hot tub. As Chris Stone told Heather Johnson in her book on the history of Bay Area studios, *If These Halls Could Talk*, "Gary decided that the most important thing was for the artist to think that he was in a living room. The greatest compliment that an artist could pay us was, 'Hey, man, I don't want to leave.'"

The Record Plant pioneered the concept of the "residential" studio, meaning artists would live and work there for a project's duration. The equipment was pretty good, too: API consoles in the two main control rooms, Yamaha grand pianos, Ampex and 3M 16-track recorders, plenty of good microphones and outboard limiters, compressors, etc.

During their August '73 lockout of the studio, the Dead didn't have to avail themselves of the guest houses to the degree that, say, George Harrison and his entourage did when he secretly came to the Record Plant—but there were times when it was easier to crash on the premises than drive back home after a particularly long and stony late-night session. The modus operandi was standard for that era: recording basic tracks with everyone playing together, then layering in vocals and instrumental overdubs. It certainly wasn't as quick as *Workingman's Dead* had been, but neither was it particularly long and tortuous.

In his liner notes for the album's 2004 expanded reissue as part of the *Beyond Description* box set, one of the Record Plant's engineers, Tom Anderson, noted that Phil Lesh "had all his gear set up in the isolation booth of Studio B, and when the project was over, we discovered we had to go into the booth and tighten up all the light fixtures and anything else that could have come loose…. The volume and frequencies generated by his bass had loosened up everything that wasn't attached to the foundation."

Another Record Plant assistant mentioned that one day when he came down to the studio, the Dead had so many McIntosh amps piled in the hallway outside of Studio B that it was hard to get by them and into the room. Owsley was on hand offering copious advice to (and hectoring) Healy, and Bob and Betty would drop by from time to time, separately, to check out the scene. There was lots of nitrous oxide and cocaine, but the work still got done and the album turned out very well, most Deadheads agreed. It was an auspicious start to the Dead's independent record-label venture—though the excitement dimmed when it was revealed that the market was awash in counterfeit albums; we'll never know exactly how many.

Suggested listening: *Wake of the Flood* featured a Biblically inspired cover by San Francisco poster artist Rick Griffin. This promo item by Griffin was sent in postcard form to names on the Dead Heads mailing list, and as a poster to record stores.

If Tom Anderson's recollection is correct, at the beginning of the *Wake of the Flood* sessions Garcia was presented with the custom guitar that would become his primary axe for the next couple of years (and intermittently for many more). Most of the year, Garcia had been playing Strats: mainly the Nash Alligator (which in '73 boasted a new bridge and tailpiece), but also, very early in the year, a rather homely chocolate-brown model with large numeric fingerboard inlays. (There are also photos of Garcia playing that guitar in his club group in late 1972.) Garcia's new axe had been crafted by a luthier named Doug Irwin, who, Rick Turner says, "came to work with me when we set up the chicken-shack factory [in Cotati]. He trained with me and eventually started making the guitars for Garcia and then split off and did his thing."

Originally from Rochester, New York, Irwin was first set on a career of some sort in biochemistry, but when he moved to the Bay Area in the summer of 1970, he abruptly changed directions, determining that he wanted to be a guitar builder. He taught himself the craft out of books under the auspices of California's Employment Development Department, and also attended night school in wood shop. By June 1971, he'd built his first flat-top acoustic guitar. Eventually, Rick Turner hired him for a half-time job at Alembic; he spent a year or more there, learning the ropes from Turner and Frank Fuller and devoting his free time to building his own electric guitar. One day, toward the end of 1972, Garcia was in Alembic's Brady Street store and spied the first guitar Irwin had made for Alembic. "He bought the guitar right on the spot [for $850], and asked me to make him another guitar," Irwin recalled in an interview.

"That first guitar was a double-cutaway made of bird's-eye maple and walnut, and it had a couple of dual-coil humbucking-type pickups. At the time, Jerry was using a lot of single-coil pickups, and when he bought that guitar, the first thing he said right away was, 'Wow, man, if I could get this with a Stratocaster pickup, maybe I could play this shit.'" (That guitar, subsequently nicknamed Eagle after the design on the peghead, might have been played a couple of times in public. It shows up sitting on a stand in a photo of the Dead's stage setup taken by Jim Santana in mid 1973 for a story about the Dead's gear in the June/July issue of *Guitar Player*.)

"So I built the next guitar for him," Irwin recalled in the same interview, "which I had actually started building at the time he ordered it; it was made out of purpleheart [also known as amaranth, a South American wood] and curly maple. It had an ebony fingerboard and mother-of-pearl inlays.... This is the one that became the 'Wolf.'" Garcia paid $1,500 for the guitar, and though it, too, bore Irwin's logo on the peghead, the body design had originally been conceived by Alembic's Susan Wickersham, she says.

The guitar didn't receive its "Wolf" moniker until later. Garcia had put a decal of a bloodthirsty cartoon wolf below the tailpiece, and after bringing it in to Irwin for refinishing between tours one year, "I knew the decal was going to be gone, so I just redid the wolf as an inlay," Irwin said. "In fact," Garcia recalled in 1978, "it was a week or so before I even noticed what he had done!"

Garcia first played the Irwin guitar on the October '73 tour. Around the same time, Phil unveiled his new axe—an Alembic custom model nicknamed the "Mission Control" bass by it principal creator, Rick Turner, and also known as the Omega bass, after its distinctive lower-body design, which slightly resembles the Greek letter. "That bass started off as a test bed for ideas, as so many things did," Turner says, "but since I was sort of given carte blanche to do whatever I wanted to do, I took my end of it as far as I could go. Then Ron, who had started out working on the electronics, turned that side over to George Mundy, who worked on it as an independent contractor directly for Phil—under his [and Ron Wickersham's] supervision, but at the electronics facility next door to the Alembic studio. George got deeply into it; he really put a lot into that instrument. I think his side of that bass probably cost something like $30,000 back then—you could buy a house with what Phil paid for that bass! Even though parts of it turned out to be somewhat unnecessary, it still was that whole thing of pushing an instrument to the ultimate limit."

On his end, Turner crafted the neck from osage orange wood (a Midwestern U.S. tree) and carved the back and sides out of Hawaiian koa. The mother-of-pearl fingerboard inlays were a series of mystical symbols, and the design on the headstock incorporated both Bob Thomas's Alembic logo and the Dead's skull-and-lightning-bolt. Two prominent inlaid mother-of-pearl stars on the lower half of the bass were each surrounded by five knobs controlling various tone settings and filters. There were also ten small push-button switches under inlaid ivory discs, which Turner says were "mostly for sending the different pickups to different places. Like on Big Brown, there were two main pickups, which were Alembics, and a quad pickup and a hum-canceler." For his part, Phil was delighted by the instrument's "better and faster switching, with buttons instead of rotary knobs." Also, Phil noted in a 2000 interview with *Bass Player* magazine's Karl Coryat, "The Guild was very fragile—it had layer upon layer of circuit cards inside it, and it was always in the shop, like a British car."

Garcia's custom Doug Irwin guitar, nicknamed "Wolf" for the sticker Jerry put on it, which was later inlaid by Irwin.

PHOTO: JON SIEVERT

Turner says that even though Big Brown had been equipped with a quad pickup, it was never used in that capacity: "I don't believe we ever really intended for the quad pickup on Big Brown to actually be sent out in quad. I think the quad pickup and the switching we set up there—which Ron really did—sent pairs of strings to different sets of stereo speakers.

"But Mission Control really did have the ability to send each string to a different stack of nine speakers. And it actually did get used that way in the Wall of Sound."

And that would be just one facet of this amazing behemoth of a sound system.

THE WALL OF SOUND

"BEAR knows."

It's a phrase I heard independently and unprompted from three different people in interviews for this book. And each time, the simple phrase seemed to be imbued with an almost mystical certitude.

Let's be frank: Bear/Owsley drove everyone crazy at some point. He was not shy about offering his opinions, and he was frequently given to non-stop lecturing about whatever was on his mind, whether it was practical matters about sound and music or subjects either more mundane or arcane. He could be caustic and condescending, quite unpleasant to be around—maybe best in small doses (pun only partially intended).

But he was probably also a genius. "His concepts were crazy," John Curl comments, "but they worked. It's true! Sometimes it's like these ideas came from some other place, like he was a channel. He was one of those natural-born leaders—always very sure of himself."

Chapter Nine
1973-1974

Rick Turner notes, "It's easy to underestimate Bear's contribution because everyone thinks of him as the Acid King. Well, yeah, he was the Acid King, but he was so much more than just that. And a lot of it was conceptual. I very clearly remember going out to the Novato warehouse in 1969, before I was officially part of the whole thing, and everyone's hanging out and smoking joints, and Bear suddenly says, 'The PA system has to be *behind* the band.' And everyone looked at him like he was out of his fucking mind. 'No, it's gonna feed back, it's gonna do this, it's gonna do that….' And he says, 'Nope, it has to be behind the band.' And by God, he was right! Of course, we didn't know how to do it then, and you know what—I'm not sure we even trusted that it was do-able. But *he* did. Bear always dreamed big."

The Wall of Sound was the work of many people, but it was Bear's idea. In fact, it might have had its origins as early as an intense LSD trip back in 1966. "I think my knowledge of sound dates back to the period of the L.A. Acid Tests—specifically, one of the rehearsals we had in the house in Watts, when I actually saw sound coming out of the speakers," he told me in 1996. "It was total synesthesia, and I'd never experienced that at any other time. It was just a unique experience. And it so completely blew my mind that I realized, 'Hey, no matter what, I've got to remember what this is doing.' I went around and inspected it very carefully, and I spent a lot of time absorbing what the sound was doing and realizing how different it was from what I thought sound did. And that became the foundation for all the sound work that I've done. It was completely three-dimensional, and ever since then that's how I've viewed sound—having real dimensionality that changes as you move around in a space."

WHY A WALL?

On a practical level, the development of the Wall of Sound was a response to the Dead playing larger venues in the early '70s. As Bear told David Gans, "When the Dead said, 'Well, we want to go to bigger shows,' I said, look, from my conversations with Wickersham and Rick and John Curl, John Meyer, and others, I believe that based on what speaker makers tell us now…we can build an integrated system where every instrument has its own amplification, all set up behind the band without any separate onstage monitors. It's a single, big system, like a band playing in a club, only large, and the musicians can all adjust everything, including their vocal level, by having a single source, by using this point-source thing."

Before we get into more details of the system, we have to give some props to a guy who never met anyone involved with the Wall of Sound, but was highly influential in aspects of its design: Harry F. Olson. Born in 1901 in Iowa, Olson studied electrical engineering at the University of Iowa, and in 1928, went to work for RCA in New York. Seeing a need in the new world of "talkies," he

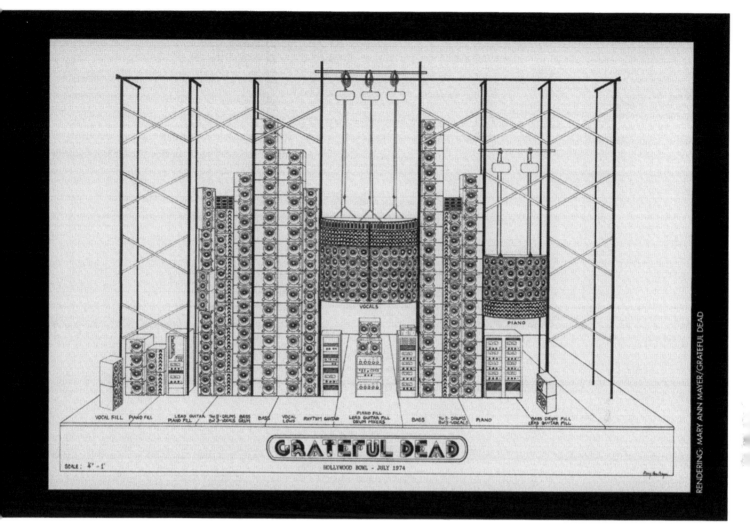

VOCALS

PIANO

VOCAL FILL   PIANO FILL   LEAD GUITAR   Th 5-DRUMS   BASS   BASS   VOCAL   RHYTHM GUITAR   PIANO FILL   BASS   Th 5-DRUMS   PIANO   BASS DRUM FILL
PIANO FILL   Bn 3-VOCALS   DRUM   LOWS   LEAD GUITAR FILL   Bn 3-VOCALS   LEAD GUITAR FILL
                                                                           DRUM MIXERS

GRATEFUL DEAD

SCALE: ¼" = 1'   HOLLYWOOD BOWL - JULY 1974

invented the first bi-directional ribbon microphone in 1931—the RCA 44A and, shortly afterward, the 77A unidirectional model, both still considered classics. In 1939 he published a book called *Acoustical Engineering*, which is still regarded as a bible in the field more than 60 years later. He was instrumental in the development of the acoustic suspension loudspeaker (1949), and a year later, with RCA's Herbert Belar, he invented the first synthesizer, the Mark I, which contained 12 vacuum-tube oscillators (the Mark II, a couple of years later, had 24) capable of electronically shaping sounds in many different ways. That instrument was the foundation for much of the pioneering work done by the Columbia-Princeton Electronic Music Center during the '50s.

That just scratches the surface of what Olson did during his 40-year career at RCA. His work was part of more than 100 patents on everything from underwater recording equipment to phonograph pickups, and another of his books, *Music, Physics and Engineering*, is still widely read. All of the great technical minds involved with the Wall of Sound bow to the accomplishments of Harry Olson.

The Dead included this diagram of the Wall of Sound in all its glory as part of the "Dead Heads"

Audio pioneer Harry F. Olson. He literally "wrote the book" about modern sound theory and applications.

"Olson's books taught legions of people the right way to think about and do things, by the simple technique of presenting the theory in the book and then building actual systems, even if they were one-offs," Ron Wickersham says. "He wouldn't just test one system; he'd do them in different sizes and say, 'Here's what the actual curves look like, and here's the theory that kind of suggests this.' Most of the books since then haven't been that instructive. This wasn't just speakers, either, but how to construct the whole sound system, how microphones worked, how the sound system interacts with the rest of the room. Actually we didn't even own a copy of Olson's book. I think it was out of print then, so John Curl borrowed a copy and then we had it photocopied and bound in Berkeley."

Again, though, the impetus comes back to Owsley's unflagging quality consciousness. "Bear would walk around the hall and listen everywhere and see what was working and how the sound was covering, and the like," Wickersham says. "He would buy gear that was expensive—exotic hi-fi kind of stuff, set it up, and either it would burn out because it couldn't take the signal levels, or maybe he didn't like the sound of it, so it would be discarded. He was always testing things, trying to find the next better step. We got into making speaker cabinets that were made out of this denser wood that would travel better and be more durable...

"Everything that went on in the sound system had to be paid attention to. He was hypercritical about building mic cables, how to coil up the mic cables; every detail. You respected every piece of gear. Bear designed some snake-cable standards that we used and even tried to promote out in the larger world, so different sound companies could pool gear for bigger gigs, and for a while had some success. He was always really into sharing ideas.

"[With the Wall of Sound] we got to the point where we wanted to take a big leap," Wickersham continues. "What do we have to do? Well, one thing was separating out instruments so they didn't get mixed together. Early on we realized, if you want to play [a system] really loud, you can't mix the stuff together and have it intermodulate. This destroys the clarity.

"There were so many problems to overcome. Bass sounds tubby in halls because it's contributing so much to the reverberant field that most of what you're hearing is the reverberation. The guy plays a note, stops the note on his bass, and about two notes later it dies. And often you can't hear bass well outside because it's being spread up into the sky. That led us back into Olson further. JBL said one thing, Altec said another, but basically what we learned was that we had to pay attention to the directivity at all the different frequencies. How do you achieve the directivity? You needed the long wavelength to launch the bass frequencies so they would not be going up to the ceiling of the concrete boxes, or up in the sky when you were outdoors, but instead were going straight back. The length of the [speaker] arrays at the frequency range they covered had to be scaled. [Don Buchla's] Banana speakers were a precursor of that idea," though, according to Bear, curved in the wrong direction.

On the issue of loudspeakers, Rick Turner says, "Harry Olson had done a lot of the calculations on point source versus line array and all that kind of stuff. My innovation in the Wall of Sound speaker-cabinet design was to calculate the cabinet dimensions so that the distances between the three pairs of walls were [multiples of] a third-octave apart in wavelength—the idea being to spread out any internal resonances in the cabinets. That theory has since been supplanted by other theories, like using the golden mean, but at the time it seemed like the right way to go. I drew up all the plans for the rectangular speaker cabinets. When it got into the curved front arrays [in the Wall], that was other people."

"Rick took what was in Olson's books and applied it to the parameters we wanted to do," Wickersham adds. "The thing you want to avoid at all costs is having one dimension that's twice another, because that will make a bigger [frequency] spike, so the response won't be as flat. With these boxes we made, we were also getting a better yield out of the pieces of wood. We used this high-grade [Finnish birch] plywood that we got from a place in Oakland. It had a lot of industrial uses, but nobody else was using it for speaker cabinets. And we were doing 14-ply, just to get something three-quarters of an inch thick. It was really durable, though. We'd had problems before with the corners [of speaker enclosures] breaking on tour."

Phil divided his time in 1974 between playing Big Brown (pictured here at the Reno show) and his new Alembic Mission Control bass (pictured in Chapter 11).

DEAD GEAR '73

It's fair to say that the Grateful Dead's sound system was always in a state of flux, but in 1973 the changes came fast and furious, though not all of them were successful. For instance, at the very first gig of the year, at Stanford University (south of San Francisco) there was a bit a of problem, as Dan Healy explained to me in a 1985 interview:

"Hometown gigs are where you experiment a lot because you're near the shop and so on, and you want to iron things out before you go on the road. On tour, typically, you take notes and notice, 'Well, this sucks,' and, 'That didn't work,' and when you come back you whip it together more. I had gone to the band in late '72 and gotten $10,000 or $12,000 to work on this idea I had. Now in '72 that was a lot of money, especially for the Grateful Dead. So I went out and got these special super-low-distortion [Electro-Voice] tweeters and all this other stuff. Just prior to that, the band had bought me this other piece of equipment, a real-time analyzer, which reads out the amplitudes of all the different musical notes. The upshot was that I equalized out the system and got it real flat, and then about three seconds into this Stanford show, the tweeters were so out of balance that they all just blew out. I smoked out $12,000 worth of speakers just like that! I thought, 'Oh, God!'—but I think the most that was said was, 'Nice going, asshole.'" (Ron Wickersham notes that this particular experiment was not related to the development of the Wall of Sound.)

Throughout 1973, the Dead's PA fluctuated in size depending on the venue they were playing, but it slowly got larger as the year went on. Around mid-year, *Guitar Player* magazine published an interview with Rick Turner that is, as far as I can tell, the first detailed technical look at the Dead's sound system. I managed to fill in some other gaps in this pre-Wall era thanks to a handwritten list in the Dead's own files, labeled "Equipment 1973."

For the musicians: Garcia "plays into a Fender Twin Reverb amp going to a McIntosh 2300 amp. This powers three Alembic B-12 speaker cabinets stacked on their sides, which provides a vertical column of speakers extending about eight feet in the air. They're stacked like this because we've found that it gives a much wider horizontal spread to the sound, with less spill going into the rafters."

Suggested listening: The two shows that make up Dick's Picks Vol. 28—*from Nebraska and Utah in late February 1973—are among my favorites from what most Deadheads agree was a great year for the band. Solid but spacy.*

Weir, who alternated between a Les Paul, an SG, and an ES-335, "plays into two rebuilt Twins, one of which powers a pair of Alembic B-12 cabinets, each with two JBL D-120s in it. He drives his extension speakers with McIntosh 2300 amps."

Phil "has six or eight Alembic B-15 cabinets, each containing two D-140 JBLs." Keith Godchaux's piano had two Countryman contact pickups on it, with half the signal going to the monitor system and half to the PA courtesy of two McIntosh 3500s. Billy was playing a Ludwig kit with a Rogers snare, Zildjian cymbals (16″ and 18″ crash; 21″ ride; 14″ hi-hat), all picked up by seven Electro-Voice RE-15s.

The monitors were a dozen A-12 "footlight" speakers, powered by four McIntosh 3500s and mixed through Ampex MX-10s. The main PA,

Turner said, was "a stereo system; the speakers on the left and the right sides are handled completely separately. In the [front of house] booth there are Ampex [MX-10] mixers, two [Altec] Acoustic-Voicette [graphic] equalizers, and a Nagra 2-track tape machine for recording the concert. Each side of the PA has a crossover network for feeding different amps. The crossover has an 18dB-per-octave slope drop-off, and it splits the signal into four parts.... Each of those then goes to a couple of McIntosh 2300s and from there as follows: For woofers [below 350Hz] there are 16 JBL 2215s on each side of the stage. The low midrange is run through 16 JBL 120s on each side. The high midrange goes into 32 JBL 2105s, which are 5″ speakers. For the highs we have 16 Electro-Voice T-350 horns."

"Why use so much gear?" the *Guitar Player* interviewer, Jim Aikin, asked. "It's not just for volume," Turner said. "Most groups could get three times as much volume as the Dead does, but that would be a distorted sound. Not that the Dead are quiet; the pressure onstage has been measured at 127dB, and that's *loud*. But it's all clean sound, not noise."

The Dead even addressed the issue of sound equipment in the "Dead Heads" newsletter that went out to everyone on the band's mailing list during this era. In a remarkably frank discussion of their growth, they revealed that 18 percent of the "Grateful Dead Dollar" went to equipment purchase and maintenance, and noted, "The physics of sound projection dictate that any given increase in the size of a hall requires exponential rate of increase in equipment capability to reach everyone in the hall with quality at volume," and then offered this little chart:

Year	Weight	Transport
1965	800 pounds	Bill's station wagon
1967	1,300 lbs.	Barney's van
1968	6,000 lbs.	Metro van
1970	10,000 lbs.	18-ft. truck
1973	30,000 lbs.	40-ft. semi

"Even before it developed to the full Wall of Sound," Ron Wickersham says today, "we'd gotten pretty good at doing the hi-fi aspect when it was still two-channel. In the intermission, people would actually sit and listen to [the recorded music playing] and applaud at the end of every song. At Winterland, the guys running the lights up top usually can't hear anything; it's just a jumble because they're up in the reverb area and all the main vocal stuff, which is directive, is below them. But they could suddenly hear fine. And at an outdoor gig, it could sound like you were in front of studio monitors, it was so clear. You could be really far away and though it was softer, it didn't sound like a scratchy transistor radio."

During much of 1973, Wickersham would travel to a venue the day before the band arrived, "and it was like we were building different sound systems for different rooms, which took a lot of design and calculating out how to get that directivity out of the gear we had. Sometimes we didn't know what would go into building the scaffolding for the stage until the equipment arrived. And different places had different problems. Like RFK stadium [where the Dead played two shows with the Allman Brothers in June 1973] could have been a disaster acoustically, but we figured out a way to actually tilt the [PA speaker] array so we didn't cover the troublesome back wall, and instead the sound went down into the audience area. We also had delay towers which delivered very clean sound to the outer reaches of the stadium." (Delay towers were also used effectively at Watkins Glen, shortly after the RFK shows; they were first used by the Dead at San Francisco's Kezar stadium in May '73.)

PHASE-CANCELING MICS

Another aspect of the Wall of Sound that was incorporated into the traveling system in the second half of 1973 was the use of phase-canceling complementary differential microphones. Turner explained the initial setup in the '73 *Guitar Player* interview: "Each of the four singers has a pair of Sennheiser microphones, mounted one above the other about three inches apart. They're hooked up out of phase, and this has the effect of canceling out the background noise. Any sound that goes equally into both mics disappears when the two signals are added together, so that all you have left is the sound of the voice, since the singer is only singing into one of them. This eliminates most of the feedback problem and cleans up the sound a great deal."

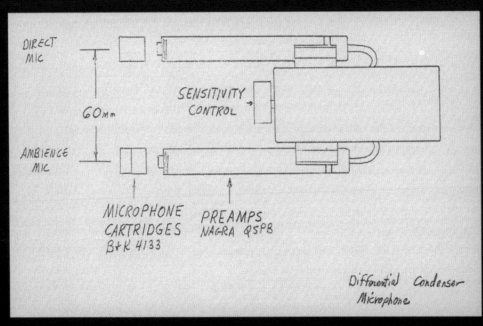

One of Ron Wickersham's diagrams outlining some of the specifics of the differential mics.

Though instituted at the behest of Owsley, who knew about them from his ham radio and commercial radio experience, this was another idea out of Olson, though he called it a di-pole microphone. However, Alembic brought it into the world of rock 'n' roll by adding a very important element: a solid-state amplification system for the differential mics, which was designed by John Curl. "Using a tube amp was not practical for what we were doing," Curl says. "I'd developed a transistor version, which other people also had in the late '60s, though we were all working independently. You can make solid-state like a tube circuit, but it will always have more distortion. So you have to use its intrinsic advantages. I started off with these FETs, which had come on the scene when I was first working at Alembic. So we were working on these really sophisticated circuits, and that's when I started working with Mark Levinson. He was commissioned by the Dead to build the circuits that I designed." (Actually, the prototypes were built by Curl and Wickersham; Levinson built the ones for the actual system. Today, Levinson is regarded as one of the pioneers of high-end amplifier design, though that reputation was built at least in part on work by Curl, Wickersham, and, later, John Meyer.) "The only way to get enough dynamic range—so we could be assured that we could be stone-quiet in the quiet times and yet handle these enormous peaks—was to design our own stuff," Wickersham says.

Curl explains some of the theory behind the amplifier circuit innovation: "The differential has been around for a long time—since the early '30s. Basically, when you hook together two devices so you have a plus and minus input, and they work together, it's called the differential connection. An op amp has differential inputs. A complementary differential is two differentials, but one is a complement of the other one—in other words, it's made of different materials [a P-channel and N-channel J-FET], so it actually works on the minus supply, while its opposite, its complement, works on the plus side. They are completely dependent on each other normally, but they add together down the line a bit and they cancel each other's distortion to a first order, because they're working in opposite phases, you might say. Then, when they tie together, you get a parallel but optimum through-path."

Though initially the mic system used Sennheiser microphones, by the time the full Wall of Sound was implemented in the spring of 1974, the Dead had switched to modified instrumentation microphones made by the famous Danish manufacturer Brüel & Kjær. (This is long before B&K made the popular pro-audio microphones so beloved by classical music engineers.) "Actually, John Curl showed B&K how to make laboratory microphone capsules have low enough noise," Wickersham says. "People assumed that when you made these smaller-diaphragm microphones that gave you honest documentary recording [which is why they were used as test mics], you had to suffer 'red' noise. But John Curl did the work at Alembic showing how there was a special class of noise that was caused by the bias resistors that brought up the polarization voltage. It was generated by the resistor itself, so we had to search out people who made resistors of higher resistance. They were encapsulated in these extremely rugged ceramic cylinders."

"We found that by just changing a couple of resistors, we could lower the noise by about 10dB," Curl adds. "In fact, Brüel & Kjær changed all of their microphones to my standard. I had to show them with my little Heathkit equipment," he laughs.

Depending on whom you talk to, it appears that another watershed event in the Wall of Sound's development occurred late on the fall 1973 tour. After the Dead's gig at the UCLA Pauley Pavilion that November, Bob Matthews talked to the band about an impending problem that would face the group when they played the tiny Boston Music Hall in a couple of weeks: Their stage setup, including the PA, was 85 feet wide, but the Music Hall stage was just 57 feet wide. However, he noted, now that the band was using the phase-canceling mics, they could increase the height of the system behind the band and eliminate the

At the Boston Music Hall on 11/30/73, the band's huge PA wouldn't fit on the theater's small stage, so for the first time the crew stacked all the speakers behind the band, foreshadowing the introduction of the Wall of Sound the following spring. *Dick's Picks Vol. 14* presents some of the best portions of the 11/30 and 12/2 Boston shows.

PHOTO: MARY ANN MEYER/GRATEFUL DEAD

side PA altogether. "Each element would have its column in the wall," Matthews says. "As for the design elements that went into the actual Wall, that wasn't me. That was Owsley and Healy and various other people."

Turner, too, remembers the Boston Music Hall episode. "The PA didn't fit, so we had to put it behind the band," he says. "Matthews was the guy promoting that idea, but it all goes back to that 1969 conversation with Bear saying the PA had to be behind the band. That's when we realized, 'We can do this! Now, what do we really want to do?'"

THIS IS A TEST

When the Dead convened at San Francisco's 12,000-seat Cow Palace at the end of March 1974 for a gig that was billed the Sound Test, Deadheads arriving for the show—myself included—could only gape in amazement at the sight that greeted them. Dwarfing the drum kit and grand piano already set up on the stage was a mass of scaffolding that held in place more than a dozen columns of stacked speakers of different kinds, ranging from clusters of 5″ Electro-Voice tweeters to 15″ JBL speakers—some 480 speakers in all, the highest of which were 45 feet above the stage. Each column of speakers was devoted to a different instrument (or, say, Garcia left, Garcia right; Lesh left, right), with the center cluster given over to vocals. This setup eliminated the need for separate monitor speakers for the musicians; indeed, they heard what the audience heard, and further, each player had control over his own volume. There was no traditional front-of-house mix position; rather, everything was handled onstage by the musicians and a busy crew devoted to attending to the musicians' needs.

Before that first show, Phil Lesh told the *San Francisco Chronicle* that the Wall of Sound "allows us to play super-loud without killing ourselves or frying those in the front—to get loud, clean sound at the back of the huge hall, and supreme musical control, because we run everything from the stage. For me, it's like piloting a flying saucer. Or riding your own sound wave." He should know. As Rick Turner says today, "With the Wall of Sound, Phil had two columns of 15″ speakers; each column had 18 D-140s driven by four McIntosh 2300s, each one driving nine loudspeakers. He could split off [his signal] so he had each string going through nine speakers. For chords and for special effects it was absolutely glorious!"

The system's clarity was truly astonishing—particularly the vocals, which had previously tended to get a little mushy in a conventional stereo PA system. Even so, Bear and the others came to believe that the B&K microphones were actually the weak link in the system: "This mic design caused a loss of low frequencies in the voice," Bear wrote in the liner notes for the 2002 Dick's Picks CD release of the Sound Test show (Vol. 24), "but it did limit spill quite nicely. Further development of the differential design might have eliminated the low-frequency loss."

Since the Cow Palace show was a "Test," it's not surprising some adjustments were made to the system before it formally went out on the road in mid May. In fact, even more speakers and amps were added, and Bear fashioned the center vocal cluster and side piano cluster into a honeycomb arrangement. "I personally designed and fabricated the piano cluster, a huge amount of work," Bear says. "Only a few bits of aluminum were welded; it was basically put together with rivets, screws, and glue. Hexcel made up the metal-skinned, kraft paper honeycomb-filled side panels to order. The larger vocal cluster was assembled of wood. That was built in our shop by Sparky Raizene to the same curved array/cluster concept."

(John Meyer, too, was somewhat involved in different aspects of the Wall's development. Early on, Bear had approached McCune Sound, where Meyer worked, about obtaining some matching AKG microphones for the differential pairs, but Meyer's research indicated they were not the appropriate mic for that sort of setup—"The charts were rather fictitious," he says. Later, when the Dead were complaining about how bass frequencies were getting lost in the upper reaches of Winterland's deep balcony, "I showed them, from Olson, that

The Wall goes up in Reno, Nevada, 5/12/74.

line arrays have a tendency to focus the sound, so there were two possibilities: You could make the line array go all the way up the ceiling, or you could curve it. So I gave Bear a design for this double-barrel-shaped thing, and they built it out of honeycomb or some expensive [material], and they loaded it with 60 E-V tweeters. [Bear] designed the barrel and the honeycomb, but it was definitely my concept for the curve." During the actual year of the Wall of Sound, 1974, Meyer and John Curl were both off in Montreux, Switzerland, at the Institute for Advanced Musical Studies, where Meyer did research on audio-transducer technology and phase-correction techniques, worked on a modular loudspeaker system, and also learned as much as he could about mastering.)

What kept the ever-growing sound and roadie crew working night and day for weeks, though, was putting together an entire *second* Wall of Sound system. The Wall was such a leviathan that it required a two-day setup (including the day of the show), and the only way the Dead could schedule a normal tour was to have one system heading for the next city on a tour so it could be set up while the other one was in use. That's a lot of speakers and amps and scaffolding, not to mention the crew to transport it and set it up. Though this practice of leapfrogging systems became common in rock 'n' roll for big tours in the '80s and '90s, it was radical at the time. "I think that whole system fit into two semis and an 18-foot," Rick Turner says, "but that's nothing compared to what I saw on the road with Fleetwood Mac last year. Now people are going out with eight and nine semis—but in the '70s everyone thought we were completely crazy."

Actually building the Wall of Sound was a long and painstaking process that involved many people. Here, crew member Sparky Raizene (with the long hair) supervises the building of part of the vocal cluster; and in the machine shop, part of that cluster in its very early stages.

Not to be overlooked in the discussion of the Wall, too, was the ultra-sturdy construction of the speaker cabinets, which truly set a standard that the SR industry could not ignore. Dan Healy: "I have to say that the Alembic and Grateful Dead cabinet shop holds the record for the finest cabinets ever made. One of the problems with the earlier speakers, the Altecs and RCAs, is [the manufacturers] didn't understand the importance of the rigidity of the cabinets—how solid they are. We developed this test where we'd synchronize a strobe light with an oscillator that we would feed into the cabinet; then you could phase-shift it so you could see the waveform coming through the speaker, and you could see these Altec speakers would bow out four or five inches on the sides. What that meant is the cabinet was costing serious efficiency. So that's how we came to understand that one of the fundamentals is you need rock-solid cabinets. That's why we started using 14-ply birchwood, which eventually went into the Wall of Sound and which John Meyer uses to this day in his speakers. That was a concept Joe Winslow and some of the other guys who designed equipment for the Dead came up with."

THE DEAD ON MARS

Before the spring/summer '74 tour hit the road, however, the Dead went into the studio to quickly record a new album, this time working at CBS Studios on San Francisco's Folsom Street. CBS was another relatively new player in the area, having officially opened in March 1971 in one of Coast Recorders' old spaces. The move to San Francisco was spearheaded by two veteran CBS-New York engineers, Roy Segal and Roy Halee; the former had already worked with such Bay Area-based CBS acts as Big Brother & the Holding Company and Sly & the Family Stone, and the latter was acclaimed for his work with Simon & Garfunkel. The duo equipped the studio with a custom 36-input console that had been in one of the company's New York studios, the best tube compressor/limiters and EQs, a fantastic selection of Neumann M49s, U67s, and KM-84s, various AKG and Shure mics, and 3M 16-tracks.

The impetus to record at CBS apparently came from Garcia. When Paul Simon had come to San Francisco in 1972 to work on a solo album with Halee (in part to give a shot in the arm to the new studio), Garcia and Simon became friendly, and in the process Garcia got to know both Halee and Segal. (When Halee brought Art Garfunkel to town to work on *his* solo album, Halee even brought in Garcia to play on a track.) "I always got along very well with Jerry," Segal, who died in 2005, told me in 1996. "He's the reason the Dead recorded [at CBS]. He liked the studio and thought it had a good sound, which it did. It had a more 'live' sound than some of the other rooms around at that time," such as the Record Plant, for example.

The Grateful Dead From the Mars Hotel was recorded in just over three weeks. "They had played most of the material live before they came in, so they were pretty tight," Segal said. "In fact, *surprisingly* tight," he laughed. The Hunter-Garcia tunes "Loose Lucy" and "China Doll" had been in the repertoire for over a year, and "U.S. Blues" had evolved from an earlier song called "Wave That Flag." But "Ship of Fools" and "Scarlet Begonias" (which musically had been inspired somewhat by Paul Simon, Garcia said) had just been introduced, respectively at Winterland in February and at the Sound Test. The other songs, including two by Phil Lesh—the convoluted epic "Unbroken Chain" and the country-ish "Pride of Cucamonga"—and Bob Weir's "Money Money," were developed in the studio. Segal remembered "Unbroken Chain" as being "very difficult; we worked on it in sections. Still, it came out very well." Garcia's

Track sheet for "Scarlet Begonias," recorded 3/30/74 at CBS Studios. Courtesy of Steve Brown.

This reel box from the Mars Hotel sessions shows the original titles of "U.S. Blues" and "Money Money."

CBS RECORDS RECORDING STUDIOS TAPE DATA SHEET					NOTE: Complete this form. Secure to box containing tape described hereon.	

CBS RECORDS RECORDING STUDIOS TAPE DATA SHEET

NOTE: Complete this form. Secure to box containing tape described hereon.

PROJECT NUMBER | STUDIO A | JOB NUMBER 105697 | REEL TWO ONE | SPEED 30 ips

DATE | SHEET NUMBER | PROGRAM Grateful Dead | MONO | 8 TRACK

☐ NEW YORK ☐ CHICAGO | CLIENT Grateful Dead Records | ☐ 2 TRACK ☒ 16 TRACK

☐ HOLLYWOOD ☒ SAN FRAN. | PRODUCER | ☐ 3 TRACK ☐ DOLBY

☐ NASHVILLE OTHER | CO. ENG. | RE. ENG. RS/MPF | ☐ 4 TRACK OTHER

TIME	MASTER NUMBER	Reel 2 PROGRAM TITLE	TAKE NO.	CODES	TIME MARK
4:40	4/16/74	U.S. GREYS	11	C	
		REEL #3			
	4/16/74	FINANCE BLUES	7	C	
		REEL #4			
✓	4/16/74	FINANCE BLUES missed kick piano over	11	C	bass end of 2nd verse—missed
	4/16/74	" "	12	C	
		REEL #5			
	4/16/74	UNBROKEN CHAIN			
	~~4/16/74 UNBROKEN CHAIN~~				

** TIME START AT MARK 000,00   ☐ FILE ☐ HOLD ☐ PICK UP ☐ SHIP

* CODES: ✓ = FALSE START, b = SHORT FALSE START, B = LONG FALSE START, C = COMPLETE TAKE, ©= MASTER

CR 724 REV 6/71

memories of the sessions were mostly rosy. He liked Segal, whom he called "Uncle Roy," and felt the record captured those songs fairly well. For his part, Segal enjoyed the Dead, and he even forgave them for spiking one of his drinks with a mild dose of LSD.

There weren't as many musical guests as there had been on *Wake of the Flood*—just Clover's John McFee on pedal-steel guitar for "Pride of Cucamonga" (Garcia having given up the pedal steel by then), and Ned Lagin on synthesizer on "Unbroken Chain." At many 1974 Dead concerts Lagin and Lesh would perform an interlude of electronic music—bass and synth—in between the Dead's two sets. It wasn't to everyone's taste, of course, but it was adventurous in the extreme and really put the Wall of Sound through its paces. Alas, little of the Lesh-Lagin music has been included on the multitude of '74 releases to emerge from the Dead's vaults (but it's commonly available among regular Grateful Dead disc traders).

The Wall of Sound began its road tour in mid May with a gig at an outdoor stadium at the University of Reno. The system drew rave reviews, of course—that

The "Mars Hotel" was a run-down building near the San Francisco studio where the album was recorded.

GRATEFUL DEAD FROM THE MARS HOTEL

happened *everywhere*—but there was at least one less-than-happy camper that day: Bill Kreutzmann.

The Hollywood Bowl concert 7/21/74 represents the apex of the Wall of Sound system.

"It was really hard to hear because there was so much sound pressure coming off all these speakers," he says. "The very first day in Reno, too, it was sort of windy, and the whole center cluster was blowing around—not a lot, but enough, and I had to sit underneath it. At first they had the drums right underneath it and you couldn't hear anything. It was like being in a tunnel with a bunch of hot-rod cars roaring on both sides of you. You were supposed to have some monitors that were going to help—ha-ha-ha. It was not my favorite time. They had done the phase-canceling microphones, and those sounded terrible. Things can look good on paper but not be so great in reality."

By the time the tour hit the Hollywood Bowl that June, the system had grown a little more and had been tweaked in various areas. The "Dead Heads" newsletter included a diagram of the Hollywood Bowl setup, a breakdown of the entire system, and this cogent explanation: "The sound system is actually a combination of six individual systems, each being electronically separate and having a specific purpose and function. No two musical 'voices' go through the same system. Thus the vocals, piano, drums, lead guitar, rhythm guitar, and bass each have their own channel(s) of amplification. This separation is designed to produce an undistorted sound, a clean sound in which qualities like 'transparency,' 'brilliance,' 'presence,' and 'clarity' are substantial musical dimensions."

SIX INDEPENDENT SOUND SYSTEMS

System	Number of Channels	Number of Amplifiers	Number of Speakers :	15"	12"	5"	Tweeters
1. Vocals	1	19	226 :	16	60	120	30
2. Lead Guitar	1	1	20 :		20		
3. Rhythm Guitar	1	1	20 :		20		
4. Piano	1	8	128 :	16	32	80	
5. Bass	4*	4	36 :	36			
6. Drums	3	10	120 :	16	20	60	24
Vocal fill		2	64 :		16	48	
Instrument fill		3	27 :	5	10	12	
Totals	11	48	641 :	89	178	320	54

* 4 in quad or 2 in stereo

THE VOCAL SYSTEM

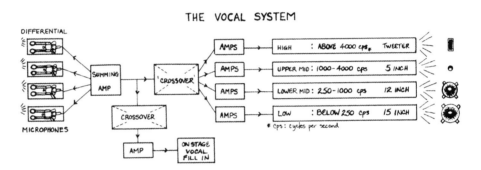

The 15″, 12″, and 5″ speakers were all JBLs, the tweeters Electro-Voice. The speakers were driven by Mac 2300s. The newsletter noted, "Our whole system operates on 26,400 watts of continuous (RMS) power, producing in the open air quite an acceptable sound at a quarter-mile, and fine sound up to five or six hundred feet, where it begins to be distorted by wind."

The Wall traveled far and wide that year, hitting out-of-the-way spots like Iowa, Montana, and Vancouver, British Columbia, as well as tried-and-true spots in the East, Midwest, and South, and in mid September, seven shows in Europe—three each in England and France and one in Germany. Bringing the Wall over to Europe was a huge and expensive undertaking, of course, and the band actually lost money on the venture.

In a 1988 *Guitar Player* article, Steve Parish described a typical day in the life of the Wall: "We'd start at 8 AM, and it would take two hours just to get all the equipment onto the stage. By noon we'd have the speakers stacked and we'd take a half-hour for lunch. Then we'd wire it and get all the amps running by 4 PM for the soundcheck. The show would start around 8 PM, and in those days the band would play until 1 AM. We left the hall around 4 AM. The next day we'd travel all night and start again." (Further complicating matters were occasional afternoon shows.)

Interestingly, Phil did not play the Mission Control bass at every show; evidently some small things had to be ironed out, so Big Brown still got a workout from time to time in '74. It was during that year, however, that a very important guest came to a Dead show and checked out Phil's new Alembic bass: "I called up Les Paul and invited him to a gig, and amazingly enough, he showed up," says Rick Turner. "Phil had the Mission Control bass, and I popped the back off and showed it to Les, and he was just gleeful; he was pretty blown away. He loved that we were doing all these high-tech things."

By the time of the Europe shows, though, it was becoming clear that for all its sonic advantages, the Wall of Sound was becoming a lead weight around the band's neck. The huge workforce needed to move it, run it, and maintain it was effectively negating the "extra" income the group was making by playing larger venues. It required *constant* upkeep on so many levels, from replacing banks of 5″ speakers that would fizzle with alarming regularity to being vigilant about the mountains of McIntosh amps being trucked from city to city. That the Wall hit the road during the Great Oil Crisis of 1974, which sent gas prices skyrocketing, didn't help matters. Neither did the fact that so many people involved on either side of the stacks were abusing copious amounts of cocaine during this period—not good for bank accounts or people's moods.

Suggested listening: The Wall of Sound year produced many excellent shows, including those captured on *Dick's Picks Vol. 7* (London, September '74) and, especially, The 5-CD *Grateful Dead Movie Soundtrack* (Winterland, October '74), which came out in conjunction with the DVD release of the *Dead Movie* in 2005.

But beyond that, some very fundamental questions were looming for the band: Has it all gotten *too* big? Is playing in stadiums really the best thing for the Grateful Dead? Do we really have to support the *dozens* of people now part of the Dead touring machine for the rest of time?

The answer they came up with was to shut the mutha down. The band canceled a proposed fall '74 tour and instead played five "final" shows at Winterland in October—filmed by a professional crew for an eventual concert movie—and then began a hiatus. There would be plenty of action during the year and a half the Dead stayed off the road—solo albums, tours by various club band offshoots, etc.—but it was the end of the road for the Wall of Sound.

"It was an experiment," Dan Healy said a decade later. "It was magnificent in its glory, and I loved every second of it—though at the same time I'm so damn glad it's gone!"

It's probably appropriate to give the last word to Bear, however: "I still consider it the best large-venue live sound performance system that has ever existed," he says. "I have a better design now, but I doubt it will ever be realized."

Dare to dream, Bear.

WHAT HIATUS?

WITH the hindsight of history, it's easy to talk about the Dead's 20-month hiatus from regular touring as a finite chunk of time, with a beginning, middle, and end, and various points of interest along the way. But when it started at the end of October 1974, Deadheads didn't really know when or if their heroes would be back. Knowing that there were going to be a variety of solo projects coming out didn't exactly soften the blow—after all, how many times had bands broken up once their members got the itch to "go solo"? Who knew whether, when it came time to record the Dead's next album, they would even want to?

Chapter Ten
1975

As it turned out, it really *was* just a hiatus from Grateful Dead touring, and nobody was sitting around idly. *Au contraire*—it was a time of great activity in many directions, especially for Garcia and Weir. And, just for good measure, every few months the Dead would come back for a one-off gig: There were four during 1975.

The onset of the hiatus did mark the end of the Wall of Sound. It led to the layoff of a number of crew members and equipment builders, as the organization adapted to life *not* on the road. This effectively ended Alembic's sound-reinforcement association with the Dead; in fact, it all but ended Alembic's involvement in that field altogether. In April 1974, Alembic had sold its interest in the Brady Street studio to a former New York-based engineer/producer named Elliot Mazer, who renamed the facility His Masters Wheels. The retail part of the Brady Street operation was sold to an outfit known as Stars Guitars. At that point, the Wickershams moved the whole operation to a renovated barn on some property they bought in the small, rustic town of Sebastopol, in Sonoma County. The part of Alembic that was booming at the time was its musical-instrument division: After an article about Alembic appeared in *Rolling Stone*, an Oregon-based instrument distributor called L.D. Heater placed an order for 50 Alembic guitars, and this helped the company through what was shaping up as a very rocky transition period. Word of mouth on Alembic instruments was so good that slowly but surely the company managed to build a faithful clientele. In the late '70s, Rick Turner and the Wickershams parted ways; Turner went on to start his own eponymous instrument company, while Ron and Susan Wickersham kept the Alembic name and have continued building distinctive handmade guitars and basses, as well as preamps, from their headquarters in Santa Rosa.

What became of the thousands of pieces that made up the Wall of Sound? The Dead kept some of them, other parts were sold, and, as Healy told me in 1985, "we ended up giving most of it away. There are probably 25 little bands running around that got outfitted by that system." Crew member Joe Winslow, electronics ace John Cutler, and some of the other people who had worked for the Dead building speakers and such for the Wall of Sound formed their own company, Hard Truckers. They would supply the Dead with speaker cabinets and other gear for many years to come.

Bob Weir was a busy guy on many fronts. A month after the Dead's final gig at Winterland, he joined a club band called Kingfish, which featured former New Riders bassist Dave Torbert, drummer Chris Herold, harmonica ace Matthew Kelly, and a remarkable young lead guitarist—who had obviously been heavily influenced by Garcia—named Robbie Hoddinott. During 1975 they played about three dozen shows in California and East Coast clubs, small theaters, and a few larger venues. Always a high-energy act, their repertoire consisted of a few originals and a truck-load of covers ranging from Marty

Robbins's "Big Iron" and Marvin Gaye's "Shop Around" to Johnny Horton's "The Battle of New Orleans" and the Coasters' "Youngblood"—an eclectic brew to say the least.

On the home front—literally—Weir had a recording studio built in a space above his garage, just steps away from his lovely Mill Valley A-frame home on the woody slopes of Mt. Tamalpais. This is where the Dead would record their next studio album, *Blues for Allah*, beginning in June 1975.

Work on what was originally designed to be a fairly modest but technologically sophisticated rehearsal studio actually began a while before the Dead started recording *Wake of the Flood* in August 1973. Weir tapped Stephen Barncard, who had recorded *American Beauty*, to set up the studio and build a custom console for the unusually shaped "treehouse" room. The studio would take the nickname of its owner: Everyone called it "Ace's."

"I had never built an entire console before," Barncard says, "though I knew how to do it. I had been inside the Heider consoles and knew I could do it as well as that. There was a company in L.A. called Op Amp Labs that made these little modules that you could string together for a console, rather than hooking up transistors, which really freaked me out; I didn't like working with individual transistors. These building blocks [were] called op amps...you could build equalizers and mic preamps and all this system stuff. And I already knew how to solder. I used the API-module width as a standard, and then I laid out modules in cans of eight. The reason I didn't want to get a commercial console is

LEFT: Garcia, Weir and Lesh recording *Blues for Allah* at Bob's new home studio.

BELOW: The custom console in Weir's studio was built from the ground up by Stephen Barncard and various craftsmen.

PHOTO: STEPHEN BARNCARD

they're big and expensive, and this was a triangular-shaped control room, so all the cabinetry had to be done custom because the shapes were so weird. In those days, there was no semi-pro market like there is today, so you either bought an expensive console or you built your own.

"I designed it piece by piece, starting with schematics, and I hired a bunch of my friends to work on different parts of it," Barncard continues. "It was really interesting—there must be five or six people who at that point in their lives had no idea what they were going to do, but this project got them on the road to doing something cool. Two of them ended up at Industrial Light & Magic: Michael McKenzie, who's a major dude in special effects—he was one of my wiring guys; and Robert Poor had a background at the Stanford Artificial Intelligence Laboratory, which also produced Andy Moorer [of Sonic Solutions fame]. Then there was this other guy named Odis Schmidt, who was a sculptor and artist and had never done woodwork. However, he really wanted to make the cabinetry, so he did, and he made this beautiful redwood cabinet. We ended up making a wooden console; it even had veneer on the surface of the panels. I bought up [S.F. retailer] Zack Electronics' entire stock of these RCA-console-type knobs from BIZ."

Another artisan who got a boost from the project was Robbie Taylor, a silversmith. "I hired him to be my soldering guy," Barncard says. "We worked side by side for almost two years. Later he became a great assistant engineer and eventually became a road manager, and he was with the Dead until the end." (And beyond: He's been a crew chief on many post-Grateful Dead tours.)

"The first recorder we bought was this nice Scully 8-track which had been in Quimby Studios in Muscle Shoals—they'd recorded Wilson Pickett and various other people on it. I actually flew to Alabama [to buy it], and I had it shipped back, but the studio wasn't ready for it, so I ended up keeping the 8-track in a San Rafael warehouse. Right when we were about to bring the 8-track in there and open the rehearsal room, Bob said, 'Uh, actually we really want to expand and make it 16-track. I'm going to buy a Stephens 16-track and the Grateful Dead are coming in to record in four or five months.' This was the beginning, of course, of *Blues for Allah*, which was recorded entirely on my console.

"So this was phase two, and I hired more people and got rid of the rotary faders and got some API light-up faders and built a new monitor panel." Fortunately, too, the module design allowed for the console's expansion.

"Around this time Dan Healy came along, and he helped out finishing some things in the studio," Barncard says. "He had been hanging out with [Carl] Countryman and suggested some op-amp circuits using monolithics. We chained together a bunch of preamp cards, and we made the deadline! That console sounded really kick-ass."

"Actually I did a fair amount of the design work on the board, too," Weir adds. "At one point I could actually read a circuit and all that. I couldn't do it now, of course, and electronics is a lot different now—I don't have the time to put into learning digital electronics. I've lost what little knowledge I had. Anyway, we were trying to do Class A circuitry."

"ALLAH" AT ACE'S

Barncard originally believed he was going to get the engineering gig to work on *Blues for Allah*, but Healy's presence changed that. When Barncard appealed to Weir, the guitarist suggested that he and Healy work on the record together—which they did for about two weeks, before Barncard departed for L.A. and a good gig at the Village Recorder, where his buddies David Crosby and Graham Nash were starting work on a new album. "Maybe I should have tried to be the producer on it," Barncard says, "with Dan engineering. But it worked out okay—I liked working down in L.A., too."

The *Blues for Allah* sessions were completely different from any the band had experienced before. Part of it was the setting—a casual, sylvan environment where they didn't have to worry about watching the clock and racking up huge sums for studio time. But also, the group's approach to the material was unique: Rather than polishing songs that had already been played out on the road, they agreed to come in with a completely blank slate and start from scratch, building the songs in the studio.

"In fact, we kind of made a ground rule: Let's make a record where we get together every day and we don't bring anything in," Garcia told me in 1991. "The whole idea was to get back to the band thing, where the band makes the main contribution to the evolution of the material. So we'd go into the studio, we'd jam for a while, and then if something nice turned up we'd say, 'Well, let's preserve this little hunk and work with it—see if we can't do something with it.' And that's how we did most of that album. What became 'Crazy Fingers' originally had a hard rock 'n' roll feel; it was completely different. A lot [of the songs] went through metamorphoses that normally would take quite a long time. We sort of forced them through."

The result of all this studio experimentation was an album that was at once jammier than their previous few studio records, yet also quite intricate and arranged in places. Stylistically it felt like *new* music: The triumvirate of "Help on the Way," "Slipknot," and

The sessions for *Blues for Allah* at Weir's studio found the group improvising extensively as a way of formulating the album's songs. The result is one of the Dead's most different-sounding and original albums.

"Franklin's Tower" moved from angular riffing to abstract explorations to gently rhythmic bopping without ever falling into any classic Grateful Dead style. There was some Latin flavor to the instrumental "Stronger Than Dirt," a nod to Bach in Weir's "Sage and Spirit," and the album's strange centerpiece, the title track, "was another totally experimental thing I tried to do," Garcia said. "In terms of the melody and the phrasing and all, it was not of this world. It's not in any key and it's not in any time. And the line lengths are all different."

Healy managed to achieve a tight, intimate feel in the recording; some of it is surely a product of the group playing in a small room that could barely contain their ideas and their energy. There's very little ambience; it's as if we're in a living room with the group—which isn't that far off from the truth. Commercial it wasn't, and of course in that classic Dead way, all of the album's songs grew and developed further once the group started performing them live with some regularity when they went back on the road in the spring of '76 (save for "Blues for Allah," which remained a studio curiosity for the most part). But the album was well received anyway, and a couple of tunes—"Franklin's Tower" and Weir's "The Music Never Stopped"—garnered decent FM radio airplay. By the time *Blues for Allah* was released in the late summer of '75, the band had decided to end their noble attempt at being a full-service record company and signed a distribution deal with United Artists—not exactly an industry powerhouse, but not in-house either, which was the point.

WEIR DISCOVERS IBANEZ

If Bob Weir's playing sounded a little different on *Blues for Allah*, it's because for the first time in a number of years, he wasn't playing a Gibson guitar. All during the Wall of Sound year (1974) he had been playing a brown and gold sunburst Gibson 335, and with Kingfish that fall he briefly switched back to a Gibson SG. Then he made a big switch: He began a long association with Ibanez guitars and for the next eight years played custom axes that he helped design.

Though the name sounds Spanish, Ibanez is a Japanese corporation, one of the first to gain a foothold with American consumers. It dates back to 1908, when the Hoshino Gakki company of Nagoya, Japan, began distributing musical instruments. In the mid '30s it started manufacturing its own guitars and other stringed instruments, but the company had little profile outside of Japan. The story jumps to America in the 1960s when a Philadelphia-area music store owner named Harry Rosenbloom, who had founded the Elger Company to make and sell guitars, decided to stop making instruments and instead became the North American distributor for Hoshino Gakki's guitars. Knowing that Japanese guitars were not looked upon very favorably at the time, the company changed the name of its American division to Ibanez USA, after a line of Spanish guitars it distributed.

One of Ibanez's early hires was a young musician named Jeff Hasselberger. As he puts it, he had been "born and raised in the shadow of the Capitol Theatre" in Passaic, New Jersey, and had worked in a music store in Ardmore, outside of Philadelphia, before being hired by Rosenbloom to build and repair guitars. At the time, Ibanez was mostly making copies of Stratocasters, Les Pauls, and Rickenbackers—decent ones, actually, but knock-offs nonetheless.

"When I went to work for Ibanez," Hasselberger says, "I could see that they were very capable of building a really good instrument; it's just that they didn't have a clue of what kind to do. This was sort of at the beginning of the whole copy business, although Ibanez wasn't the first company to knock-off American guitars. Actually, before that, the Japanese were building their own designs, but a lot of them were quite bizarre and they didn't sell very well—although oddly enough, some of them are collector's items today. So at some point somebody made the suggestion to knock-off Stratocasters and Les Pauls. I think the first instrument I came into contact with was the Univox from the company that became Korg, on Long Island. I had some old Les Pauls myself, so I started to incorporate some of my experience with those guitars into the ones I was making, but I was always hoping we could get into some more original designs. We were all young guitar freaks who were maybe a little embarrassed to be working for a Japanese company, and we wanted to turn it into something legitimate, although we didn't have a clue how to do that in the beginning."

A meeting with Bob Weir gave him the chance to do just that. "On the Dead's last tour with the [Wall of Sound], one of the guys who worked in the [Ibanez] shop, Jim Fisher, was a real Deadhead, and he said we should go down and see them at the Philly Civic Center," Hasselberger recalls. "I'd never seen them before, never really paid much attention to them. We were starting to make some of our own designs, and we were also copying one-off guitars. John McLaughlin [of the Mahavishnu Orchestra] had this great doubleneck guitar that Rex Bogue made. I had contacted Rex, who was kind of like a surfer/skateboard dude out in Glendale [California], and asked him if we could rip off his guitar design for that doubleneck guitar, and he said sure; he was flattered. So we made a copy of that, and it was probably the most expensive guitar we'd ever made at that point. Anyway, somehow Jim Fisher got us into the Dead show early, and we ran into Bob and Jerry and the rest of the gang, and Bob and I hit it off immediately.

"It turned out that Bob was like a fountain of ideas when it came to guitars. I caught the sense that he was looking for somebody to take those ideas and run with them. So we showed him the Rex Bogue doubleneck guitar [copy], and he played it through the system after the show. He was pretty fascinated by the whole concept, so he asked if we could make a single-neck guitar—he had no use for a doubleneck—but take the shape and do this or that with it,

Bob Weir's association with Ibanez was mutually beneficial. He got guitars that he loved and Ibanez got a celebrity endorser. Here he is on the cover of the company's 1978 catalog.

Bob playing one of his prettiest Ibanez axes, at Oakland Stadium, October 1976. Jerry has his Travis Bean, and Phil the Alembic "Mission Control" bass.

'and I always wanted to have a sliding pickup that I could move in increments.' So we agreed to build him a guitar. I think we both understood that it wasn't going to be just one guitar and that would be the end; it was going to be an ongoing thing. Of course I was really excited to have a guy of Bob's stature buy into an idea like that, and I think he was thrilled to have somebody make the offer."

Was Weir dissatisfied with the 335? Hasselberger offers, "He thought the tone was a little too dark, which is true—it's a thick-sounding guitar, very good for soloing and all, but in the context of the Dead he needed something with a little more cut and a little more top end and clarity."

When it came to pickups, Hasselberger says, "Bob liked the thickness of the sound of [the Gibson] humbuckers, but he also wanted a little of that clarity and top end that Jerry was getting from the single-coil, so I said, 'There's no law that says you can't put some of each on the same guitar, and then we can devise a switching situation where you can use them in any combination." This had been done before on a thinline Fender Telecaster, but it certainly wasn't common. "So with that guitar we took the double humbucking concept, which Bob was familiar with, and we made a movable Stratocaster-type single-coil pickup that could be placed anywhere in between those two. There was three and a half inches of space between the two humbuckers, and it was a matter of figuring out a way to make the pickup slide in there." The guitar body was made of ash, and the maple neck was modeled somewhat after the 335 neck.

That blonde Ibanez custom was Weir's axe of choice when the Grateful Dead made their first hiatus appearance in the spring of '75 at a benefit concert at San Francisco's Kezar Stadium. And it's the guitar he used for most of the *Blues for Allah* recording—although the second iteration of that design, with a slightly different neck and a few other tweaks, arrived toward the end of those sessions and also made it onto the finished record. As Hasselberger predicted, it would be an ongoing relationship that would cover many years and encompass several different Ibanez guitars, as well some other pieces of gear, as we'll see shortly.

THE GARCIA FRONT

Meanwhile, Garcia was working almost non-stop during 1975. Besides working on *Blues for Allah*, he toured incessantly with the latest incarnations of his solo group: The jazzy lineup with Merl Saunders, John Kahn, Elvis drummer Ron Tutt, and reeds player Martin Fierro finally got a name, Legion of Mary; by the fall, however, he'd dropped Saunders and Fierro and hired British piano ace Nicky Hopkins in the first group to carry the Jerry Garcia Band moniker. Garcia helped Keith and Donna make their lone solo album, which was largely recorded at the couple's house in Stinson Beach, Marin County, using a Neve console that Bob Matthews installed in their basement. Jerry (and scads of other top S.F.-scene singers and musicians) played on the very strange record of "electronic cybernetic biomusic" by Ned Lagin called *Seastones*. He played some guitar on the superb album by the Diga Rhythm Devils, an ensemble of percussionists from different cultures spearheaded by Mickey Hart, who was also formally welcomed back to the Dead fold during this period. And Garcia produced a bluegrass album called *Pistol Packin' Mama* by the Good Ol' Boys—Chubby Wise, Don Reno, and Frank Wakefield. All were Round Records releases, as was an Old & In The Way live album, culled from Owsley's wonderful stereo tapes of a 1973 performance by the short-lived group.

The other project that took a lot of Garcia's time was the Grateful Dead movie, filmed over the final five-night run at Winterland before the hiatus. Nine camera crews—some veterans from *Woodstock*, *Gimme Shelter*, and other top rock films—captured every note onstage and dozens of hours offstage, too: the setup, Deadheads waiting in line, vendors in the hall, folks boogying during the show, the whole gamut. Garcia was the director, and he became intimately involved with every aspect of the post-production, which was done at a house in Mill Valley (dubbed the "Film House") with editor Susan Crutcher leading a small crew. The first order of business was syncing up the hundreds of hours of footage to an audio track; then came the long and difficult job of choosing what to include and what to leave on the cutting-room floor.

At the Dead's Kezar Stadium benefit concert appearance that spring, a new tube amplifier showed up amidst Jerry gear: a Mesa Boogie Mark 1. Mesa was another Northern California company with humble origins: Founder Randall Smith started out in the late '60s hot-rodding little Fender Princeton amps by putting in a circuit for a 4×10 tweed Bassman. "The trick," Smith wrote in his informal history of the company, "was to get all the high-power electronics, big transformers, and a JBL 12 built reliably inside a package that was intended to house a 10″ speaker and produce 12 watts! But it was worth the

Suggested listening: To celebrate the release of *Blues for Allah*, the Dead played a rare club gig in San Francisco at the Great American Music Hall on August 13, 1975. The show was broadcast on the radio nationwide, and in the late '80s it was remixed by Dan Healy and released as *One From the Vault*—definitely a keeper!

The Grateful Dead ®

cordially invite you

to a

rare and important musical performance

at

The Great American Music Hall

859 O'Farrell Street

Date: August 13, 1975   Time: 9:00 p.m.

This invitation admits one

effort. The quote from one of the hottest local guitar slingers, Carlos Santana, was, 'Man, that little thing really boogies!' Thus the name was born." In fact, that amplifier (originally called the Super 60) became an integral part of Santana's sound and helped launch the company, which quickly became known for its powerful, compact amps. The Mark 1 had two channels—one clean (some have compared it to a classic Fender amp sound), the other high-gain (the overdriven sound Santana liked best). Garcia played through a single Mark 1 throughout 1975, but by mid '76 he had two onstage, as did Weir. In the fall of 1976, however, Garcia goes to a dual Twin Reverb head setup, housed together in a Twin combo cabinet.

Garcia also switched guitars during the second half of 1975—a somewhat surprising move, as he had expressed no real dissatisfaction with the Irwin "Wolf" guitar. Apparently, however, a new kind of axe caught his eye, and he fell in love with it: a Travis Bean guitar.

Originally a motorcycle racer, Travis Bean got into the musical-instrument business in the early '70s after he was injured and could no longer ride competitively. While working at a Burbank music store he met Marc McElwee, who did repairs. "Doing guitar repairs over the years, Marc built a couple of guitars himself, and at the same time my interest in playing was starting,"

The Travis Bean aluminum-necked guitar was the only electric guitar Garcia ever formally endorsed, as shown by this ad from the March 1976 issue of *BAM* magazine.

Bean told *Vintage Guitar*'s Willie G. Mosely in a 1999 interview. "I had a natural tendency to tinker, so I decided to build a guitar; I got a couple of Gibson [humbucking] pickups from the store....

"I'd spent hours watching Marc fiddling with necks and adjusting them, and in my simple and naïve way of looking at things, I said, 'I can solve that.' I had very little experience in metalworking, but I knew wood backwards and forward, and I didn't want to implant a trussrod into a piece of wood, so I literally whittled the neck out of a piece of aluminum. That's how it started: I was trying to fix some problems in a completely naïve way, but once we got down the road a ways and the thing worked, the lesson of not knowing enough not to do it wasn't lost on me," he laughed. "Being hung up by convention is really stifling for me." It should be noted that, Bean was not the first person to experiment with aluminum as a neck material, but in 1974 he did become the first to make a production model that way. The thinking, of course, was that wood was both a more flexible and absorptive material than aluminum. As a 1978 Travis Bean brochure noted, "The ideal material is durable enough not to warp, twist, or break, but is resonant enough so that just the pure string tone without coloration is produced."

Garcia's first Bean was a model 1000A, the body of which was made of carved koa wood painted white. The single-piece forged (Reynolds) aluminum neck ran from the headstock (with its distinctive hollowed "T" design) down through part of the body to the bridge, which mounted onto the neck itself. So did the pickups, which in that guitar were a pair of Alnico-magnet humbuckers. The company literature also crowed that "we've hollowed out the base of the Travis Bean neck assembly and tapered it to form a chassis for the length of the string. It is this patented chassis that makes the Travis Bean guitar what it is—an instrument that has become the most dramatic breakthrough in electric guitar technology in 50 years." Well, what's a little hyperbole between friends?

At a free concert in Golden Gate Park in September '75, Garcia plays a Travis Bean, Phil has a Big Brown and Weir shows off his Ibanez.

PHOTO: CRAIG TREXLER

It's possible that Garcia tested his Travis Bean during a handful of shows with the Legion of Mary the third week of September 1975. But the first photographic evidence of him playing it comes from the big September 28 free concert in Golden Gate Park with the Jefferson Starship (who were at a commercial peak following the success of their *Red Octopus* album), the last of the four shows the Dead played that year. Evidently he liked the experience enough that the Bean (actually two different models) became his everyday guitar for the next two years, and in 1976 he actually appeared in ads endorsing it. In a 1978 *Guitar Player* interview (ironically, *after* he had gone back to playing the Wolf) he enthused, "I'm the kind of player who generally plays one guitar at a time so I can learn its idiosyncrasies, and ideally the guitar that doesn't have idiosyncrasies is the one I like. I have a couple of Beans, and they are virtually identical in terms of their setup, neck, and fingerboard, so there's no question of regaining chops in the event that one breaks down on the road or something. No other production guitar is like that—they're all completely different. That level of consistency in the Beans means a lot to me…. As far as I'm concerned, the Travis Bean is the finest production guitar on the market."

For the record, some of the other instruments and gear onstage at that Golden Gate Park gig: Weir—Ibanez custom, a MusicMan head (probably an HD-130 Reverb), an MXR Phase 45 or Phase 90; Lesh—Big Brown (he'd played the Mission Control bass at the Dead's Great American Music Hall club gig earlier that summer, a promotional radio broadcast hyping the release of *Blues for Allah*); Keith: Fender Rhodes; Billy: Ludwig set with one tom missing; Mickey: Rogers set. For the occasion, the Starship rented the sound system from FM Productions, the sound wing of Bill Graham's organization. Everyone agreed the Dead played very well on that cold, foggy afternoon. Deadheads were cheered by the notion that the band would return to touring, but it would be another nine months before the Grateful Dead touring machine revved up again.

COMEBACK

ONE thing that happened during 1975, which at the time seemed fairly unimportant but turned out to be quite significant, is the Dead leased a warehouse space less than a mile from their main office near downtown San Rafael. Nicknamed Le Club Front, or just Front Street (it was located on Front Street in a slightly depressed area of anonymous warehouses, a funky marina, and, right across the street, a seedy hotel populated by hookers and ne'er-do-wells), it would become the Dead's rehearsal space, equipment storage facility, and band and crew hangout spot. Within a year, it would also become the group's main recording studio.

Chapter Eleven
1976-1977

Before that studio became a reality, however, the band members were forced to keep working at commercial facilities, or at home studios like Weir's or Mickey's. Garcia, too, had a modest home-studio setup in Stinson Beach, but when the Film House was set to work on post for the Dead movie, most of his studio equipment went to that operation. He chose His Masters Wheels— the former Alembic Studios—as the site of his next recording project, a solo album called *Reflections*. Half of the album was cut using his solo band with Nicky Hopkins, but when that group was dissolved at the end of 1975 because of Hopkins's erratic behavior, Garcia decided to fill out the rest of the album with tracks cut by the Grateful Dead, including three Hunter-Garcia songs that had been in the Dead's live repertoire for several years—"They Love Each Other," "It Must've Been the Roses," and "Comes a Time"—and a rollicking new tune about the Dead's trans-Canada train trip a half-decade earlier, "Might As Well." When he was done with those sessions and the album was in the can, Garcia kept on recording tracks at His Masters Wheels with Keith and Donna, who replaced Hopkins in the Jerry Garcia Band early in 1976. One of studio owner Elliot Mazer's staff engineers, a Scotsman named Robert "Smiggy" Smith, was behind the board for most of the Garcia solo sessions, many of which reflected the group's turn toward lazily paced, harmony-heavy gospel-style material.

Meanwhile, Phil Lesh and Bear were given the task of putting together a live double-album from the October '74 Winterland "farewell" concerts. The shows had been recorded by Billy Wolf, one-time bassist for the Fugs and engineer on the overwrought debut album by the Rowan Brothers (produced, under a pseudonym, by their pal David Grisman), and as Bear told *BAM* magazine in December '77, the tapes were not in good shape: "Donna's tracks were missing, Phil-Lagin [the electronic duet segment] wasn't recorded, and there were weird noises all over them. Phil and I hated that stuff, but Ron Rakow [president of Round Records at the time] insisted that we had to have them mixed in nine days, which was inconceivable. We worked for 18 days [mixing at the Burbank Studios] and tried using delays, filters, tricks to overcome the sound— but the job was next to impossible. I'm very fussy with quality, and I thought the finished work was garbage."

It didn't help, too, that the records were encoded for Q-S quadraphonic reproduction which, Phil told *BAM*, "sounded good on tape but didn't translate onto the disc." However it wasn't just the discs' sound that was so disturbing. On an artistic level the album was a disappointment, too. Lesh's selections and sequencing were unusual, to be generous. *Steal Your Face*, as the mess was named, was a resounding critical and commercial failure. (Nearly 30 years later, however, Grateful Dead vaultmaster David Lemieux and engineer Jeffrey Norman, who together have shepherded so many of the Dead's archival releases, put together an exceptional five-CD set from those same Winterland shows, all but erasing the bitter memory of the *Steal Your Face* fiasco.)

The Garcia Band and Kingfish were playing in the Bay Area and heading out for short tours during the first few months of 1976. Then, in May, the Grateful Dead re-convened for rehearsals for their comeback tour of small theaters, set to begin in June. The Dead that returned from the hiatus was quite different from the group that had "retired" at Winterland in fall of 1974. The biggest difference was that Mickey Hart was back full-time. Re-introducing a second drummer to the mix proved to be more challenging than anyone probably anticipated; being a band wasn't exactly reflexive at that point. Songs needed to be re-arranged and rehearsed, some were dropped from the repertoire altogether, and a spate of exciting new tunes that took good advantage of the two-drummer setup were introduced: Weir's dynamic take on the old blues spiritual "Samson and Delilah"; his own combination of "Lazy Lightning" and "Supplication," which he'd been playing with Kingfish; Garcia's "Might As Well" and "The Wheel" (five years after it was recorded!); and of course the new material from *Blues for Allah*, which was very well received by Deadheads. In general, the tempos were slower than they'd been pre-hiatus, and the jams, while occasionally quite spacey, lacked the exploratory genius and explosive fire of the best '74 improvisations. Not that Deadheads were complaining, particularly. They were just happy to have the band back, and there was no question that the Dead ramped up their playing with each successive tour in 1976, and hit a new peak in the spring of 1977.

AFTER THE WALL

A new era for the Dead's touring operation called for a new approach to their sound-reinforcement needs. Still feeling the financial pinch of the Wall of Sound era (a strain aggravated by the Dead staying off the road for so long), they decided to go back to renting their sound systems. "When we went back on the road, we decided no more albatrosses," Healy told me in 1985. "We had a year to get to miss touring [actually a year and a half], and we had time to reflect on what a truly valuable, precious thing we had. And we wanted to keep it economical so that it would survive."

In February 2006, I asked Healy if going back to rental systems felt like a step backward, since the Wall of Sound had been spectacular on so many levels. "Of course it did," he replied, "but sometimes you have to cut your losses and go with what you can to preserve a bigger part of the picture. By then, everyone was starting to make their own stuff instead of just using old RCA and Altec designs. The writing was on the wall, and everyone was moving in the direction we had been for a while.

"Look, the Wall of Sound served its purpose—it did what it was supposed to do. I thought it did it really well; it completely scrapped and rewrote the rules of sound reinforcement. Basically, everything up until then was based on Western Electric [ideas] for motion-picture sound in 1927, so all the horn designs and speaker-cabinet designs were really from the '20s. They had new coats of paint, figuratively speaking, but it was the same kind of stuff. So the Wall of Sound, and all the work that went into it in the years before it, was really the first time that a major departure had happened, and as we saw later, a lot of those ideas stuck and were influential. So even with the sweat and the expense and all of it, it was still completely worth doing."

On that first tour of theaters in June '76, the Dead stayed true to their old hi-fi roots. They combined a pair of rented systems—one from Jeff Cook in Southern California (primarily for vocals), the other from Bearsville Sound in upstate New York (for instruments)—into one powerful and very clear system. Healy described Cook's creation as "an incredibly interesting and obscure sound system that was sort of like the Wall of Sound. It was sort of styled after it, in fact"—only much, much smaller, of course, and with a left-right PA configuration and traditional monitors.

Harry Popick became the Dead's monitor engineer on that tour, after a number of years in sound reinforcement on the East Coast working with everyone from the Bee Gees to Foghat to the Garcia Band. "Cook's system had these *beautiful* Sansui amps," he says, "and his speaker system, when it was on, was so amazing that you could literally walk up to the thing and it was what we call 'black'—you couldn't hear any noise, no amplifier hiss, *nothing*. It was pretty incredible, especially at that time. He had 5″ speakers in these very large cabinets, which were sand-filled maple—he put sand in them to dampen them; they were heavy as hell. And he had two per side. It had subwoofers with these giant 'W' cabinets—the baffling looked like a 'W' lying on its edge. And

Hangin' with some of the GD crew, 1976: (L-R) Betty Cantor-Jackson, Ram Rod, Steve Parish, Harry Popick (kneeling), Kidd Candelario and John Hagen.

PHOTO: SNOOKY FLOWERS

then Bearsville had much smaller cabinets with 5″ speakers, so Healy decided on hiring both of the companies together, because neither [system] could supply as much sound as he wanted.

"It was funny—one of the things Healy wanted to do was tilt the speakers back, and Jeff Cook just went ballistic, because to do that you had to nail the cabinets together. Jeff was like, 'You're *not* putting a nail in my furniture,' because it was really gorgeous furniture-level stuff. It was like an unbelievably big hi-fi. Bearsville said, 'Do whatever you need to do.' I can't remember how we resolved that issue, but we figured something out.

"Cook had these monitor cabinets that were also loaded with 5's and made out of the maple, also beautiful. And they worked very well with the Sansui amps. I believe the console was a hand-built unit that he made. There might have been two house consoles, one from each company."

Healy scrapped the B&K mic pairs that had been a key component of the Wall of Sound, and he also decided not to return to the old Electro-Voice mics that the Dead had used throughout the early '70s—"They were good for singing, but their transient response wasn't that good," he says today—and instead mixed and matched various brands, including several models by Sennheiser and Shure. "Philosophically, I'm not one of those die-hard and particular microphone types," he says. "I changed microphones like people change their shorts. Here's my logic: What's good one day at one barometric pressure and one temperature gradient is not good at another. So I chose microphones based on the time of year and what was going on. It always worked out okay."

Despite making noises about keeping the Dead scene small and manageable during the comeback, it was no surprise when, after the initial theater tour, the Dead were forced to jump back to larger venues—mostly sports arenas and small stadiums—to meet the extraordinary demand for tickets and to keep their finances in order. This required a different sort of sound system than the Cook/Bearsville hybrid, so they rented a system from FM Productions, which was the sound-reinforcement wing of Bill Graham Presents. Like most of the production companies of the day, FM built and maintained its own proprietary equipment—both loudspeakers and consoles.

FM got its start around 1970, originally to handle lighting for bands coming through San Francisco, but then little by little the company got into sound. "Originally, FM was literally in the basement of what had been an auto garage, and then we moved into several different buildings," says Stephen Gagne, who had done sound work at the Fillmore East beginning in 1969, but came out to San Francisco to head up FM's audio end toward the end of 1971. "When I got there, there was some sound gear but not much, and it was mostly based out of Winterland. The Fillmore [West] had closed already."

Gagne knew the Dead from his Fillmore East days, and as a person interested in sound during the early '70s, he followed the evolution of the Dead's sound system with much interest. "We were having a great time watching them," laughs Gagne, who is a successful filmmaker these days. "Their Wall of Sound filled a few semis, and it had a crew large enough to build a Guatemalan village, so they were clearly not paying the same kind of attention to what it cost versus output that most other employers on the planet were. And I admired them for their courage and their pluck and their inventiveness. My own personal hit was that it sounded fascinating, but I wasn't so sure it sounded *better*. The instruments sounded great, but I wasn't that impressed with how the vocals sounded. In terms of being influenced by it, though—it didn't make me want to try it; let's put it that way.

"What fascinated me, and my main energy at FM, was going into developing studio-like sound in a concert environment that was moveable—that you could afford to put up. And one of the things that was wonderful about working for Bill [Graham] was that he cared about the audience on a level that no other promoter in the country did. You wouldn't think that if you saw his stage persona, but in fact he was willing to spend money to send good sound to the cheap seats, and nobody else was. And he was willing to allow me to do the research and design to develop sound systems that projected in a 20,000-seat coliseum or a 50,000-seat outdoor stadium—that projected to the distant balconies with whatever fidelity was possible.

"So I started developing things like high-velocity tweeter projectors. As you've probably noticed, when a jet flies overhead, treble drops away dramatically over distance and bass does not, which is why when you're close to a jet it's a scream, and when you're far away it's a rumble. So I started developing these highly directional treble-projection units that would completely bypass the main floor in an amphitheater or coliseum, or the field in a stadium, and get treble to the back seats. And then we also had intermediate projectors and then close-field wide-dispersion projectors. Bill gave me money to have good test gear and to hire crews to do tests. So I got interested in building custom speaker arrays and designing my own horns and cabinets to affordably throw sound around in controlled ways."

"Most of the drivers in the FM system were JBL if I remember correctly, but it changed constantly," says Dennis Leonard, who started working with Hard Truckers in 1976 and did some spot sound work with the Dead again beginning in 1977. "That system was always evolving, so in that sense it was like a continuation of the way the Dead had always worked. I remember a lot of different configurations. I think it was the first regularly flown system that we'd ever used, and this was in the dark ages of flying systems. So that was something new and really exciting, because there were a lot of advantages to getting [the PA] off the ground and being able to point speakers more easily in the areas you wanted to cover, rather than balancing them and schlepping them into scaffolding. In a way, it was better than most of what was going on. The FM system was also the last system where you hung midrange boxes in a cluster, so in some ways it was borrowing from the Wall of Sound in that there was an attempt to keep high-frequency elements together and mid-frequency elements together. That's a much better approach for intelligibility than what became the standard around this time: the Clair Brothers' approach, which was to build a standard box—theirs was the S-4, which was a four-way, but then Electrotec [another top sound company] had its version, a three-way, and so on. For the time, FM's system was pretty hi-fi, which is obviously a reason it appealed to the Dead."

"I used components from all over the place," Gagne says. "I used arrays of these great ribbon tweeters—Heils. I had Heil build me custom high-level drivers and put horns around [them]. I remember showing those to Healy, and he was pretty excited about that. I also had some drivers from JBL and some from E-V. We also designed our own folded bass horns. Healy and some

The empty stage at Oakland Coliseum Stadium awaits the Dead, October 1976, when they were co-billed with The Who for two concerts; quite a pairing.

PHOTO: SNOOKY FLOWERS

Suggested listening: The intimate sound of the 1976 Dead is well represented on *Dick's Picks Vol. 20*, two shows from their September East Coast tour.

other people came over and listened to [the system], and they thought it was the best-sounding thing out there, besides their own—but their stuff was bankrupting them. So they decided to hire us.

"At that point I had a four-way system with electronic crossovers. I wanted to know what the amplifiers are doing [during a show], but of course they're onstage and I'm out in the sound booth—so the other thing I developed, which as far as I know no one had even thought of, was a switching system that would send me feeds from every power amp on the stage at low current, back to the sound booth through a matrix array. I hooked that up to an oscilloscope so I could actually monitor the waveform of every power amp in the system. I wasn't the first one to be monitoring amps with a scope, but it was my idea to have a matrix where you sent [the signals] 300 feet up to the sound booth. This way they knew what their power amps were doing, when they were clipping, and so on."

Gagne and John Chester of FM also designed a parametric EQ console: "At that time there wasn't even parametric EQ in the recording studios, except for outboard units—like, Orban had come up with a giant one- or two-channel unit. But most of them didn't sound that good, and no one had them at a console size," Gagne says. Gagne left FM near the end of '76 and got involved in both film and dolphin research, still his passions. "I was having some problems dealing with sound—I didn't think the industry needed a deaf soundman," he chuckles.

Onstage at Oakland Coliseum Stadium, Phil unleashes the thunder with his "Mission Control" Alembic bass; October 1976. During 1976, Phil's speaker setup often included a 3x15 cabinet. By '77 he was using a 3×15, a 4×12 and a 2×18.

One sad note from the summer of 1976 was the tragic death of long-time crew member Rex Jackson in an automobile accident near rural Marin County's Shoreline Highway in the beginning of September. Jackson had been elevated to tour manager when the band returned to the road in June, and his loss was deeply felt throughout the Dead organization.

AXE VARIATIONS

Through all of 1976 and most of '77, Weir and Garcia stuck with versions of the new guitars they'd picked up during the hiatus. After going through three iterations of the original blonde Ibanez, Weir moved to a different custom model. "Then he wanted a solidbody guitar with the neck through the body, and looks-wise he wanted something that was a symmetrical double-cutaway like a 335, although you wouldn't make a solidbody that big," Jeff Hasselberger says. "We made the body slightly bigger, and he also wanted a larger headstock: He thought a large mass in the body and a large-mass headstock would help the guitar's sustain, and I think he was onto something there; it definitely changes the sound to have more inertial mass at both ends of the string." This was Weir's famous brown sunburst "Cowboy Fancy"— so named because the intricate inlays were somewhat reminiscent of the type that could be found on the guitars of the great singing cow-boys of the '40s and '50s. (The Tree of Life vine "growing" up the neck had originally been used by Ibanez on the John McLaughlin doubleneck discussed in the last chapter, and it became something of a signature for the company. The inlay is actually quite similar to vines found on various Weymann banjos from the first third of the 20th century, including one of Garcia's.)

Hasselberger says that Weir always liked to have as much control as possible over pickup switching— being able to go between the hum-buckers and the single-coil in different combinations—and the

A nice view of Weir's "Cowboy Fancy" Ibanez from the early '80s. Versions of this guitar are still sold in limited numbers.

PHOTO: CLAYTON CALL

Cowboy Fancy also had phase switches, "so Bob could throw the pickups out of phase, which would give it a very odd sound." On that guitar, too, Weir got away from the moving middle-pickup concept: "After about a year of having guitars that had that, I realized [the sliding pickup] hadn't moved in months," Bob says, "so we measured where it was, and that became the [fixed] placement for the middle pickup. I thought I would want to use that more than I ended up using it." (Today, a very limited number of new Cowboy Fancy guitars are produced and sold in the U.S. The list price as of 2005: $6,666. That *is* fancy!)

During '76 and '77, too, both Garcia and Weir became increasingly interested in effect boxes. At least some of the impetus for this came from Hasselberger, who worked with both guitarists in developing various devices. "Bob always liked his toys," Hasselberger says, "and pretty quickly our relationship expanded beyond guitars and into electronics, as well. He was a big influence on a lot of the stomp boxes and gizmos—he called them "zoo-zoos"—that I made. I had an electronics engineer working R&D with me at the time, so we were designing things and trying to come up with new things, and we'd feed them over to Japan. Bob had a lot of input into the electronic effects he could use. For example, the Ibanez analog delay was originally a concept here in the States; we made a couple of prototypes in Japan, and Bob had a look at it and made some suggestions—and then it wasn't a stomp box anymore, it was a rack effect. The AD-230 kind of came from that; in fact, I think the Dead still have a couple of those in their studio. Bob helped me work out the control panel. I think it was one of the best-quality analog delays ever made. It had some idiosyncrasies that made it a very useful studio tool. Garcia used just the stomp-box version; he actually preferred the lower tech.

"The other thing that both Jerry and Bob influenced highly was the UE-600 Universal Effects [device], which had a compressor and a distortion unit and a phase shifter. The idea was to have one rackmount box with the kinds of effects these guys wanted to use—it was one of the first rackmount multi-effect units. We actually made a cheaper version, the UE-400, too. But it was an interesting piece of gear, because if you drive a compressor into a distortion box, it's totally different from a distortion box driving into a compressor; a lot of people didn't understand that the sequence [of effects] really made a difference. The UE had a rotary switch that allowed you to select the position in the chain."

In the summer of '76 Garcia switched from a Travis Bean TB1000, which had humbuckers, to a TB500, which had single-coil pickups—the Bean single-coils have been likened by some to the old Gibson P-90s. Garcia reportedly received one of the first ten 500s produced, and it became the test bed for electronics that would completely revolutionize Garcia's approach to guitar effects. It had a unique effect loop which Garcia himself conceived, and which was added to the guitar by John Cutler and Dan Healy: "One of the best ideas I ever had," Garcia told David Gans and me in a 1981 interview. "It's really easy. The modifications are nil—all you have to do is a put a jack in there [on the guitar]."

"It allows me to have all my effect pedals wired to the guitar with the ability to bypass them all with a switch," he had elaborated to *Guitar Player* in 1978. "I use a stereo cord, and the signal goes from the pickups to the tone controls and pickup switch and on down the 'A' side of the cord to a network box that controls [the different effects]. The signal goes through the devices, back into the network box, and up the 'B' side of the cord, back into the instrument *before* the volume pot, and then out to the amp.

"All those gadgets are voltage-sensitive. If you have them after the volume control, their behavior is affected by the loudness setting on the guitar. With my system, on the other hand, the effects always see the guitar as if it had full output voltage…. The whole thing is so stable that it's completely repeatable in every situation, and I never run into any weirdness of any sort. I'd used effects in recording before, but they were always too unstable for me to use onstage until we came up with this."

Another innovation that made the effect loop more efficient and reliable was a unity-gain buffer devised by Cutler. It converted the signal to low impedance, so the signal's fidelity didn't degrade over the long cable runs the loop required. (It was a smashing success, and to this day Cutler's invention is sold through CAE Sound of San Mateo, California.)

That final incarnation of the TB 500, which Garcia played for most of 1977, had a decal that read THE ENEMY IS LISTENING.

Jerry evidently likes the sound coming through the effect loop on his Travis Bean guitar: Winterland, March '77.

CLIVE AND ARISTA

When the Grateful Dead's distribution deal with United Artists ended late in 1976, they signed a lucrative deal with Clive Davis's Arista Records. Davis was a longtime fan of the Dead, particularly Garcia—in fact, Garcia is the main reason he had signed the New Riders back in 1970. And though he claimed he would leave the Dead alone to make the kind of records they wanted, he also made no secret of his desire to be the record executive who finally squeezed a bona fide hit single out of what had always been an "album" band. For their part, the Dead were remarkably open to taking advantage of their new situation by trying something different. And so, at Davis's suggestion, the Dead agreed to work with an outside producer for the first time since poor ol' Dave Hassinger had run out of the studio in terror during the New York *Anthem of the Sun* sessions a decade earlier. The names of a number of big producers were tossed around (and there were, not surprisingly, a couple on Davis's list who had no interest in working with the Dead), but fairly quickly they settled on their man: Keith Olson. One of the hottest producers in rock at the time, Olsen had helmed Fleetwood Mac's eponymous multi-platinum breakthrough album in 1975 and worked on their next album, *Rumours*, as well (which would become one of the biggest sellers of all time). "In November or December '76," Olsen told me in 1996, "I had a meeting with Clive Davis, and at one point he said, 'I've just signed a band that I've wanted to have for years and years, ever since I was at Columbia. I finally signed the band I always wanted to sign.' I said, 'Who's that?' He says, 'The Grateful Dead.' I said, 'Oh, that's interesting.' He said, 'I need a commercial record out of them,' and I said, 'Nawwwww!' He said, 'Give it your best shot,' so I said I'd go talk to them."

"When you're producing a group," Garcia told Adam Block in the December '77 issue of *BAM* magazine, "you're dealing with the interior dynamics of the group. There's a lot to it. You have to be psychologically involved; you have to be emotionally involved. You have to know what's going on, and you have to be on top of it. Olsen is a real *good* producer, as far as I'm concerned...."

"What [he] did, and the only way he could have worked with the Grateful Dead, was this: He spent some time with us while we were rehearsing [at Front Street]. He didn't call rehearsals; we were rehearsing. He came up and hung out and got high with us—listened to the music. He carefully notated what was going on, paid attention to what was going on, learned the changes, learned our music. Then we would go over the tunes, and if there were things he felt were conflicting or contradictory, he would make suggestions.... He provided an exterior uninvolved ear."

Olsen certainly had an interesting batch of songs to deal with, key among them a suite of tunes by Hunter and Garcia called "Terrapin Station" (which became the album's title) and an exciting 7/4 reggae-rock tune by Weir and

Barlow called "Estimated Prophet." The actual sessions for the album, which began in the winter of 1977, took place at Olsen's studio in Van Nuys (near L.A.), Sound City. The two-room complex was loaded with state-of-the-art equipment, including Neve consoles, Studer multitracks, scads of fantastic Neumann, AKG, and Sennheiser microphones, a Hammond organ, two Steinway grand pianos, and a wide range of outboard gear including EMT and AKG echo units, Lang and Pultec EQs, and much more. The cutting of the basic tracks took six weeks (longer than tracking *and* mixing for *Wake of the Flood* and *Mars Hotel*), mostly because Olsen was such a perfectionist. "We didn't get one basic for the first three weeks we were there," he told me in 1996. "I kept throwing them away, saying, 'It ain't good enough, guys.' Garcia would say, 'Really?' And I'd say, 'No, Jerry, it's not good enough.' Bobby would say, 'But we don't play any better than this.' And I'd say, 'I'm going to make you play better. It isn't too late!'" he laughed. Olsen had a particularly difficult time dealing with two drummers—so, working with Mickey and Billy, he actually orchestrated the drum parts: "'Okay, Billy, you get the hi-hat, kick, and snare, and an occasional cymbal. Mickey, you get all the tom fills, all the flash, all the color.' And they did it. That's the way we recorded."

As for Phil Lesh, "He had this really weird bass that I think was one of the first Alembics," Olsen said. "It basically sounded like somebody took a washboard with a broom handle and put one piece of rope on it. But he was really into it: 'It's low impedance.' I said, 'It sounds like crap—got a Fender?' He didn't like that. But I dealt with it." In the end, many Deadheads agree that the *Terrapin Station* bass sound is actually better than on many other Dead studio albums.

The album gave Garcia the opportunity to try out a couple of new "toys," though only one of the two would become part of his live setup. On the instrumental climax of the title song of the side-long "Terrapin" suite, Garcia augmented some of the contrapuntal guitar lines with textures from one of the early guitar synths, the Slavedriver, by the Southern California company 360 Systems (founded in 1972 by former USC film student Robert Easton). The Slavedriver was not a full synthesizer per se, but a guitar-to-control-voltage converter; i.e., the guitar could be used to drive a keyboard that had a CV input, such as the popular Minimoog or Oberheim SEM. The interface allowed Garcia to color his guitar lines with hints of other instrument timbres, something he'd long desired. As he noted in a 1978 *Guitar Player* interview: "There are times I wish I were a combination of a French horn and an oboe. Anything that will give me more possibilities, I'm a nut for. The other side of that is there has to be no hassle; the guitar should be predictable and repeatable." Later, in the same interview, he noted, "My technique fits well with [guitar synthesizers]. A synthesizer likes to hear a cleanly noted sound, and I think it responds better with a guitar that's set up like mine—with sort of a high and stiff action. It shouldn't be too difficult for me to make the transition...."

PHOTO: ED PERLSTEIN

Keith's onstage setup in '76 (when this rehearsal shot was taken) and '77 included a Steinway grand piano and Fender Rhodes.

Evidently the Slavedriver didn't pass the "no hassle" test for Garcia. Neither did another unit he tried, the Zetaphon, by Holt Electro-Acoustic Research of Berkeley. Later he said that he found the triggering on all the early guitar synths he tried to be disappointingly slow and unreliable, and it would be more than a decade before he once again explored that area seriously, when he (belatedly) embraced the possibilities inherent in a MIDI guitar system.

A box that really *did* grab Garcia—and which became an integral part of his arsenal beginning on the killer spring 1977 tour—was the Mu-Tron III envelope filter, developed in the early '70s by an engineer named Henry Zajac for a company called Musictronics. (Subsequently Zajac formed HAZ Laboratories and acquired the rights to the Mu-Tron III.) Sometimes known as an "auto-wah," the envelope filter gave a distinctive "wah" or "thwack" to every note, with the effect's shape determined by the intensity of the picked note. This was the sound at the center of Garcia's guitar work on Weir's "Estimated Prophet" (played at 51 of 60 shows that year), and also a new Hunter-Hart song, sung by Garcia, introduced that spring: "Fire on the Mountain." The effect also occasionally found its way into a number of other songs, ranging from "Sugaree" to "Not Fade Away"—when Jerry liked a new effect, he wasn't shy about using it. It's interesting to note, too, that as Garcia increased his use of the envelope filter and, just a little later, a Mu-Tron octave divider (which "split" a note's frequency in two, creating a second note an octave or two below the original), he started to all but phase out his traditional wah-wah pedal, which had so defined his early '70s sound. It's a small but significant shift in his playing style, surrendering the subtlety and variability of the real-time foot-controlled wah-wah for a device that was effectively controlled by the picking hand instead. Over the course of the next year, too, Garcia added MXR analog delay, Distortion+, and Phase 100 units to his onstage pedal collection.

"Jerry and I would go to music stores, or he'd send me out, looking for new pedals," Steve Parish says. "Once he found the ones he liked—the Mu-Tron and MXR stuff—he stuck with them for a long time. The thing with Jerry, though, is he didn't need a lot of effects. His hands could do a lot of tricks, and of course he understood his equipment so well, he could do an amazing amount of stuff with just his amps and the [volume and tone] knobs and pickups on his guitar. He was a master at getting subtle things out of his equipment."

During this period, Phil was playing his Alembic custom through an Alembic F2B preamp hooked up to a McIntosh 2300 stereo power amp driving a pair of Hard Trucker cabinets filled with Gauss speakers—one with four 15s, the other with three 12s. Both Weir and Lesh had switched to Gauss speakers because they could handle so much power (though they also needed a lot of power to run them), and also because, for a time, the quality of JBL speakers became somewhat inconsistent. It wasn't a huge stretch to switch to Gauss, either: Ed May, a respected and influential design engineer for JBL from the mid '50s until '69, helped establish Cetec Gauss as a major speaker manufacturer during his tenure there in the early '70s. It was May who introduced the concept of dual spiders for Gauss's bass drivers.

MOVIE MAGIC

The Grateful Dead Movie (actually just titled *The Grateful Dead*) was released around mid-year to unanimous raves from Deadheads in the few cities where it actually played. Everyone agreed it was an artful and exciting depiction of many different levels of the Grateful Dead experience (including a hilarious sequence looking inside Phil's Alembic bass). Rather than relying on conventional movie sound systems, which in the mid '70s ranged from mediocre to just plum atrocious, the Dead sprang for small, dedicated PA systems to be brought into theaters where the film was playing, to better reproduce the concert experience. The sound was painstakingly mixed at MGM studios in Los Angeles at the same time the Dead were completing *Terrapin Station* with Keith Olsen.

Suggested listening: Though overwrought, the Keith Olsen-produced *Terrapin Station* still is worth checking out. There are numerous strong 1977 releases in the *Dick's Picks* series, including Vol. 3 from Pembroke Pines, Florida, 5/22/77; Vol. 15 from the Dead's mammoth gig at a racetrack In Englishtown, New Jersey, 9/3/77; and *Dick's Picks Vol. 29*, which contains two complete shows—Atlanta 5/19/77 and Lakeland, Florida 5/21/77. A great year for Dead music!

The movie had required a massive effort up until the very end, as Garcia and Dan Healy tweaked the five-channel sound in L.A. in hopes that the film experience could somehow approximate the feeling of being at Winterland. "What we wanted to do," Garcia noted, "was create the illusion of broad-spectrum sound. We wanted to create the illusion of volume, although what we're dealing with [in movie theater sound systems] is like 40-watt amplifiers. Any rock 'n' roll guitarist has more power in one guitar [amp] than a theater has. So dealing with these givens, how do you get maximum efficiency out of a really second-rate system, utilizing what's there?"

"We chose to mix the sound down at Warner Bros. in Burbank, because on their biggest stage they had a great Neve [mixing console] and it was a formal feature [film] stage," film editor Susan Crutcher told me in 1995. "We had three mixers, all of whom were very brave to work with us. We brought in a ton of outboard gear and hooked it into their board, which actually they had never done. It was music-processing stuff that you'd commonly find in a recording studio, but never on a film soundstage in those days. So we were mixing, and it was all going fine—long hours and tedious, but good. We got to the last night of the last day; Jerry was going on the road for the weekend and didn't want to have to come back on Monday. We were already in overtime, heading for 'golden time' [triple time]. We were trying to get the last reel done, which was going to be really hard to do in one day.

"So when we made that decision at midnight to go for golden time, everyone hit the coffee. There was also some tequila around. Anyway, a person who shall remain nameless decided that it might be even more exciting, since we were all exhausted, if we were dosed—so he dosed the coffee and the tequila but didn't tell anyone. At about 1:30, one of the union guys in the loading room had to be carried out. At that point I didn't know what was going on; I was paying attention to the work. I knew things were weird, but I thought everyone was just tired. It wasn't until I was driving back to the motel with my three editors that I started to notice that I was hallucinating. At one point my friend Pat [Jackson] mentioned she wanted an ice cream cone, and I looked at her and I saw an ice cream cone on the end of her nose and it was dripping down her face. That's when I felt, 'I must be really, really tired.' Later at the hotel, when I started laughing uncontrollably, I realized, 'Oh fuck, we've been dosed!' I'd never taken acid before, so I didn't know what to expect. I spent the next two days laughing. It was intense. In the end, Jerry came back on Monday, and we finished it then."

Terrapin Station was released in July to mixed reviews, both in the press and among Deadheads. Most agreed that the "Terrapin" suite and "Estimated Prophet" were knockout tunes, but many were put off by the decision to have British arranger Paul Buckmaster orchestrate and add a choir to the former. The move had been fully endorsed by Garcia and Weir, though the extent of the orchestration—particularly on Mickey and Bill's "Terrapin Flyer" percussion duel—seemed to catch everyone off-guard. Mickey, in particular, was apoplectic about Olsen's handiwork, and though Garcia initially was completely supportive of the Olsen touches, he later admitted he thought the arrangement was "overripe." Clive Davis didn't get his hit single from *Terrapin Station*, though three Weir-sung tunes—"Estimated," "Samson and Delilah," and a punchy pop-rock tune by Phil Lesh and Peter Monk called "Passenger"—did get a fair amount of radio play. As a result, sales of the album were higher than for (the far superior) *Blues for Allah* two years earlier.

That summer, too, Garcia began work in earnest on a new solo album with the Jerry Garcia Band (with Keith and Donna), *Cats Under the Stars*. Rather than working at an established studio, however, the Dead's Front Street rehearsal hall was transformed into a recording environment.

"What happened," says Betty Cantor-Jackson, "is Jerry went into Front Street with his band to rehearse before going into His Masters Wheels to do a solo album, and I came in with my Ampex [MX-10] mixers and my Nagra [recorder] and recorded the rehearsals. They listened back to the tape and [JGB drummer] Ron Tutt loved my drum sounds, so Jerry said, 'You can have a 16-track here tomorrow, right, Betty?' 'Sure Jer, whatever.' [The 16-track Studer recorder] had been up at the Film House because we had been using it on the movie, but that was finished, so I packed it up and moved it down to Front Street and set it up with my MX-10s. I'd use two microphones in different positions and pan them, because there were no pan pots available, and the album started that way. Then we decided we needed a board, so I talked to Bob [Matthews] about that, and we got together and ordered up a Neve 8058. It was a wonderful board! Jerry bought it. I remember it arrived in these two huge crates with a whole book of schematics and nothing to tell you how to put it together, so we just worked slowly and eventually got it together. We recorded all the basics for *Cats* there." The album was also mixed there, by Bob Matthews. Betty did the mastering.

Unlike conventional studios, Club Front did not have an isolated control room; rather, the Neve, the recorders, and the outboard gear were off on one side of the large, high-ceilinged rehearsal room. Monitoring had to be done using headphones, as loudspeakers would interfere with recording. (Not surprisingly, the Dead also had fantastic monitors for playbacks and mixing.) Betty Cantor-Jackson, for one, didn't care that there was no control room. "I liked the openness of it. We brought in theater curtains to deaden the room a little, and we put foam and plastic almost to the ceiling, and we had Sonotubes

PHOTO: ED PERLSTEIN

Engineer Bob Matthews at the Dead's newly built Club Front recording studio, 1977. That's their first Neve console, and a Studer 16-track is visible in the background.

[a type of large tubular baffle or gobo] to shape the sound. We'd put bars between them, and we'd hang curtains from them and move them around, depending on what was being done."

It was funky, to be sure, but it *worked*, and over the next 18 years it would be the site of many recording sessions for both the Dead and various solo ventures.

BELLY OF THE BEAST

BEGINNING with the fall 1977 tour, Garcia stopped playing Travis Bean guitars and went back to the Irwin Wolf, which a little earlier had been retooled to include the effect loop and unity-gain buffer that had worked so well in the TB-500. Garcia never expressed any particular dissatisfaction with the Beans; perhaps he just liked the woodier feel of the Irwin axe. It was at this time, too, that Doug Irwin inlaid the "Big Bad Wolf" (as Jerry called it) on the spot where an identical sticker had been.

Chapter Twelve
1977-1979

(For the sake of completeness, we should also note that while the Wolf was having new DiMarzio humbuckers installed in June '78, Jerry briefly played an Ibanez Musician similar to one that Weir favored for a short time during 1978. It had an asymmetrical, more Strat-like body than the regular Bob Weir and Cowboy Fancy models. Garcia's axe, of course, was fitted with his onboard effect loop, too.)

Meanwhile, on the sound-reinforcement front, the Dead switched from their hometown FM Productions to the giant East Coast company Clair Brothers—then and now the most successful sound company in the U.S. Founded by Roy Clair and based in Lititz, Pennsylvania (originally it was situated in an old barn), the company was always on the forefront of live sound innovation, building its own proprietary house and monitor consoles, loudspeakers, and even outboard gear. By the time the Dead contracted their services, Clair Bros.' main PA box, which they would fly as needed (Clair was actually the first company to a fly a system), was the S-4, which Dennis Leonard describes as "a four-way system consisting of two 18s, four 10s, two

Donna watches Jerry wailing on his refurbished "Big Bad Wolf," 11/24/1978. Bill is playing Sonor drums by this point.

PHOTO: JAY BLAKESBERG

[JBL 2405] compression drivers, and two of these old silver bullet tweeters, all in one behemoth box. They were about four feet by four feet by 20 or 24 inches deep. They were a *motherfucker* to handle," he laughs. Though Clair Bros. has traditionally not revealed details of their systems' components, they have had a more than three-decades-long association with JBL, so the Dead were in familiar territory there. The primary power amps Clair used were Phase Linear 700s, originally designed by Bob Carver (later of the well-known Carver Corporation) in the early '70s and used by Pink Floyd and many other groups through the years. Phase Linear even developed a special "700B" specifically for Clair, which ordered hundreds in the late '70s and early '80s.

"An interesting thing that happened with Clair Bros.," Leonard says, "is that when we took [their PA] out for big Grateful Dead shows, we found that about 30 percent of their speakers were out of phase. They had been struttin' their stuff, snapping their suspenders: 'Our shit? It's *together!*, And Healy says, 'Okay, let's just check the phase.' Well, they scurried around with their tail between their legs after that. They were so ashamed; we busted them so badly. But it was forgivable. We didn't throw it in their faces; these things happen. Hopefully they then revised what they did to make sure that [the system] was cohesive. It was good for the company and also for all the bands that used their stuff after that."

Clair also had its own remarkable front-of-house console, which was designed by Bruce Jackson (later mixer for Bruce Springsteen) and Ron Borthwick in the early '70s. "It was unique on a number of fronts," Jackson wrote in *Live Sound* magazine. "The control surface folded right out of the case—no heavy lifting up onto a table. It was the first console to have plasma-bar graph meters, which also displayed simultaneous RMS and peak levels. And the meters were conveniently located beside the faders, right where you tend to look. In addition, it was the first live mixing console to have parametric EQ."

At the beginning of the Dead's association with Clair, Harry Popick was using a monitor system he had built earlier. "I took part of the Wall of Sound—they had 12″ speakers and 5″ speakers—and I cut those cabinets down into floor-wedge monitors, and I had sidefill cabinets, too, probably three of them stacked up on each side. Then I had these double-wide racks made with four McIntosh's in each one—and they're 130 pounds apiece. So I had over 500 pounds just in amplification in there, plus the rack itself, which had to be strong enough to carry it all. It was huge; it was like a locomotive." Eventually, however, he went over to Clair gear for both the Dead and the Garcia Band.

Club Front saw lots of action in 1978. The Garcia Band's *Cats Under the Stars* was completed and released that spring. It was Jerry's own favorite solo album and contained a number of excellent songs, including "Rubin and Cherise," "Gomorrah," "Rhapsody in Red," and the title song. From listening to it, you'd never guess it was made in a studio that was still under construction; indeed, if any criticism is to be leveled at this generally fine work, it's that it sounds *too* slick and studio-crafted, a far-cry from the messy, wires-everywhere, down-home ambience of Front Street's early days.

For their part, the Dead elected not to repeat the Keith Olsen experiment a second time (though Weir did make his second solo album, *Heaven Help the Fool*, in L.A. with Olsen); instead, they enlisted Little Feat leader Lowell George to produce their next album, *Shakedown Street* (the ultra-funky title track of which was inspired by places like Front Street). This must have seemed like a good idea at the time: George was a wonderful spirit, an extremely talented guitarist and bandleader, and certainly a fellow traveler, as they say; it was a mutual admiration society. But the fact is, Little Feat's best albums had been produced by Ted Templeman, not Lowell (indeed, Feat guitarist Paul Barrere and keyboardist Bill Payne were often more involved in the studio than Lowell was), and he didn't really understand how to work effectively with a band as unfocused and anarchic as the Grateful Dead could be when someone wasn't riding herd on them. Working at Club Front was maybe a little too comfortable for the Dead, too: There was more partying than recording most nights (another weakness George shared with the group, especially during this era), and in general, not a helluva lot got done for a number of weeks. Originally Arista had hoped to have the album in the stores during the summer of '78, but that deadline came and went with barely the basic tracks being completed by the end of August. Lowell George had to leave the project at that point to return to Little Feat, and the Dead had an important set of shows looming in mid September…in Egypt, of all places.

PYRAMID POWER

The Dead's Egypt adventure—three shows at the tiny Sound and Light Theater at the foot of the Sphinx and the Great Pyramid of Giza—could be a book in itself, but for our purposes here it's more an interesting aside than an important and cosmic stopping point. For one thing, the Dead didn't bring the Clair sound system over to the desert; instead, Healy rented one from a company in England called Turbosound. Same with the recording truck, which was a mobile unit used by the Who. The Dead hoped to make a live album from the trip to defray some of the costs, just as they had in Europe six years earlier.

Even without those two huge elements, however, the Dead still shipped many tons of equipment to Cairo. However, something that *didn't* make it over to Egypt turned out to be a critical omission: Before the trip, Keith Godchaux's piano tuner had a falling out with members of the crew and stayed back in the U.S.; as a result, Keith's piano did not sound as good as it should have on the show tapes.

In the summer of '78 Keith switched to a Yamaha Electric Grand piano. Phil is playing Big Brown again in this shot from the Capitol Theatre in Passaic, New Jersey, 11/24/78.

The instrument Keith played beginning that summer was not one of his beloved Steinway grands. Instead, he shifted to perhaps the most popular "electric grand" piano of that era, the Yamaha CP70B. Yamaha was yet another venerable Japanese musical-instrument manufacturer, dating back to the 1880s, when Torakusu Yamaha began selling reed organs. By 1897, he'd started the Nippon Gakki musical instrument company, which many years later changed its name to Yamaha to honor its founder (who had passed away in 1910). Yamaha has been successful in virtually every aspect of musical instrument and audio manufacturing it has attempted, from guitars to keyboards of every variety (acoustic pianos to the DX7 synthesizer) to mixers, loudspeakers...you name it.

The CP70 (the "B" model added balanced outputs) was quite a revolutionary instrument for its time. It took up much less space than a true grand, and at close to 300 pounds, was a fraction as heavy (though certainly not as light as

GRATEFUL DEAD
DANE COUNTY COLISEUM, MADISON, WI 2/3/78
UNI-DOME, UNIVERSITY OF N. IOWA, CEDAR FALLS, IA 2/5/78

Suggested listening: My favorite of the official releases featuring 1978 Dead are *Dick's Picks Vol. 18* (two blistering shows from the February Midwest tour) and the epic *Closing of Winterland* show (12/31/78), which is also available as a fantastic DVD. I can't recommend the studio album *Shakedown Street*, particularly, but the expanded remastered edition does include two hot tracks from the 9/16/78 Egypt show: "Ollin Arageed" into "Fire on the Mountain."

a Rhodes or Wurlitzer). It had 73 wooden keys and a complex internal design that was essentially like that of a real baby grand piano, complete with strings and hammers and a solid frame. However, rather than having three strings for each upper and midrange note and two for the lower notes, Yamaha's engineers figured out a way to assign just two shorter strings per upper and midrange note, and a single string for the lower notes. Under each of the strings was a piezoelectric pickup that amplified the note; this made it unnecessary to design the piano with acoustic projection in mind, so it could be kept on the smallish side. It was probably the most natural- and best-sounding electric piano until electronic units with sampled piano sounds came in vogue a number of years later. Other features of the CP70B included a built in three-band equalizer, tremolo, volume, and jacks for external effects. However, like a "real" piano, it did have to be faithfully kept in tune, and it was notoriously difficult to manage the pitch in great heat—like in Egypt.

As it turned out, the piano sound on the Egypt tapes wasn't the only problem; the shows in general were not strong enough to warrant an album release. This was not a great time for the band overall: Garcia was sliding into serious drug dependency, Phil was drinking heavily, Billy had a broken hand, and Keith had become a veritable cipher onstage, rarely playing anything interesting, as he battled his own demons. Still, talk to anyone in the band or crew or family and they'll tell you Egypt was one of the greatest events in the Dead's storied career—it's just that its magic was mostly outside of the music.

There was one sonic aspect to the story that's worth a little ink, however. One night before the first show, Garcia, Dan Healy, Mountain Girl, David Freiberg (of Quicksilver and Starship fame), and John Cutler went into the King's Chamber of the Great Pyramid after hours (with special permission, of course) and spent the entire evening singing and om-ing and jibber-jabbering. "The sound was incredibly rich and full," Healy related to his friend Cookie Eisenberg and me a month after the trip for a story in *BAM* magazine. "Also, the King's Chamber has a giant sarcophagus in it—a rectangular coffin about seven by four by four feet—and it, too, had a particular resonance, so each of us took turns lying down inside of it and humming notes. When you found the resonant note, the softest you could hum would reverberate so much in that frequency that it would massage your whole body. And if you hummed at the level of a reasonable talking voice or louder, it hurt your ears."

"It was about one-quarter mile from the stage to the Great Pyramid, and we had high-quality FM radio transmitters to span that distance. So we put a transmitter down at the stage and sent the signal from there up to the outside of the Great Pyramid, where we had a receiver. We couldn't put the receiver directly in the King's Chamber because it is deeply imbedded in the stone structure, so from the outside we ran wires from a receiver into the Pyramid, down the Grand Gallery, through the Queen's Chamber, and into the King's Chamber, where we hooked the wires to a speaker. We also put a microphone in there, ran the wires back the same way…and sent the signal down to a receiver onstage that was plugged into our console in the form of an echo return. The object, of course, was to send voices and instruments up through the radio link to the King's Chamber, where it would play through a speaker, be picked up by the microphone, and sent back down to the stage.

"Unfortunately, we hadn't brought enough cable with us [from the U.S.], so we ended up buying some Italian cable from a local telephone company. But it was inferior. Our other problem was that we had to run it through the Grand Gallery's walkways, and we believed the cables would be damaged by being stomped on by the tour groups that tramp through during the day."

Alas, the hookup was ultimately unsuccessful. "Some suggested that perhaps, cosmically, it wasn't meant to happen and that's why it didn't work," Healy said. "I don't buy that. I think it didn't work because from a technical end we didn't have it together."

(For the record, Owsley, who went over to Egypt several days before the band arrived, independently arrived at a similar notion of wiring the pyramids, only he concluded that the King's Chamber was "an acoustic nightmare" and that the interesting resonances worth capturing were in certain other subterranean chambers. "I began to realize that it was like a gigantic organ, or it was like the cavities in your head," he told David Gans, "It had certain frequencies that were almost imperceivable to the ear, but you could feel them." In the end, he was bitterly disappointed that others did not share his view of how and where to wire the pyramid. "If they'd done it the way I thought they should do it, it would've been dynamite and everything would have worked," he said with typical self-assurance.)

One final note on Egypt, from Harry Popick: "When we tore down the [PA] system the day after the last show, we tried to get the stuff out of there, and it was so hot that the speakers had literally welded themselves to each other! They had epoxy paint, and in the 120-degree weather they bonded to each other. I swear to God, we were using crowbars to separate them." (During the last of the three Egypt shows, Popick announced to road manager Richard Loren that he was so fried from two-plus years of round-the-clock work with the Dead that he was quitting. "I was like an old manuscript paper that was burnt brown on the edges," he says with a chuckle. He did, in fact, leave the organization for more than a year.)

Upon returning to America, the Dead threw themselves back into the completion of *Shakedown Street*, with John Kahn helping out in the studio with production and also adding various keyboard textures because Keith was rarely around. The album came out in mid November to generally lukewarm-to-negative reviews from Deadheads, despite the presence of such concert favorites as the title cut, "Fire on the Mountain," Weir's "I Need a Miracle," and the intended single, "Good Lovin'." It remains perhaps the least distinguished entry in the Dead's catalog of studio albums.

NEW BLOOD

Despite the lack of excitement over the album, the Dead continued to draw more and more people to their shows, and they got a major boost when they appeared on *Saturday Night Live* in November '78; it turned out producer Lorne Michaels, John Belushi, and writer/performers Al Franken and Tom Davis were serious fans of the band. It was the largest audience the Grateful Dead ever played for. On New Year's Eve that year, the Dead (and the world) bid adieu to Winterland with a marathon, locally televised concert, which also featured opening sets by the New Riders and Belushi's serio-comic R&B revue the Blues Brothers. By mid February 1979, however, the band's festering dissatisfaction with Keith and Donna led to a mutual parting of the ways, and the Dead brought in a new stud to the keyboard chair, Brent Mydland.

Like his predecessor, Brent was a product of the suburban East Bay: a small town called Antioch, about an hour east of San Francisco, and then, a little closer, Concord. He started piano lessons at age six and studied classical piano through his junior year in high school. "In late high school," he told me in a 1987 interview, "I got into playing rock 'n' roll with friends, and it was almost like I had to start from the beginning, because if I didn't have a piece of music in front of me I couldn't do much. I changed my outlook on playing real fast after that." He also played trumpet in the high school band. Brent was in a succession of short-lived bands with friends, first playing "a little Thomas organ that you could barely hear. A couple of years later I got a Gibson Kalamazoo, which was sort of like a Farfisa, and I was really happy."

The day after he graduated from high school, he and a friend moved to L.A. try to get a music career going, but after a while he retreated back to his parents' home. He was in a variety of Top 40 and bar bands, but eventually he landed a gig through a bass-playing friend (Rick Carlos) to be a part of the backing group for the duo Batdorf & Rodney. When that dissolved, he and Carlos put together a soft country-rock group called Silver, which cut an album for Arista Records in 1976. Mydland played a B-3 and a Fender Rhodes in that group. That band broke up before cutting a second album, and within six months he and Carlos had joined the Bob Weir Band, which also included guitarist Bobby Cochran (another Ibanez advocate) and drummer John Maucer. When Keith and Donna left, Weir gave Brent a call. One blues jam session at Front Street later, he was invited to join the band. He officially joined on April Fool's Day 1979 and made his debut on April 22 at San Jose's Spartan Stadium.

One thing that appealed to the Dead is that, unlike Keith, he was open— even eager—to use synthesizers onstage and on records. His first synth (in his pre-Dead days) was a Minimoog, which, following its 1970 introduction, was the first synth to be widely embraced by touring rock and jazz musicians. The

Two views of "new guy" Brent Mydland in 1979. Brent's stage setup included a prominent Hammond B-3 organ (that's the innards of a B-3 in the daylight shot from a show in Rochester, New York, 9/1/79), a Rhodes, a Prophet 5 synth and various other synth modules. The indoor shot is from Pittsburgh, 12/1/79.

instrument was a product of the fertile mind of Robert Moog (1934–2006), who got his start in the mid '50s building Theremins with his father but co-developed the revolutionary Moog Modular Synthesizer in the mid '60s with Howard Deutsch. The Minimoog was specifically developed to be portable. Encased in walnut, it had 44 keys and many of the same controls available on the much larger studio synths of the day. It had three oscillators to produce pitched tones, one source for unpitched sounds, and a mic preamp for bringing in live signals. Mixer controls allowed the user to balance the different signals, and there were also various sound modifiers and controllers ranging from a lowpass filter (with its own contour generator) to wheel controls for pitch bend and modulation— directly to the left of the keys for easy access. The back of the control surface was equipped with jacks for sequencers, foot pedals, and a joystick. Unlike many later synths that became known for their uncanny ability to mimic strings and other instruments, the Minimoog's sounds were original and distinctive; you couldn't miss 'em!

PHOTO: JAY BLAKESBERG

Of his first Minimoog, in 1982 Brent told Bob Doerschuk of *Keyboard* magazine, "Things would just start happening to it—I'd be playing along, and then for no reason the modulation would kick in [like a siren], so I took it back to the store. But they wouldn't do anything except tell me where to take it to get it fixed. I took it back to that place for repairs so many times that I ended up writing to the Better Business Bureau and to the Moog people. Between the two of them, I eventually got a new Minimoog, but by then the repair people had talked me out of using it, so I said, 'Okay, keep it in the crate, just give me credit'—which I used to buy an Arp 2600. I had that 2600 for about two years, and I wish I'd kept it for some studio stuff—but at the time I needed money, so I sold it for real cheap and got a Minimoog again. I really like the Mini now. The filter sound is so ballsy and thick, and I love how the wheels are set up."

When Brent joined up with the Dead, they also bought him a Prophet-5, which had been introduced the previous year by inventor Dave Smith's company, Sequential Circuits, and which had the distinction of being the first popular programmable polyphonic (five-voice) synth. Although the Prophet was inarguably a fine-sounding instrument that would be as influential in its own way as the Minimoog, Brent found it was not as well suited to his live performance needs with the Dead. As he told *Keyboard,* "The problem is our music is so spur-of-the-moment, I might hear something that gives me an idea to change to a different program, but by the time I'd come up with it, they'd be off to something else. I don't like to be left back there trying to figure out what to come up with. It's not the kind of group where you can work things out in advance, like, 'Okay, here I go to [preset] 22.'" He did use the Prophet in the studio, however, and later he purchased a Prophet-10 ten-voice synth, which he used both onstage and in the studio.

Still, Brent's greatest strength unquestionably was as a B-3 player; in the pantheon of rock keyboardists, he is greatly underrated in this regard. Kidd Candelario, who was Brent's roadie (as he had been Keith's), recalls, "When he came into the band, he brought his B-3 that he'd been using with Weir and with Silver before that. But he didn't really want to use his, so I went out and bought three of them. They were surprisingly cheap then, because everyone was pulling them out of churches and going digital, so they were everywhere. I found a guy in L.A. and I bought 12 Leslies, and we got those in here and totally modified them. Brent was always blowing out tweeters, so we found this little 15-amp Electro-Voice tweeter that worked better with the organ. We also put in all new relays and a whole new system with a big connector so it was easy to actually set and daisy chain [the Leslie cabinets]."

Wait a minute—*12* Leslies? "Actually, he only used ten at a time, with two as spares," says Peter Miller of San Mateo-based CAE (Custom Audio Electronics), who came onboard as an organ tech in 1980 and went on to work with the Dead for the rest of their history, designing all sorts of big and small electronic devices, often in conjunction with John Cutler, with whom he often still works to this day. "Those were the days of the volume wars onstage, so every guy needed two cabinets to hear the organ." Kidd adds, "Brent had four Leslies behind him, Jerry had two or three near him, Kreutzmann and Mickey had two in the stack, and Phil had one out at the very end. Believe me, Brent needed all that. I thought it was pretty magical; he was quite the organist, and in those early days he was the nicest, sweetest guy you'd ever want to meet. He was so fun to hang out with."

In 1981, Garcia told Gans and me that he thought Brent was "an excellent musician, a great choice for the band…. What we always wanted was someone who would produce color. The thing of having another percussion instrument [i.e., piano] in an all-percussion band was really too much of the same thing. The effect that the piano had on the ensemble was something we could accomplish with guitars, so what we were really looking for was that sustain—you know, we were all *hungry* for color. Real hungry."

Brent's hiring had an immediate impact on the Dead's sound. Not only did he bring new, fuller keyboard textures to the music, but his vocals also blended better with Garcia and Weir than Donna's had, and visually he was a striking and animated presence.

Suggested listening: *Dick's Picks Vol. 5,* from the Oakland Auditorium, 12/26/79, shows the power Brent brought to the group just a few months into his tenure. The whole second set is killer.

A WORLD OF DRUMS

The other big difference in the group beginning with that Spartan Stadium concert was also plain to see: On the back of the drum riser along with Mickey's and Billy's kits and their assortment of timbales, congas, and other instruments, was a giant metal ring—perhaps seven feet off the ground—on which were suspended five *huge* drums. This setup was nicknamed The Beast. And under the ring were a number of other unusual percussion instruments, including Rototoms and what looked to be a long plank strung with piano wire. That was The Beam. Both were brought to the Dead's stage by Mickey Hart and became an important part of the percussion arsenal for the rest of the band's history, in the process completely re-defining what a "drum solo" could be.

Mickey had always been immersed in the world of drums. As a teenager he was entranced by Olatunji's *Drums of Passion* album, which popularized African drumming in certain circles. Likewise, he loved the tabla playing of Ustad Alla Rakha on Ravi Shankar's records, and once he was in the Dead he even studied with the master—Alla Rakha's instruction to Mickey about playing in unusual time signatures, in part, influenced the Dead to tackle 11/4 time for "The Eleven" and, a little later, 10/4 time for "Playing in the Band." As we saw earlier, he was among the first rock drummers to use gongs and various

Latin percussion instruments onstage. In 1975 he was a part of the all-percussion Diga Rhythm Band, which included Zakir Hussein—Alla Rakha's son—and several other fine players, and they made one of the first true "world music" percussion albums, fusing African, Latin, and Asian ideas into a seamless whole.

"Around that time," Mickey says, "I started getting into all these rhythmic cycles and translating boles [vocal mnemonics that mimic the tones of the tabla—e.g., *takka-takka-ta-ta-takka-ta-ta-takka-takka-ta*, etc.], transposing these rhythm patterns onto the drum set, so I needed *more* drums because with tablas you have dozens of sounds—you can mute them, hit different parts of the drum, all these things, as opposed to a regular drum kit where you have only a few. So that's when I started enlarging my set with the Dead and adding more drums behind me, and then it just kind of got out of hand," he smiles.

The whole Egypt adventure had a profound effect on everyone in the band, but perhaps Mickey most of all. He had already been exposed to Egyptian folk music and percussion back in the Bay Area through his friend Hamza El-Din, with whom he had studied the tambourine-like, single-membrane hand drum called the tar. Each night at the Sound and Light Theater, the show's second set had begun with a troupe of Nubian singers and percussionists (including Hamza) playing a rhythmic song called "Ollin Arageed," during which the other members of the Dead would slowly filter onto the stage, add their tuneful electric accompaniment, and slowly move into a jam before ending up at a

A fraction of the many percussion instruments assembled by Mickey and company for soundtrack sessions for *Apocalypse Now* at Club front.

Grateful Dead number. After the shows, Mickey, Hamza, and engineers Brett
Cohen and John Cutler journeyed into Upper Egypt—even visiting Hamza's
home village of Tuska—to play with the musicians there and capture their
indigenous music for posterity on a Nagra recorder and either Sennheiser
shotgun condenser mics or Neumann KM-84s. When he returned to America,
Mickey began to regularly incorporate the tar into the drum solo segment,
adding yet another musical weapon in his expanding arsenal.

What really sent Mickey into the drum stratosphere, however, was his
involvement in the soundtrack for Francis Ford Coppola's incredible Vietnam
epic, *Apocalypse Now*. During a Dead concert at Winterland in the fall of 1978,
after their return from Egypt, Coppola—who was in the throes of what would be
seemingly endless post-production on the film—was enthralled by the glorious
percussion jam in the second set, and shortly afterward he approached Mickey
about helping create a percussion underscore for his film. (There were already
plenty of other musicians involved in the soundtrack, from various synthesizer
specialists—Bernie Krause, Pat Gleeson, and others—to Coppola's classically
trained father, Carmine.)

"Francis wanted me to paint a picture of the jungle with my music," Mickey
told me in an interview shortly after the film opened in August 1979. "He kept
telling me, 'Make the jungle come alive!' Well, when I started out, I didn't have
all the colors to make the picture Francis wanted, so I went out and *made* them.
He wanted a cosmic orchestra. This was to be music of the spheres."

So Mickey commenced assembling a percussion jungle of his own. He already
had a substantial collection of hand drums and mallet instruments from around
the world, but this gave him an excuse to obtain more. He recalled in the winter
of 2006, "We built all those wild Harry Parch instruments—the 43-to-the-octave
Chromelodeon, and various others. [Parch is a maverick composer famous for
constructing his own instruments, from specialized marimbas to "cloud chamber bowls."] We built scratchers, we had a glass harmonica—everything imaginable." Hart called upon his many percussionist friends, including Zakir Hussein
and the great Brazilian drum master Airto Moreira, to supply what they could
and to help him out when it came time to record. Then he and Ram Rod, who
was his drum roadie, enlisted the help of Willie John Cashman and Danny
Orlando at FM Productions to build the giant drums that would become the
heart of The Beast. It's no surprise FM would be sympathetic to Mickey's project: Not only did Bill Graham love Mickey and the Dead, he appeared in one
particularly surreal *Apocalypse Now* scene as the emcee of a jungle concert.
Talk about typecasting!

"We built the big drums for the air strike at the end of the movie," Hart says.
"We conned Bill into giving us this place [FM's San Francisco warehouse] to
work at night—just for a few days, we said, but we ended up staying there for
weeks building these giant drums. We based the big drums on [Japanese] Taiko

drums, but instead of making them out of wood, we went to Alcoa and bought this steel, and me and Ram Rod and everyone rolled the steel into drums."

Mickey says the notion of hanging the drums off a metal frame was already in place: "Before we built the big drums, we put tom-toms up there, we put congas up there, to see what it was like to hang drums and play them. The idea was to make a battery of all these different colors, because when Francis showed me the movie I thought, 'Holy shit, you can't get that many drums in one place in proximity.' Plus, you need air to propagate. So the idea was to make a circle and be in the middle of it."

Once that first version of The Beast was completed, Hart and the crew moved all the percussion instruments over to Club Front and set them up in different groupings around the room. Then he invited his percussionist friends—Zakir, Airto and his wife Flora Purim, Billy, Michael Hinton, and various others (plus Phil Lesh)—over to the studio, and the real journey began: As the tape on the Studer A-80 16-track rolled (the principal engineers were Brett Cohen, Betty Cantor-Jackson, and Dan Healy), "We'd move around the room playing whatever inspired us," Mickey says. "You'd go over here and play bowls; go over

Mickey in heaven: surrounded by drums of all sizes, 1979.

PHOTO: SNOOKY FLOWERS

there and there are shakers; over there is The Beast. Francis didn't want this score to be done scene by scene. His idea was for me to go inside the Heart of Darkness [the title of the Joseph Conrad novel that inspired the film], to go up the river in search of Kurtz [Marlon Brando's renegade colonel character], so every time we did the music, we would start from the beginning of the movie and go all the way to the end. When the napalm comes, you jump on The Beam and here comes napalm! It was all very spontaneous and laborious and self-indulgent in a way, but wow—what great results!"

The Beam deserves a special mention here. "The Beam is based around the Pythagorean monochord," Mickey says. "It's not a musical instrument as much as it's a vibration, and it's all low end. It has 13 bass piano strings all tuned to the same note—*D*—and it's extremely resonant. I built my first one from a piece of Stinson Beach driftwood." However, the Beam that was constructed for *Apocalypse Now* (and subsequent versions) was made from an aluminum I-beam—all the better to generate all sorts of interesting tonal reflections that were captured by magnetic pickups and then blasted through loudspeakers. Sounds could be conjured by plucking the strings, scraping them with different textured metal shafts, pounding them, tapping harmonic points on the strings, or even hitting the aluminum part of the instrument—the whole apparatus was so sensitive and the sound was so exaggerated, everything came out outsized and strange. "It was perfect for that film," Mickey says, "and later it was perfect for the Grateful Dead." (Hart gave the *Apocalypse Now* Beam to basketball great and World's Tallest Deadhead Bill Walton. Walton also has a duplicate Beast…in his living room!)

For ten days and nights, the group worked informally under the name the Rhythm Devils, and at the end of their sessions, Mickey mixed the tapes down to two tracks and delivered them to the sound crew mixing the film at Zoetrope Studios in San Francisco—the one-time home of Columbus Recorders. Though ultimately not that much of the percussion score made it into the finished film (more came out on a fine album called *Rhythm Devils Play River Music: The Apocalypse Now Sessions*), Mickey was transformed by the experience, and he brought some of the project's energy to the Grateful Dead beginning that spring. The percussion-solo portion of the second set even became known as the Rhythm Devils segment, and Bill Kreutzmann became an eager co-conspirator in navigating the new tangle of instruments behind their traps.

Back in the 1970s, Mickey and Billy were very rarely interviewed by the music press, but there was one excellent interview in the August 1979 issue of *BAM* that not only got deeply into their drumming technique, but also gives us a thorough snapshot of their gear at the time: At Billy's urging, for their main kits they had both switched to Sonor drums, their first major move away from Ludwig and Rogers kits. Sonor is a German company that dates back to 1875, when a Bavarian drum maker named Johannes Link started his company in Weissenfels. It's been said that William Ludwig Sr. was influenced by Sonor drums' design and construction; whatever the case, Ludwig easily eclipsed Sonor in Britain and the United States during the rock drum boom in the last quarter of the 20th century. Still, Sonor did have its faithful followers, including Sonny Payne—one of Mickey's influences—and jazz great Jack DeJohnette, who was an endorser in the mid '70s. "How I got into Sonor," Kreutzmann says, "is Jerry was rehearsing his band at home and he didn't have a drummer or drum kit, so I needed a little set I could play over there. I found this little cocktail or jazz set, and I fell in love with how it sounded. Then I convinced Mickey we should each get a set, so that's what we did.

"The Sonors made a real difference in our sound," Billy continues. "Over the years we had changed from using skin heads and then plastic heads to these even *more* plastic heads [on the Sonors] that were made out of this bullet-proof material you could hit the heck out of and still get a great tone. [These were special heads developed by Joe Pollard, developer of the Syndrum.] The drums were really thick—an inch or more—and had a great tone and they were also *really* loud, which of course Mickey liked," he laughs. The shells were made of a rosewood/beech/rosewood lamination; according to Mickey, the drums

Red Rocks, 8/12/79. The Beast has already expanded since its debut in April '79. Billy and Mickey play Sonor drums. Jerry had just started playing the Irwin "Tiger," Bob was still on an Ibanez, and for the moment Phil was back to playing Big Brown.

PHOTO: BOB MINKIN

weighed a third more than any other commercial set on the market. The drummers didn't like the Sonor hardware, however, and changed over to Rogers hardware shortly after buying them.

One innovation the duo brought to their kits, also suggested by Billy, was to mount a third tom over the 24″ bass drum: "We took their floor tom off of a cocktail set and put it above to make three tom-toms, just to get another note up there," Billy says. "Then, when other companies saw the three drums like that, [the arrangement] started turning up in all the drum catalogs."

So, Mickey's traps set in 1979 consisted of a 14×7 snare; 8×12, 8×13, and 8×14 rack toms; 18×18 and 20×20 floor toms; a 15″ hi-hat; a selection of 18″, 19″, 20″, and 22″ Zildjian cymbals; and a 20″ prototype of an ungrooved Zildjian "Earth Cymbal." Billy's set was similar except his floor toms were 16×16 and 18×18, and he had three fewer cymbals.

Among the drums behind the kits were timbales and Remo Rototoms—drumheads ranging in size from 6″ to 14″ that can actually be tuned while playing by rotating the drum by the rim, which increases or decreases the tension on the head, thus changing the note. There was also what Hart termed his "electronic desert": a wooden slit drum, kalimba, and marimba, which were hooked up to a preamp, stereo mixer, and various effects ranging from a Morley wah and phase pedals to an Ibanez AD-230 stereo delay. And, of course, there was The Beast.

"The Beast changed everything," Hart says. "It allowed us to go off on these...*excursions* that were totally different from anything we had done before, and to get into some very deep and strange spaces. In the old days, our 'space' was when we all got confused, and we'd be trying to get the feedback going—the guitarists were shoving the guitars into the speakers," he laughs. "But that got old, because a lot of it was just screeching—like creatures coming out of the speakers, which was kind of cool, I guess. But once everybody got more sophisticated and then we developed The Beast, 'space' became a place for us to really do some interesting stuff in a musical context. This was a totally new kind of playground and, as we learned, it was really limitless. We would keep adding new things and it changed constantly, so it always sounded fresh."

EYE OF THE TIGER

There were other significant instrumentation changes in the Grateful Dead during 1979, including the arrival of Garcia's second custom axe from Doug Irwin, nicknamed Tiger for the stunning mother-of-pearl and brass inlay of a growling beast in an oval under the bridge. Garcia first played the guitar at a pair of shows at the Oakland Auditorium—which was the de facto successor to Winterland—at the beginning of August that year.

According to an interview with Irwin, he actually began work on this guitar shortly after he'd presented Wolf to Garcia: "He liked the Wolf so much when I delivered it that he said, 'I want you to make me another one, but I don't want you to hold back—I just want you to go for it.' He said, 'I'm not going to tell you what I want; you can just make it the way you want.' I really made an effort to make it my best effort. It's a guitar unlike any one I've ever built since then. It's got a lot of detailing on it. I actually put over 2,000 hours directly into working on that guitar." Tiger cost Garcia $5,800.

Unlike Wolf, which had a golden-brown hue, Tiger was a deep reddish color because its top layer was South American cocobolo, "dragged out of the jungle on muleback," Irwin said. The body also consisted of a layer of vermilion, a stripe of maple, and a flame-maple core. The layers were expertly glued together and further bound by a thin line of brass following the body contour and across the front. The neck was western maple with a padauk inlay, the fretboard ebony with a brass binding. It had a Schaller bridge and a custom tailpiece.

The electronics included three pickups: a single-coil DiMarzio SDS-1 Strat-style in the neck position, and two DiMarzio Dual Sound humbuckers in the middle and bridge positions. (In 1982, he would switch the Dual Sounds for a pair of Super Distortion IIs.) The pickups were controlled by a five-position selector switch and two three-way toggles for coil selection on the humbuckers (hum-canceling/hum-canceling dual/single-coil). "I can [also] use the half-positions, in and out of phase, and with the humbucking and single-coil switch on each pickup," Garcia said in a 1988 interview with Jon Sievert. "So right there, that's like 12 discrete possible voices that are all pretty different. And the whole thing with guitar and effects is getting something where you can hear the difference. That gives me a lot of vocabulary of basically different tones. And that's just the electronics; the rest of it is touch. I mostly work off the middle pickup in the single-coil setting, and I can get almost any sound I want out of that."

Another toggle was an on/off for Garcia's beloved effect loop/unity-gain buffer setup. Like the Wolf, there were two output jacks—one running in mono directly to Garcia's Fender Twin, the other to the effects rack and back, as described earlier.

Garcia would play this guitar almost exclusively for the next 11 years, the most of any of his axes. What made the Irwin guitars special to Garcia? "There's something about the way they feel with my touch—they're married to each other," he told Sievert. "The reason I went with his guitars in the first place was they just fell into my hand perfectly…. I'm not analytical about guitars, but I know what I like. And when I picked up [his first Irwin guitar], I'd never felt anything before or since that my hand likes better."

PHOTO: BOB MINKIN

The rest of Garcia's setup in '79 was similar to what he'd been using for a while: two Fender Twin preamps (one Silverface, one Blackface) into a McIntosh 2300 power amp out to a Hard Truckers 3×12 cabinet with JBL120 speakers. Effects were unchanged: Mu-Tron envelope filter and octave divider, and MXR analog delay, Distortion+, and Phase 100, all wired through a custom foot controller and effect-switching unit designed by John Cutler, and an Ernie Ball volume pedal.

As for Bob Weir, he was still playing an Ibanez guitar (as he would for the next few years), through an Intersound IVP (Instrument Voicing Preamplifier). Sometime in 1978, though, he had started using a Godzilla power amp, made by a short-lived entity called Great American Sound (GAS), which was originally founded in 1974 in Chatsworth, California (near L.A.), around the high-power "Ampzilla," designed by James Bongiorno. The later Godzilla was a Class-A solid-state amp that delivered 400 watts per channel through Bob's

Garcia takes his new Doug Irwin-designed axe, "Tiger," through its paces at Red Rocks, August '79. Note that Jerry's effects pedals are sitting at hand-level in two rows, rather than on the floor.

Hard Truckers cabinet, which contained eight 12″ Gauss speakers. Pedals and effects included a John Cutler-designed wah/phaser that could run either or both effects at once, Ibanez AD-202 analog delay and UE-400 multi-effects unit, Furman RV-2 reverb and parametric EQ, and an Ashly SC-50 compressor/limiter. (Other accounts also put an Ibanez AD-9 Auto Filter and an Ibanez Tube Screamer in his setup.) Weir, too, had the custom switching and controller units.

Beginning with the Oakland shows where Garcia first unleashed Tiger, Phil made some changes as well. For those shows and the short tour that followed, he went back to playing Big Brown again. By the time the November-December '79 tour of (mostly) the East Coast rolled around, however, he'd switched to a Doug Irwin bass that looked remarkably like Garcia's guitar. "[Irwin] happened to have one in stock for me, though Garcia's was custom-made," Phil told *Relix* in 1980. "It has a beautiful inlay [on the back]...a black panther or something. That's obviously his image."

HALFWAY ANNIVERSARY

THE AUGUST 4 and 5, 1979, shows at the Oakland Auditorium were notable for reasons other than the first appearance of Tiger. A couple of new songs were introduced: the loping Hunter-Garcia tune "Althea," and Weir and Barlow's moody "Lost Sailor," both of which would turn up on the Dead's next album. And Hamza El-Din showed up the second night to lead the crowd in rhythmic handclapping on "Ollin Arageed," a little Egypt flashback for the assembled throng. But probably very few in attendance that night (including your humble narrator) noticed that the Dead employed a completely different sound system that night, and the experience would end up having a profound impact on the Dead's future sound-reinforcement direction.

Chapter Thirteen

1979-1983

At this point in our story, you need to meet Don Pearson and Howard Danchik. Born and raised in Chicago, Pearson (who died unexpectedly during surgery in January 2006) cut his audio chops in D.C.-area recording studios in the late '60s and re-located to the Bay Area in the very early '70s. He briefly worked in SR for Jefferson Airplane; then he moved over to Hot Tuna, working as a roadie and soundman. That's where he met Howard Danchik, who was Tuna's front-of-house mixer. Howard had grown up around D.C. and once ran his own studio there, called Rutabaga Recording, before heading West in 1972. Together, Pearson and Danchik "developed a sound system with a company called Star-Fine Sound, who had bought parts of the old Grateful Dead Wall of Sound," Pearson told John Dwork in *The Deadhead's Taping Compendium, Volume II*. "So we worked on configuring that into a sound system for Hot Tuna tours throughout the '70s. During one of those periods [1975] Dan Healy called the owners and asked to take the Tuna system out on the road to use on an Ace [Weir], Keith & Donna tour." Pearson helped Healy put the system together for a show in St. Louis, "and from that point on, Healy and I became friends, and we started doing projects together.

"At the end of that Hot Tuna era, which was around '76 or '77, we got really involved in various projects. Healy and I would work on these projects all year long, which always culminated on New Year's, at whatever venue it happened to be—during those years it was Winterland. Every New Year's Eve, we would take the experimental things we were working on and try them." Pearson helped Harry Popick set up his custom monitor system in 1978, and on New Year's Eve that year—the Closing of Winterland—Pearson and Healy put together their first time-aligned PA system: "We built a very elaborate custom crossover that allowed us to have individual control of each of the sound system's sections: the woofers, the low bass, the mid-bass, the mid-high-end, and the tweeters," Pearson said in the same interview. A friend named Dennis Fink, who worked for UREI, "customized a delay unit so we could individually correct the arrival time of each of the system's components. That made it so the arrival time of sound at the user's ear was one, rather than being a smear. It was the first time a PA sound system had ever been aligned in that way…. It was five-way stereo, a very elaborate thing, but it was nothing you could ever take on the road. It was pieces and parts from five different companies, but it was quite a powerful system."

MORE PA CHANGES

Which brings us back to the Oakland Auditorium eight months later. Dan Healy picks up the story: "Those shows were basically like one-offs, and we didn't think they warranted bringing Clair Bros.' stuff out from Lititz, Pennsylvania; there wasn't enough money to do that. So we had a band meeting and Jerry asked, 'What do you think, Dan—can you scrape something together?' I said, 'I'll take a shot at it.' So we put together this big system, bumming equipment from all these different places. I had some stuff of my own, and we had some Grateful Dead stuff—some bits and pieces of the Wall of Sound. Donnie Pearson had some of his stuff left over from working with the Starship and Hot Tuna, too. We had some old Altec and JBL horns and these great Heil tweeters—it was like a big pile of different stuff that we divided into two and put on each side of the stage, and somehow we got it to sound really good."

"We got the vocal cluster and the piano cluster from the Wall of Sound and filled them with 12″ speakers," elaborates Dennis Leonard, who had been working with Hard Truckers, which morphed into being part of Pearson and Danchik's new San Rafael-based company, Ultrasound. "This was a collaborative effort between FM, John Meyer, Ultrasound, and Dan. We had a day that was just hanging the system and de-humming it, and then the next morning we had tuning, and I believe there was a one o'clock call for band gear; then they sound-checked that night, and the next day was the show.

Phil with his Irwin bass, September 1980. His love affair with the instrument was relatively short-lived, however.

"If you get a look at the vocal cluster and count speakers, there was one row that was not filled—we didn't use any of the 5's, and then the piano cluster was 32 12s, and we put half of the vocal cluster and half of the piano cluster up on scaffolding, and that was the midrange for the system. Then FM had these wonderful hot-rodded 4×15 ported cabinets [with JBL speakers], and we stacked four of those up per side. So we're talking about just over 40 12″ speakers per side in these spherical enclosures, and four of these 4×15 cabinets stacked vertically. Then outside of those were eight of the new single-18 cabinets John Meyer had made for the *Apocalypse Now* premiere. We also had a rack of Harbinger Fiberglas 90-degree horns—a really compact horn—and on those there were Gauss 2″-aperture high-frequency drivers. Ten of those horns were in an aluminum rack, and they were articulated a little like the way a line array would be articulated now. The wonderful icing on top of this cake was 16 ESF Heil ribbon tweeters [heavily modified by Healy and FM's Willie John Cashman]—they weighed

PHOTO: SNOOKY FLOWERS

like 25 pounds each, and it was all Alnico magnets; the ribbons were four inches tall by an inch wide, and they were in this graduated, line-array style. All of this stuff was hung way up and downstage so that it could be mechanically time-aligned first, and there was rudimentary UREI delay. Everything was run by Mac [2300] amps, and the tweeters were run by tube Macs [3500 vacuum-tube amps].... It was a really great-sounding system, and we put it together again for the New Year's shows at Oakland Auditorium that year, too."

As Leonard noted, John Meyer returns to the picture around this time. When we left him during the Wall of Sound era, he had gone off to Switzerland for about 18 months. When he moved back to the Bay Area, he did some consulting for McCune and others but mostly spent his time developing a new generation of loudspeakers, which would be sold by the company he and his wife Helen started, Meyer Sound Laboratories. The first product Meyer made, the ACD studio monitor, had its genesis in Switzerland in 1978 and in fact was built there and imported. Not surprisingly, the Grateful Dead were among the first clients:

"We did a demo in Berkeley at General Electronics, and Bear was there," Meyer remembers. "I hadn't seen him in a long time, and he said, 'Oh, this is *the kind*. You've got to bring this out to the Grateful Dead studio and show it to them.' He gave me the address on Front Street and gave me a time. So I went there and knocked on the door and it's, 'Who are you?' 'I'm John Meyer—I'm here to show some studio monitors.' 'We don't know about this!' 'Bear didn't tell you?' 'Oh, if it's from Bear, of course nobody would know. Since you're here, why don't you bring them in.' I didn't hear anything for a couple of days, and when I went on Monday morning to pick them up, they came out on their hands and knees and said, 'You can't take them!' So they bought some," he laughs. From that point on, Front Street would be equipped with Meyer monitors (replacing the UREI 813s that previously resided there), including the 833s (patented in 1986) and still-beloved HD-1s, which were patented in 1989.

Meyer claims that Bear liked the ACD so much that he decided to give it a try as a stage monitor for the Starship, with whom he was closely associated in the late '70s, "but it wasn't quite powerful enough or loud enough, and also it was too big," Meyer says. However, Bear disputes that he ever tried the "bulky, fragile" speakers in that capacity, noting that the band actually used another Meyer creation, McCune's JM-1s. "Don Pearson [who worked with the Starship at the time] tested every available stage monitor and those were the best-sounding, but they just weren't loud enough," Bear says. And so, at Bear's urging, and spurred by Paul Kantner's desire to have the smallest monitor box possible onstage, Meyer developed the UM-1 UltraMonitor, "which was specifically built to solve the low-profile issue but had the heavy electronics to be able to handle bass and all that stuff," Meyer says. The first two went to Frank Sinatra, and the next four, in 1980, to the Starship.

The compact UltraMonitor contained a proprietary 12″ low-frequency driver (instead of a 15, as in the JM-1) and a high-frequency horn/driver in a custom box designed in conjunction with Pearson and Danchik. But what truly differentiated it from other systems was the separate M-1 Control Electronic Unit (CEU), which, the company's literature at the time crowed, "provides electronic crossover, speaker protection, phase and amplitude correction, subwoofer interface, and specialized user/setup controls…. [It] is the last component in the signal chain before the user's power amplifiers." Basically, it was a highly efficient way of electronically managing powerful speakers through the constant monitoring of the RMS power, with limiting and other functions provided as needed, resulting in much lower distortion and wear and tear on the speakers. (Shortly after the UM-1 came out, Meyer followed with the UPA— UltraPA—which employed similar electronics, woofer, and driver, but with a wider-dispersion horn better suited to PA applications.)

That UltraMonitor was also designed to be used in conjunction with one of Meyer's subwoofers of the era, such as the model 650, a 110-pound box with single 18″ driver (plus the CEU) that was developed originally as a way of delivering massive low end for the 70mm prints of *Apocalypse Now*. Tom Scott of American Zoetrope (Coppola's production company) had heard Meyer's ACD reference monitor and accessory subwoofer and tasked Meyer with the job of coming up with a system that could convey the bone-rattling sounds of war. "Coppola wanted the sound of the napalm explosion to be felt in the audience, so we worked for three months on that, trying different subwoofers—stereo subwoofers, mono subwoofers, quadraphonic subwoofers [using San Francisco's Northpoint Theater, which was already equipped with a set of five Altec A-4 speaker systems]. I worked with Walter [Murch, sound designer on the film] on that until he was happy." Originally there were plans to equip some 50 theaters nationwide with top-flight systems including the Meyer subs, and he believed this was going to be his entrée into the movie business. But there were problems with some of the E-V drivers—"They started burning up," Meyer says—and by the time a company in Italy was found to adequately replace them, Warner Bros. had canceled the sound upgrades in all but seven theaters. FM Productions, which had subsidized the speakers, was left with a warehouse of the subs, but they would find their way into many systems—the Dead's included, as described earlier—and through Bear, Meyer was also able to audition the speaker for Phil Lesh, who was, of course, intrigued.

Kidd Candelario recalls, "I remember John [Meyer] brought over a single 650 to demonstrate for Phil, and we set it up at Front Street. Phil played a couple of big notes, and the speaker popped out of the diaphragm and extended totally. Meyer looked at the technician who was with him and said, 'Oh, I guess we need *two* speakers in that cabinet,'" he chuckles. (Meyer subsequently introduced the 650-R2, with a double-18.)

IT'S GODZILLA!

Another factor that added to the beefiness of Phil's bass sound was his adoption of GAS Godzilla amps like Weir used. What did he like about them? "Sizzling-fast transient response and gobs of power!" is Phil's simple reply. (Back in 1982, Phil had enthused to David Gans about the amps, "All I know is that now I can be as loud as Garcia—and that takes some doing.")

Peter Miller remembers that when the Dead called upon him in the very early '80s to do some repair work on one of the amps, "I didn't know anything about it. They told me John [Cutler] doesn't want to touch it," he laughs. "We didn't have any schematics, and we didn't know other people who had them. Out of the 25 Godzillas ever made, the Dead had five of them. All we had was the designer's name, so I had to track down Andy Hefley, who at the time was working at Hughes Aircraft designing electronics to go on satellites. It was a great amp, though. The specs were incredible: 1,000 watts into two ohms per channel stereo.

"A little later," Miller continues, "Phil had Andy build him four custom [amplifier] units—the only four ever built—and those were under the PIE name: Precision Innovative Electronics. It was a derivative of the Godzilla amplifier, and Phil had him name it the M87 [after a huge elliptical galaxy discovered in the late 18th century by astronomer Charles Messier—a typically Phil touch]. I was the host of the meeting when Phil and Andy came to my store here in San

One of Phil's legendary custom PIE amps. At 4,000 watts, this baby had some serious punch.

PHOTO: ROBERT MINKIN

Mateo, and we settled on the specifications he wanted, and then Andy went away and built them. They were totally hand-made. Andy was a brilliant designer who'd had a lot of contact with the space industry; one of the really cool things in it was this fan that was out of one of the missiles they sent into space. It was modulated by temperature, so when you first switched on the amp the fan would be turning real slowly, kind of lumping along, and then as the amp got hot it would speed up to the point where, when it was cranking, it was pretty noisy. [The PIE amp] was 4,000 watts mono; it weighed in at something like 180 pounds, and he used two at a time. The Ultrasound guys used to tease Phil that he had more power for the low frequencies [in his rig] than they had for the whole PA, though I don't know if that was true or not."

The Dead started work on their first studio album of the Brent era at Club Front in the summer of '79. This time out they chose British producer/engineer Gary Lyons to sprinkle a little commercial magic dust on them—he had previously worked with the likes of Queen, Alice Cooper, Wet Willie, and perhaps most famously, Foreigner. An amiable sort of chap who was particularly known for capturing good guitar and drum sounds, he wasn't intimidated by the prospect of taming the band he joked "had the reputation as being the Bermuda Triangle for producers."

In a 1995 interview Lyons told me that when he started the album, which would later be titled *Go to Heaven*, "They had the songs but they hadn't had a chance to develop them much onstage at that point, which I gather is not the way they generally worked. So they'd come in and everybody would have all sorts of suggestions about tempos and feel. Jerry more or less had his things worked out, so it became a question of capturing that magical moment, which was not easy. We must have recorded 'Althea' a hundred times. We'd do it ten or 15 times and then go on to another song, and come back to it later or the next day or whatever. Eventually it fell into place and it came out quite nicely.

"Bobby, on the other hand, might have the basic idea for a song, but he might not even have the melody worked out. We'd get the tracks down and he'd still be working on the melody and lyrics. Bobby took a little more advice from me; we collaborated a little closer, and we became good friends on the project."

Weir's contributions to *Go to Heaven* included "Feel Like a Stranger" and the connected pair of "Lost Sailor" and "Saint of Circumstance." Brent had a pair of tunes as well, which he'd originally written with the Bob Weir Band in mind, before he joined the Dead: "Easy to Love You" and "Far From Me." The "new guy" got to contribute a variety of synth textures to the record, including a pitch-bending Minimoog lead line on Garcia's sprightly rocker "Alabama Getaway," and a combination of Minimoog and Prophet-5 on "Feel Like a Stranger." Betty Cantor-Jackson was the album's primary engineer.

Suggested listening:
Recorded before most of the
material had fully ripened,
Go to Heaven still showcased
some fine tunes by both
Garcia and Weir, including
"Althea" and the dynamic
combo of "Lost Sailor" and
"Saint of Circumstance." To
hear what live dynamos the
songs on *Go to Heaven*
became a little later, check
out *Go to Nassau*, recorded
In Long Island, 5/15–16/80.

The studio work was staggered over several months because of the Dead's touring commitments, and Lyons noted that "when they'd come back, the songs would have changed a bit. But it was actually fine having the breaks [in recording]. I was trying to do an Aerosmith album [*Night in the Ruts*] at the same time, so I'd be two weeks in New York with Aerosmith, who were going in one direction, and then a couple of weeks on the West Coast with the Dead, who couldn't have been more different. In New York it was all doing lines of coke and running around, and in California it was smoking pot, being laid-back, and everything was cool. It was a strange combination.

"Peter Thea, my assistant, would work with them while I was back doing Aerosmith. He'd be sending me cassettes of the overdubs and I'd make comments. Then I'd go out to California and be with the Dead, and Peter would go to New York and take over the Aerosmith record. Finally, I finished the Aerosmith album and then could devote more time to the Dead."

Eventually, though, work on the album bogged down to the point where the Dead booked time at Mediasound Studios in New York when they were on the East Coast, fitting in overdub work there whenever they could. "Jerry was so great to work with," Lyons recalled. "He was very curious and always interested in what I was doing. And in general he was very patient; he didn't get frustrated if things didn't happen easily. Sometimes he'd do solos and there'd be good bits and bad bits, so we'd compile a solo from different performances. I'd combine all the best licks into one great solo."

However, Betty Cantor-Jackson told me this story about one of Lyons's attempts to construct a Garcia solo for the record: "One day Gary said to me, 'I want to play you this combine I did of all these different guitar tracks, like five tracks of guitar leads.' So he played it for me, and I said, 'He wouldn't play it that way.' He said, 'What? What's wrong with it? He played all of it.' I said, 'There's nothing *wrong* with it; he just wouldn't play it in that way.' So Jerry comes in later and Gary says, 'I want you to listen to the combine track I did.' And Jerry listens to it and says, 'I wouldn't play it that way,'" she laughs. "It was true, because his style had a certain logic, and there were certain ways he put together notes—the sequence of notes, which had to do with the way he thought about music. So to cut that up, it no longer sounded like the way Jerry thought."

Go to Heaven was completed in the late winter of 1980 and released at the end of April, several months behind Arista's timetable. Another *Saturday Night Live* appearance and copious radio airplay helped make "Alabama Getaway" a minor hit, but the album as a whole was not as commercially successful as its two Arista predecessors. Typically, the Dead shrugged it off—by this time their attitude toward studio albums was, "Oh, well, too bad…maybe *next* time."

GD: ACOUSTIC AND ELECTRIC

That fall the Dead decided to celebrate their 15th anniversary by adding an acoustic set to their already long shows. They were booked into San Francisco's 2,000-seat Warfield Theatre for a whopping 15-night run stretching from the end of September to mid October; then, following two shows in New Orleans, the action shifted to New York's sumptuous art deco palace, Radio City Music Hall, for eight shows, culminating in a closed-circuit telecast to select East Coast theaters on Halloween night. All in all it was quite a month.

An acoustic set at the Warfield Theatre in San Francisco, 10/13/80. Garcia is playing a Takamine, Phil his Irwin bass, and Weir an Ovation.

PHOTO: JAY BLAKESBERG

The Warfield is set up for one of the Dead's acoustic sets, September–October 1980. The white instrument next to the piano is a harpsichord. The hanging speakers are Meyer JM-10s.

The acoustic sets were a wonderful treat for Deadheads. They included a number of old folk, country, and old-time songs outside of the band's usual repertoire—George Jones's "The Race Is On," Elizabeth Cotten's "Oh, Babe It Ain't No Lie," the Memphis Jug Band's "On the Road Again," et al.—and also several Dead songs played in acoustic arrangements for the first time, such as "Cassidy," "To Lay Me Down," "Bird Song," "China Doll," and others, always culminating in a grand ol' sing-along on "Ripple."

For these acoustic sets, Weir chose an Ovation, which he notes "were all the rage for a while. They're good guitars, too; they work. That one had a nice, rich, full sound, and it blended nicely with Jerry's guitar." In a 1981 interview, he had also noted, "I tried a FRAP [Flat Response Audio Pickup, a minuscule transducer-preamp combo] on my Martin 000-21, but I couldn't get the feedback down to an acceptable level, even though it sounded good."

It's true that Ovation did take the acoustic music world by storm beginning in the late '60s when Glen Campbell played one of the guitars every week on his popular television variety show, *The Glen Campbell Goodtime Hour*. The company was founded in the mid '60s by Charlie Kaman, whose aviation company, begun in the '40s, designed and built helicopters—these days, Kaman Aerospace is part of a billion-dollar company called the Kaman Corporation. Charlie was also an avid guitarist on the side, and in 1964 he put together a team of aerospace engineers and technicians—some of whom also had woodworking experience—to design a new kind of acoustic guitar. He believed that a traditional flat back hindered both the tonal balance and the projection capabilities of the instrument. What the team came up with, and began marketing in 1966, was a guitar with a wooden top and neck, but a rounded back of molded fiberglass.

When Campbell asked Kaman to electrify his Ovation, the engineers designed a piezo pickup—and with that, the Ovation became the first popular electric-acoustic guitar. Certainly, Ovation guitars have a very distinctive sound (which is not to everyone's taste): The combination of the molded back and wood top (Weir's was from the era when they were using Sitka spruce) gave the instrument a big, resonant—but not particularly woody—sound. No one would ever confuse it with a choice Martin, but it proved to be an excellent and surprisingly rugged live-performance guitar for many, many performers. It remains very popular to this day.

Garcia played a Takamine F-360 guitar, perhaps because it, too, was one of the few brands at that time that had a built-in piezo pickup. Based in Sakashita, Japan (and named for a mountain there), Takamine started as a small family business and over the course of several decades grew to be an internationally successful company. Beginning in 1978, some of the Takamine's acoustic models included a pickup consisting of six piezo transducers embedded in the bridge plate. The best guess of the exact model of Garcia's guitar is 1978–80 F-360, sometimes nicknamed the "lawsuit dreadnought" because of a popular rumor that Takamine had been sued by Martin over the guitar's uncomfortable similarity to a 1938 "Dreadnought" Martin D-28. (There was no such lawsuit.) The top was spruce, the back and sides rosewood. Copy or not, the guitar sounded great, and Garcia was happy enough with Takamine's electric-acoustics that he later got a single-cutaway model.

Except for Phil, who played his Irwin bass, the other band members altered their setups for the acoustic sets as well. Mickey and Billy would switch back and forth between a tiny kit—snare, hi-hat, and 18″ kick—and a small setup of Valje congas: Valje, founded by Tom Flores, was a renowned L.A.-based maker of hand-made Cuban-style congas and bongos from 1954 until 1983. Brent had a rented Steinway baby grand piano and, just for the haunting "China Doll," a harpsichord. "I never did feel comfortable with that thing," Brent told *Keyboard* in 1982. "I kept missing the sustain

Suggested listening: The 1981 two-record set *Reckoning* was drawn from the acoustic sets of the band's multi-night runs at the Warfield Theatre in San Francisco and Radio City Music Hall in New York City.

pedal and the control of dynamics. You try to hit something soft and it doesn't come out soft."

Adding to the festiveness of the Warfield and Radio City runs was the fact that all 23 shows were recorded for possible inclusion on a pair of live double-albums that came out at different times the next year: *Reckoning* brilliantly captured the magic of the acoustic sets, while *Dead Set* was an uneven but beautiful-sounding recording of the 1980 electric Dead—the group's first official live release since the woeful *Steal Your Face*.

A lot had changed in the Dead's live recording setup since Bob and Betty were dragging the ol' Ampex MM-1000 and MX-10 mixers around Europe. Healy designed the recording system, and Betty Cantor-Jackson supervised the recording during the show and mixed it all later at Club Front. Paramount to Healy this time out was to create a nearly holographic sound image to give a sense of the music existing in a three-dimensional space.

This was accomplished, Pearson explained to John Dwork in *The Deadhead's Taping Compendium, Vol. II*, by devising a unique recording setup: "Two Studer 16-tracks were recording the live mics from the stage, while [four Ampex ATR] 4-track machines were [capturing] different microphones' positions spaced out through the room—we had some at the stage, some a third of a way out, some halfway out, and some by the mixing board. Each of those was on a separate 4-track recorder. Two of those tracks were for the microphones, and the third was the SMPTE [timecode] track [which allowed the 16-tracks and 4-tracks to stay in sync]. So when we went to play it back, using a [SMPTE] resolver, we could take the multitrack tapes and then move the room mics up and back and forward in time until there wasn't any echo. So you had all the presence of the mics onstage and the ambience of the room, but the ambience was in time with the stage mics. That's why those live shows have that sound—because we had the ability to move the room mics backward and forward in time until it sounded acoustically the way we wanted it to."

At the Warfield, a basement room that had been a speakeasy during Prohibition became a makeshift control room, with the Neve console from Front Street brought in for the occasion, a similar second rented console added, and Meyer ACD monitors and smaller Hard Truckers full-range speakers set up in front of the boards. For the Radio City shows, they rented two Neves and had them carried up several flights of stairs to the seventh-floor Plaza Sound Studio—after considerable trouble. "They had to knock out part of an overhead stairway because they couldn't get it up the last flight of stairs," Betty told John Dwork. "Finally they said, 'Oh, the hell with it!' and they brought out a sledgehammer and started knocking out the wall." Needless to say, this did not go over well with the powers-that-be, as the stunning art deco theater is a bona fide historical landmark and protected by law. But the fact was, the Dead had sent ahead blueprints of the Neve to Radio City, and the mistake—a mere two inches of clearance—was on their end; later, the person who had made the miscalculation was fired. At least the potentially long cable run to the seventh floor wasn't an issue: Radio City had its own built in tie-lines linking the studio to the stage.

Another problem Betty faced in New York was that the Neve's monitor section got blown out by a mod done to another part of the board. "I had no monitoring, so to listen to my mix—well, to listen to anything—the only monitoring I had was out of the tape machine's electronics," Betty said. "I was plugging my headphones into each track. I had one ear to each track, and that's how I mixed them . . . . Sometimes it got to be a little much. After all, I was doing two stereo drum kits, and I could only listen to one half of each of those drum sets in one ear at a time."

A touch that seems quaint in retrospect but was actually fairly bold at the time: Don Pearson also brought an Apple II computer to the studios to assist in cataloging tapes, keeping track of mic and effect assignments, and printing out song lists, among other things. Within a decade, of course, computers would become ubiquitous and indispensable.

During this period, the Dead were using a Clair Bros. system for most of their tours, but on the West Coast they often relied on the sort of integrated patchwork system they had pioneered at the Oakland Auditorium. At both the Warfield and Radio City shows in the fall of '80, instead of the Clair S-4s, the PA consisted of a pair of Meyer Sound Labs three-way JM-10s—a huge cousin to the JM-3—supplied by McCune Audio (each side had 12 12″ woofers, six midrange horns, and 30 tweeters); six JM-3s for front fill; FM Productions' System 80 hanging center cluster, which incorporated Meyer modified woofers, horns, and Heil tweeters; and a dozen UltraMonitors provided by Ultrasound. Additionally, Phil tried out a prototype of the 650 double-18 subwoofer.

PHIL SWITCHES AGAIN

It was during 1981 that Phil stopped using his Irwin bass—"It didn't sound right, and the balance was too peghead-heavy" is all he recalls today about his dissatisfaction—and for a very brief period switched to a Fender Jazz Bass for the first time since the summer of 1967! "That was a classic Jazz Bass, with concentric volume and tone knobs, that I bought from a neighbor in Fairfax," Phil told me in 2006. "It disappeared from the GD warehouse after Jerry's death, probably into some roadie's collection. Great instrument—wish I still had it."

However, he didn't like it enough to actually keep playing it. Within a couple of months he'd moved on to a G&L L-2000, which was not a radical departure, certainly: It had a Fender lineage. G&L took its name from George Fullerton and Leo Fender, who had worked together at Fender from the late '40s (when

George helped Leo develop the Broadcaster) until 1970, five years after Fender sold the original company to CBS. Beginning in 1975, George and Leo developed instruments for Music Man (itself a spin-off of Fender started by two ex-employees, Tommy Walker and Forrest White), but by 1980 the two old chums had started G&L, trying to update and improve on their classic designs. Stylistically, the L-2000 was certainly in keeping with the look and feel of '50s and '60s Fender instruments, and the fact that it was a few pounds lighter than the Irwin was certainly a plus.

Once he stopped using the Irwin bass, Phil switched back to a Fender Jazz Bass for a brief period. This is from the Greek Theatre in Berkeley, September 1981, backdrop by Courtenay Pollack, who was responsible for the tie-dyes on the band's amps in the early '70s.

PHOTO: RON DELANY

One aspect of the G&L instruments that Leo Fender was particularly high on was that the neck was a single piece of maple, rather than laminated: "It's one piece of wood with the same expansion factor from humidity change, since it all grew in one place in one tree," he told David Gans in *BAM* in 1980. "The cell structure is the same all the way through, so if there's any humidity change, it's going to react uniformly." Another feature was that the base of the frets actually cut through the fretboard and were anchored in the neck itself, which segmented the rosewood fretboard and eased the tension that's sometimes created by having a single-piece glued-on fretboard pulling the neck.

Internally, it had G&L TriTone active/passive electronics, and Phil appreciated that "it's louder and it has more tone controls than the Fender, and it has a master volume," he told Gans in 1982. "On the Jazz, when I wanted to change the volume, I had to use two fingers, and I couldn't do it very rapidly. The G&L also has treble boost and bass boost and humbucker-to-single-coil switching. I always use the single coil, because the humbuckers sound so choked. I don't quite understand that, because other humbucking pickups don't sound like that." Other components of his sound during this era included the Intersound IVP preamp, the aforementioned Godzilla power amps, and eight Meyer loudspeakers: four 18s and four 15s.

Phil played the G&L until the end of 1982, when his long love affair with Modulus graphite-necked basses began. The roots of Modulus are in the U.S. aerospace industry, and, indirectly, the Grateful Dead. Geoff Gould, who developed the neck, was already a fan of the Dead when he saw his first concert in 1969 while he was a freshman at the University of California at Santa Barbara. This was shortly after he'd bought his first bass, a 1964 Fender Jazz, and needless to say he was mightily impressed by Phil Lesh when he saw him live. Gould eventually left UCSB, moved back to the South Bay region where he'd grown up, and took a job as a technician at Philco-Ford Aerospace in Palo Alto. One of the projects he worked on while he was there was the Voyager space probe— as a materials technician for the antenna.

Gould picks up the story. "In October 1974 the Dead played five nights at Winterland right before they took their break [the hiatus]. I was always interested in what Phil was up to, and that night I noticed he was playing this bass with a big, woolly strap—that was the Alembic with the George Mundy electronics in it. I thought, 'Huge strap—that bass must be heavy.' And that got me thinking about whether some of the materials I'd been working with might be good for a neck, because when you're making stuff to put into space, it's all about weight and strength.

"Not long after that, I heard an interview on KSAN with Rick Turner, I think it was, talking about Alembic equipment, and after talking to my bosses, I took a few samples of various doo-dads made of various composite materials up to the place that became Stars Guitars on Brady Street, next to the Alembic studio.

PHOTO: JAY BLAKESBERG

Phil with his G&L bass at Frost Amphitheatre at Stanford U. in October 1982. If it looks like a Fender it's because the "L" in G&L stands for Leo Fender. The pickups and controls differed from the Jazz Bass, however.

They had what they called a 'war council'—it must have been a board meeting or something—and they thought the stuff was pretty cool, so we arranged for them to come down and visit [Philco-Ford]—I remember it was the day *Blues for Allah* was premiered on the radio [in the summer of '75]. So we talked about working together on something; they were pretty excited.

"What happened next is Alembic replicated the short-scale bass that Stanley Clarke was playing; he was a big customer of theirs. And then we made a neck mold down at the aerospace place, and we made the neck out of graphite; it was a through-body with a short-scale neck. I think it was April of the following year that we finished the first prototype. There was a Return To Forever concert at Berkeley Community Theater with the classic lineup of Chick Corea, Al DiMeola, Clarke, and Lenny White, and at the soundcheck, Stanley played his regular Alembic bass and then he played our bass—and you could *really* hear the difference. There was much more presence; it seemed more focused. Everything about the two basses was identical except for the neck, so it was pretty eye-opening. Stanley was very impressed and interested.

"So we took this bass back to the satellite factory and kind of ran it up the flagpole. It went up a couple of levels [at Philco-Ford], and a guy finally said, 'Well, this is really nice. But we're in the business of building satellites, not guitars'—so it was dead in the water. If we were going to do this, we had to figure some way to do it."

Shortly after that, Gould started Modulus Graphite (now Modulus Guitars) and hooked up with Alembic for a co-venture, making Fender-style graphite necks. In January 1977 he was awarded a patent for carbon-fiber musical-instrument necks. The graphite necks were lighter than the traditional Alembic wood-laminate necks and also both stiffer and denser than wood, "so the energy stays truer and in the string; it's not sucked up as much, and the overtones are purer," Gould says. "Wickersham and I even measured it. In the beginning we used ebony fingerboards, but they were very unstable and had a lot of problems, so we ended up using what you might say was an ebony substitute—a phenolic laminate, which was like paper layers impregnated with black-dyed phenolic. When Steinberg came out with the same thing later they called it ebonol," he laughs.

When the relationship with Alembic came to an end, Gould kept Modulus moving forward, building custom 5- and 8-string basses for the likes of John Entwistle of the Who, Greg Lake (of ELP fame), and many others. But it was a photo of Gould himself holding a 6-string bass in an issue of *Guitar Player* that prompted Phil Lesh to call him out of the blue late in 1982. In a magazine article published around that time, Phil had talked about how he was working with Doug Irwin on another bass, "but I don't think they got very far with it," Gould says. "So I delivered a bass to him, and he played it for the first time at the Christmas run in 1982 [at the Oakland Auditorium]. My wife, who was very pregnant, and my five-year-old son, got to be guests behind Phil up on the stage, and Kidd gave us a bunch of Steal Your Face stickers. Then the next day my wife had a baby. The new era was on.

"That initial 6-string bass had a 35″ scale and was actually built on a 4-string neck, so it was pretty tight [string] spacing. We made two or three different variations on that one." The pickups were active Bartolinis, similar in many ways to Alembic pickups. When I asked Phil in the spring of 2006 what he liked about switching to 6-string after so many years playing 4-string basses, he noted, "Mostly it enables me to extend my thoughts in both high and low registers. The biggest problem was adjusting to the narrower string spacing," though obviously he quickly overcame that. The larger appeal of the Modulus bass for Phil, though, was "the tremendous sustain from the carbon-fiber through-body neck, and massive low notes."

BOB GOES GRAPHITE, TOO

The following summer, Bob Weir ended his long association with Ibanez and started playing Modulus instruments as well. Weir's first Modulus guitar, which was black, was a through-body Strat-style made of koa, and had a Floyd Rose bridge. "I fell for the Modulus guitars right away," Weir says. "I really liked the

PHOTO: JON SIEVERT

Modulus founder Geoff Gould with one of the early graphite-necked guitars, circa 1983.

rigidity of the necks—that plus the fact that you take the guitar out of the case and it's the same guitar you put in the case, no matter what climate changes there have been. With some wooden necks, you could spend a whole soundcheck just getting it to feel right again, and then if it's warm out, like an outdoor gig, it might still not feel right when you get to the gig. The Modulus neck solved that problem completely."

Weir played a long succession of Modulus-necked guitars for the rest of the Dead's history, sometimes using two or more at a show and using so many, "I have no idea exactly when he used what," Gould says with a chuckle. As we go through the '80s and '90s we'll look at some of them in a little more detail.

Brent acquired a Yamaha GS1 polyphonic synth at the beginning of 1983, and that became a staple of his sound for the next couple of years. "That was like a piece of furniture," Kidd Candelario says, and he's not kidding. Weighing some 200 pounds and built primarily for studio use, the GS1 had a wood frame that made it look like a cross between a baby grand piano and a B-3. It had a full complement of 88 keys and a fairly extensive library of 32 pre-programmed voices, with space for other custom ones. "It was pretty temperamental," Kidd recalls, "but it had some nice sounds. It had a [magnetic] card reader and these teenie strips that were about four inches long by a half-inch wide. You could go down to the Yamaha store and get sounds from them [on the strips], and then we started making some of our own programs, too." One of Brent's favorite textures on the GS1 was a woody timbre that sounded almost like a combination of a Rhodes and a marimba, but he managed to coax many other interesting noises from it before he moved on to other instruments in the late '80s (such as the Yamaha DX7, one of the GS1's more popular successors). Other instruments in Brent's setup at this time included the B-3, Rhodes, Minimoog, and Prophet-10. He had a Biamp Systems mixer that all his instruments and Leslies were run through, McIntosh 2300 power amps, and mostly Gauss speakers—10s and 12s for the mids, 15s for the lows—and ESS/Heil air-motion transformers for the highs.

By 1982–83, the Dead had finally disassociated themselves with Clair Bros. once and for all and had switched over completely to a Meyer PA supplied by Ultrasound. There had been a time in the early '80s when they still used a

Clair system in the East and Midwest, but after a point Healy wanted to make the switch—especially after Meyer introduced the MSL-3, which consists of two proprietary MS-12 low-frequency cone drivers, an MS-2001A high-frequency driver, a 70-degree modified radial horn, and the Meyer CEU. As usual, Meyer devised the system with the clarity of classical music and opera in mind, but it was quickly embraced by sound-conscious rock artists: Frank Zappa was the first to buy stacks of MSL-3s for his traveling PA, and Ultrasound wasn't far behind.

"[Healy] did a shootout between Clair and the [Meyer] MSL-3s up at the Greek Theater [in Berkeley in 1981]," Meyer reveals. "We were on one side and Clair was on the other side…and after that, they ordered more speakers [from us], so I guess we won. I guess [Roy] Clair was really mad at losing that account. Bear claimed that Roy had a picture of me that he threw darts at, but with Bear, you never know," he laughs.

Healy notes, "I remember at one point going back to talk to Jerry and saying, 'I cannot go back to Clair Bros.' God bless them—I love them all, and they were all wonderful to us and I was eternally grateful that they were there when we needed them, but they were looking at hundreds of bands operating worldwide, so for them to take the time to customize sound equipment for any one band was stretching them; it wasn't in the scope of their business. There were so many things we wanted to try—we were always testing something or looking up the road to see what we could do next—and Clair just wasn't the company that was going to allow us to do that. But Don [Pearson] and Howard [Danchik] were right there with us, so it was easy to go with Ultrasound."

It should be noted, however, that before Healy took that ultimate step, he asked Clair Bros. to purchase some MSL-3s from Meyer. "Dan said, 'Please buy these MSL-3s and I'll rent them from you," Howard Danchik says. "But Clair said, 'Sorry, we only do in-house.' So Healy said, 'Well, it's up to you, boy,' and that was it."

In the early days of the Meyer system, the Dead used a setup that included eight MSL-3s per side, but that quickly escalated as the band needed more power for bigger venues. Also, the MSL-3's original design included a bank of four piezo tweeters (Meyer says that Frank Zappa's engineer had turned him on to that notion), but according to Howard Danchik, "we didn't like the piezo tweeters and disconnected them and just ran the cabinets two-way." Meyer loudspeakers would be a part of the Dead's sound until the end. Ultrasound's power amp of choice in this era was the Crest 3500 (from New Jersey-based Crest Audio, founded in the early '80s by John Lee), which delivered 475 watts per channel in a relatively compact two-rackspace chassis—although with the numbers the Dead used, the 3500s could barely be considered space-savers! Crest, too, would be on the Dead's gear list until the story ends.

Suggested listening: There have been relatively few official releases from the early '80s, but two that are worth hearing are *Dick's Picks Vol. 13*, from Nassau Coliseum 5/16/81 (famous for its jam after "He's Gone") and *Dick's Picks 32*, a solid outing from Alpine Valley, Wisconsin (8/7/82)

Another part of the sound puzzle was solved in 1983 when the Dead started using Gamble consoles for both the front-of-house (Healy) and monitors (Harry). The company is the namesake of Jim Gamble, who grew up a surfer dude at the beach south of L.A. but at a young age got involved in the sound world and started his own PA company, Audio-Tech. Eventually, however, he merged with one of his competitors and became part of Tycobrahe (named for the Danish astronomer), for whom he built custom consoles and loudspeakers—whatever was needed. In fact, in 1974 Tycobrahe provided the PA for the opening act—Maria Muldaur—at a Santa Barbara show featuring the Dead and their Wall of Sound. "They offered to let me use the Wall with Maria," Gamble says from his Lake Tahoe headquarters, "but I didn't want to, and I really didn't want to use their dueling microphones—the concept was fabulous, but in reality you couldn't rely on the musicians to hit the spots. So I said, 'No, we're not using your shitty PA—we brought our own!'" he laughs. "Actually, they ended up being pretty amazed that the little amount of gear we brought went so loud."

Many years having passed, Tycobrahe is a distant memory for Gamble; now he's devoting himself completely to building high-quality consoles. "Don Pearson came by one day and he really liked what we were doing, so he bought a Gamble HC-40 for the house, and then they bought an HC-32 stage [monitor] console. They were *real* happy to run into me. They said, 'Forty channels? Oh, my God, we've never seen that many!'"

Harry Popick adds, "Don had his finger in so many pies everywhere all over the country, if there was something new, Don knew about it. He educated all of us about so many things, and the Gamble was one of them."

What set Gamble's console apart from others on the market (which in the early '80s were still few in number)? "Well, for one thing, it had all-digital VU meters, which was kind of different at that time," Gamble offers. "It also had a built-in digital spectrum analyzer with digital tenth-octave filters that you could switch over to and look at the whole spectrum on that same display. So that was pretty cool. It had full parametric [EQ], which was unusual. It also had higher-class ICs than anyone else was using at the time.

"I didn't cut any corners; we used great capacitors and great topology, and we were really careful about *everything*. It's something you can do, but which most people don't do. We knew we were never going to get rich doing this, but it doesn't matter. Our philosophy was, let's do it the best it can possibly be. And that's an idea that Don Pearson and all the people at Ultrasound supported, and which Dan Healy and the Grateful Dead supported, so it was great that we found each other."

"Jim [Gamble] had a great ear," Harry says. "He didn't just put components together and say, 'Okay, here's a preamp.' I consider him famous for his 70-percent rejection rate—he would actually send back 70 percent of the parts he bought. What that did was yield a consistency and sameness through each output, each stage of his console, and I think that enabled him to make the best console out there. Nobody else took the time to do that.

"Then, on the other side, you have Ultrasound handling the consoles, and they would modify them, tear them apart. They would fix the grounding, improve things. They would measure things most other sound companies wouldn't bother with. Pearson helped Jim make them more road-worthy, and Don was also in touch with every single person who owned one; I mean *everybody*. So once we got the Gamble consoles we were happy; it was one less thing to worry about. Between the Meyer [sound system] and the Gamble consoles, we had some stability in our main [system] that we really hadn't ever had before. Of course we never really stopped messing with things," he adds with a laugh. Indeed.

A TOUCH OF SUPERSTARDOM

THE EARLY and mid '80s were an interesting time for the Grateful Dead. Unfortunately, hanging over the band during this period was Garcia's severe drug addiction, which definitely seemed to put a damper on his personal creativity: He wrote very few songs from 1980 through 1985, and he expressed little interest in recording—this after reliably pumping out one studio album after another from 1967 through 1979. By 1984 he was frighteningly pale and obese, and his once-bubbly stage demeanor had changed dramatically. Still, the early '80s was a period of tremendous growth for the Dead's fan base. They regularly packed arenas throughout the country, and this is the era when the colorful Deadhead bazaar *outside* of shows sprang up and became an attraction itself. It helped, too, that the band started playing more interesting venues during this time: the Greek Theatre in Berkeley, Palo Alto's Frost Amphitheater, the County Fairgrounds in Ventura (on the coast north of L.A.), Alpine Valley in rural Wisconsin, and Colorado's Red Rocks (which they actually first played in '78), to name just a few—places that became destinations rather than just concert sites. No wonder more people than ever before followed the Dead on their tours.

Chapter Fourteen
1984-1987

And despite Garcia's alarming physical condition and Phil's occasional, obvious bouts of ennui (he once referred to that era as "the Heineken years"), the Dead could still get it goin' in a big way pretty consistently. Brent settled into the keyboard chair nicely. Ever the showman, Weir was always willing and able to step into the breach when Garcia was not at full strength. And show after show, Mickey and Billy delighted and amazed the crowds with their incredibly varied percussion assault: The Rhythm Devils' solo in the second set was reliably *great* every night—a trip worth taking! A few new original songs got added to the mix, too, among them Hunter and Garcia's anthemic "Touch of Gray" and the slinky, bluesy "West L.A. Fadeaway," and Weir and Barlow's anti-political rant "Throwing Stones" and the driving rocker "Hell in a Bucket." Plenty of interesting cover tunes were introduced, too, including "Dear Mr. Fantasy," "Gimme Some Lovin'," "Why Don't We Do It in the Road" (!), and "Keep On Growing," among others.

In February 1984, the Dead made a very tentative stab at recording a new album when they convened at Berkeley's Fantasy Studios on and off for a couple of weeks. This change of scenery had been Weir's idea—he was hoping that perhaps being in a new environment, rather than Club Front, might light a fire under the band. However, not much got done. Garcia was out of sorts the

The Greek Theatre in Berkeley was one of several great new venues the band played regularly during the '80s. This shot is from 5/23/82. You loved the "Scarlet" that night.

PHOTO: JAY BLAKESBERG

PHOTO: BLAIR JACKSON

entire time, the drummers were upset that Weir brought in a drum machine to try to ensure a steady beat to rehearse his tunes, and eventually the sessions just sort of petered out due to lack of interest. For their part, Arista didn't seem to care particularly; the Dead's albums had never done *that* well for them. Clive Davis liked the prestige of having the Dead on his label, though by the mid '80s even that was debatable.

The following year, however—the Dead's 20th anniversary—they decided to try something new: During the third week in April, they secretly booked the tiny (2,000-seat) Marin Veteran's Auditorium in San Rafael (where they had played shows in the fall of '83 and spring of '84), and spent three long days recording a wealth of material onstage in the empty theater, as a battery of video cameras captured them in action. Len Dell' Amico, who had directed the live videos that were made at Radio City Music Hall in 1980 (the Halloween simulcast, a Showtime special, and a commercial release called *Dead Ahead*), worked from a video truck parked behind the auditorium; meanwhile, John Cutler handled the audio end, sequestered in Le Mobile, a remote recording truck operated out of L.A. by a charming French Canadian engineer named Guy Charbonneau, who aided Cutler in the recording. In what can only be considered a miracle of stealth, Deadheads never caught wind of the Marin sessions. Cutler had supervised a number of Grateful Dead broadcasts by this point and was considered an excellent live mixer.

John Cutler at the board in the Le Mobile remote recording truck for the "secret" Marin Vets sessions, April 1985.

The band was set up on the stage as if it were a concert, except the vocal mics were facing inward so the singers faced each other and the drummers rather than out into the empty hall, and there was no PA. However, Cutler hung several mics throughout the auditorium to pick up the sound of the music coming off the amplifiers out in the room. The group rolled though both new and older songs, sometimes stopping in the middle if there was a flub, or performing two or three takes of a song consecutively. At this point, it wasn't clear exactly what product would emerge from these sessions, but everyone agreed that Cutler and Charbonneau succeeded in capturing the band's sound well on the Studer multitrack recorders through the truck's Neve console. For his part, Garcia seemed to be interested and engaged in the proceedings; he always had a soft spot for visual projects. And at a 20th Anniversary press conference backstage at the Greek Theater that June, Garcia said he hoped that the video project—whatever it ended up being—would be out by that November. In fact, the band got together for four more days of audio/video shooting at the Marin Vets in November, and talk shifted to putting out the video in early spring 1986.

It was not to be, however. Other projects and commitments came along and knocked the video into the background temporarily. Then, in the summer of '86, Garcia nearly died when he was unexpectedly felled by a diabetic coma. Months of Dead shows were canceled, as Garcia slowly recuperated—his brain was so scrambled that he had to essentially re-learn the guitar, and it took a long time for him to regain his strength. But the Garcia that came out on the other side of this near-death experience was a changed man: grateful (no pun intended) for having been given a second chance, completely drug-free for the first time in years, and determined to make the most of every waking hour. It's not like Garcia was exactly a slacker before this, but once he was healthy, he seemed to have nearly boundless enthusiasm for all sorts of projects. Really, the return of the band to performing at the Oakland Coliseum in December 1986 marks the beginning of the next Golden Era of the Grateful Dead.

A LANDMARK YEAR

First on the agenda, in what turned out to be a landmark year for the Dead, was recording a new studio album—their first since *Go to Heaven*. Garcia and company had been so happy with Cutler's recordings for the video that the band went back into the Marin Civic, set up as before, and spent a couple of weeks recording basic tracks on eight songs, including a couple of Hunter-Garcia tunes that had been premiered at the December '86 shows: "Black Muddy River" and "When Push Comes to Shove." The others went back as far as 1982 and included "Touch of Gray," "Throwing Stones," "West L.A. Fadeaway," "Hell in a Bucket," Brent's fine "Tons of Steel," and the Weir-Barlow number "My Brother Esau." Once again, Guy Charbonneau and his Le Mobile remote recording truck were on hand to capture the action.

"These guys have an awful lot of experience recording and a lot of life experience, and I think all of us are getting a little more, shall we say, 'mature,'" John Cutler told me in an interview in the spring of '87, before the album, *In the Dark*, was released. "We did basics in two weeks. A few years ago [1984] they went to Fantasy, did a month-long lock-out, and got nothing. The Dead is most successful as a live band. There's no reason why they can't be successful as a recording band, but I think it's apropos that they do their basic tracks in a live situation—as if they were playing live—because that's where their expertise lies. We had them set up onstage in the same places they would be for a concert, and I think that helped a lot. But it's definitely a studio recording."

This marked the first complete album to be recorded using Dolby's new SR noise reduction system. "When we were going to start this project," Cutler said, "I'd heard some rave reviews of the Dolby SR from the friends of mine at the Power Station [a top Manhattan studio] and other places. Then I talked to Guy about it, and he raved about it. So we got a couple of cards from Dolby and tried them out at Front Street while recording some rehearsals, just 2-track. We were favorably impressed, so one day Mickey Hart and I did an experiment with his drum kit—because my complaint with the old Dolby A is it squashed drums a bit, although it was good for other things. I had Mickey play on his kit and I mixed to mono, but to two tracks—one with SR, one without. When we played it back we could hear virtually no difference between them except that the SR track was a lot quieter. And it wasn't squashed—it didn't mess with the drums—and that's what finally sold me on it."

Using the SR also allowed Cutler to move from 16-track (long the Dead's preferred format) to 24-track, "because you don't have to record as hot," he said. "The nature of the system is such that crosstalk between channels is reduced, and its dynamic range is increased. So I don't have to pull two tape machines all the time, which means you use half as much tape, which is nice economically.... It *is* transparent."

After the basics were done, the action switched over to Club Front for fixes, overdubs, and mixing on the Dead's new Neve VR console. And while the song-writers—Jerry, Bob, and Brent—essentially supervised their own songs, Garcia and Cutler were the über-producers and ultimate decision-makers, with Cutler managing the workflow and keeping tabs on the overdubs, including a whole mess o' percussion parts Mickey Hart recorded both at Club Front and at his home studio to 16-track slave copies of the songs (so he wasn't constantly play-ing the master tapes).

An important new face comes into the Dead scene around this time: Bob Bralove, who would help the Dead members navigate the tricky waters of MIDI (Musical Instrument Digital Interface) and become an important, permanent part of their sound crew up until the end.

BRALOVE ON BOARD

A native of suburban Scarsdale, New York, Bralove grew up playing several instruments and enjoyed classical, jazz, and rock music. After studying psychol-ogy at Hampshire College in Massachusetts for a while, he transferred to San Francisco State, where he added a second major in music composition—at the time he wrote mainly chamber music. After college, the always technologically inclined Bralove got involved in the world of computers, working as a consultant and also landing a gig with (now defunct) Osborne Computers. It was through Osborne, strangely enough, that he got into the music business: Osborne user

Stevie Wonder hired him to develop software that would allow his computers (and later, his musical instruments) to speak to him through a speech synthesizer, a fairly radical idea at the time. This led to Bralove learning about the intricacies of MIDI technology, and touring with Wonder to make sure his battery of electronic keyboards were working at all times.

In 1985, at a Grammy Awards "Keyboard Summit" event that included Wonder and other top players, Bralove met Merl Saunders, who at the time was working with the Dead (sans Phil) on music for *The Twilight Zone* TV series, which had been recently revived. Saunders was the musical director for the show, and Mickey Hart became one of the main effects designers. When Saunders invited Bralove over to Club Front to check out some of the work being done for the series there, Bralove hooked up with Mickey and began assisting him in searching for and recording odd sounds and then processing them in unusual ways. "Mickey and I shared a vision almost immediately," Bralove said in a 1992 interview with Steve Silberman and me in *The Golden Road*. "There was something happening in the weirdness end of life that we saw in each other. Getting weird sounds and making them work—the spirit of that was clear to us right away."

At that point, Bralove was recording sounds to a Sony F-1 digital recorder and then loading them into an Emulator II sampler and manipulating them. "We went sampling crazy!" Bralove says today. "We were recording Mickey's Tibetan bowls [actually Nepalese bowls procured by Bear in Kathmandu in 1983] and all these other percussion instruments he had—really, anything that sounded cool and weird. There was a kind of anechoic back room at Front

Bob Bralove became a key player on the Dead's technical team. Here he is backstage with his racks of gear in the early '90s.

PHOTO: SUSANA MILLMAN

Street—really dead—and we'd set up there and record." Over a period of more than two months, Bralove commuted back and forth between L.A. (where Wonder lived) and the Bay Area, and he also did some recording work with Mickey at Russian Hill studios in San Francisco—and at another more unusual location: "At one point Mickey had back surgery," Bralove says, "but you know Mickey—that didn't stop him. So we actually kept recording things in the hospital!"

Almost two years later, when *In the Dark* came around, Bralove got another call to help out in the studio. Again he worked with the drummers on various sampling and processing tasks (such as re-pitching Vibraslaps and shakers and the like), and he also worked extensively with Brent, helping him navigate two new keyboard samplers that Kidd Candelario had purchased for him—an Emulator II and a Kurzweil K250 (both of which Stevie Wonder had used extensively).

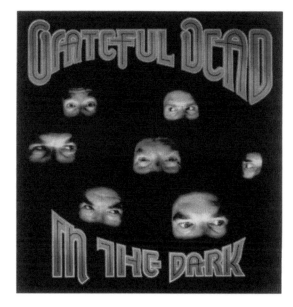

The fact that we lionize Leo Fender and Les Paul and other innovators of the electric guitar is a function of that instrument's long and colorful history, plus the fact that guitars really *do* seem to have personalities of their own. But how many people know about Dave Rossum and Ron Dow, or Ray Kurzweil? All three have had an enormous impact on today's music.

Rossum was a Cal Tech science brainiac who went to U.C. Santa Cruz in the early '70s, where he became obsessed with a Moog 12 synthesizer there and decided he would try to build his own instrument, just for the hell of it. It was 1971, and the sign on the door where Rossum and a couple of his buddies were doing their work read, STARSHIPS AND SYNTHESIZERS, SINCE 1984—which is what got a friend from Rossum's junior-high years, Scott Wedge, intrigued enough that he wanted to help out on the synth quest, too. That year, they built their first prototype synthesizer—called the E-mu-25, "after our favorite drug [LSD-25]," Rossum told *Polyphony* magazine a decade later. They sold that one, put the money into making a better modular model, sold that one, too, and by November 1972 had started E-mu Systems (while both still held other jobs). The company's first breakthrough occurred in 1975, when Ron Dow approached Rossum about helping finance the development of a custom VCA (voltage-controlled amplifier) chip. Rossum elected not to get involved at that time, so Dow went to SSM (Solid State Music), and they put out the chip. Soon after that, however, Rossum did become involved with Dow, and working both independently and together, they developed a series of voltage-controlled chips for SSM—a second VCA, an oscillator, a filter, and a transient generator.

Suggested listening/viewing: *In the Dark*, produced by Jerry and John Cutler, was the biggest seller of the Dead's career; *View From the Vault IV*, a CD and DVD release from 2003, contains two complete Dead shows from summer '87 tour, 8/24 (Oakland) and 8/26 (Anaheim). Alas, the Dylan-Dead sets from those shows were not included.

These chips and the ICs they came on became the foundation for an entire new generation of multi-voice analog synthesizers—and not just ones made by E-mu (like the Audity), but influential instruments like the Sequential Circuits Prophet-5, the PPG Wave 2.2, and the Korg Poly 6. The other companies paid royalties for the ICs, which helped finance E-mu's growth.

Then, in 1981, E-mu introduced the Emulator sampler. In sampling, an analog audio signal—anything from a recorded note of a musical instrument to sounds without traditional pitch (in other words, *anything*)—is converted to digital; it can then be played back and manipulated in various ways using some sort of controller, usually a keyboard. The Fairlight CMI was the first keyboard-based sampler, and it was widely regarded as a fantastic invention. However, at more than $30,000 for a system, it was out of the reach of most musicians and even some high-end recording studios. So Rossum went to work and figured out a way, using a new technology known as Direct Memory Assessing (DMA) chips, to pack many of the Fairlight's best features into his Emulator, which sold for roughly one-quarter the price. The Emulator was an instant hit, and in June 1984 Rossum and his team of engineers topped themselves with the Emulator II, an eight-voice polyphonic digital sampling keyboard that included an 8-track sequencer, custom DSP (Digital Signal Processing) chips, and 12- to 14-bit playback resolution of 8-bit samples. By current standards, the Emulator II was not a powerful machine—its floppy-disk memory was just 512MB (though for another three grand you could add a Winchester hard disk)—but the quality of the samples was obvious, and it found its way onto many, many albums during the '80s (and beyond).

As for the Kurzweil 250—well, that's just a blip on the resumé of a man who is one of the great inventors—and thinkers—of our time. As a child growing up

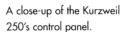

A close-up of the Kurzweil 250's control panel.

The Kurzweil 250 features an 88-key touch-sensitive keyboard with extensive sound programming capabilities and impressive preset resident sounds. An expandable 12-track sequencer and optional user sampling program make the Kurzweil 250 a powerful creative tool for performers, composers and arrangers. (Kurzweil Music Systems, Waltham, MA).

in Queens, New York, Ray Kurzweil invented a computer that could compose music in the style of Mozart and Bach. He attended M.I.T but spent nearly all his time working on various inventions—he missed so many classes he earned the nickname "the Phantom." Later he developed the first flatbed scanner and also came up with speech-recognition software and a text-to-speech reading machine for the blind (which explains why Stevie Wonder was an early user of Kurzweil instruments). The K250 was widely praised for having the best acoustic music samples of any '80s instrument. "The Kurzweil grand piano sound was the best grand piano sample out there, and that's what Ray was committed to," Bralove says. "That was the connection with Stevie: Ray's whole premise was making that convincing dynamic range happen."

PHOTO: BRUCE POLONSKY

Brent had some familiarity with synthesizers when he joined the band, but in the second half of the '80s, Bob Bralove schooled him in digital synthesis and MIDI.

The K250 contained a 16-bit sampler, a 12-track sequencer, samples of 96 acoustic instruments, and 341 presets. It had a full 88-key keyboard and was MIDI-friendly. A number of years ago Kurzweil sold his interest in the instrument company that bears his name; these days he is best known as a futurist and author of many books. He's an expert on nanotechnology and robotics and foresees a world where the human lifespan can be doubled or more. As he wrote, "An analysis of the history of technology shows that technological change is exponential, contrary to the common-sense 'intuitive linear' view. So we won't experience 100 years of progress in the 21st century—it will be more like 20,000 years of progress (at today's rate)." That hurts my head.

On top of that, Bralove added a few more ingredients to Brent's setup, including the Yamaha TX816. This large rackmount module was the equivalent of eight of Yamaha's extremely popular 16-voice DX7 digital synthesizers—more than 150,000 DX7s were sold between its 1983 introduction and 1987, and it was used by everyone from Kraftwerk to Talking Heads to U2 to Herbie Hancock to (yes) Stevie Wonder. More than perhaps any other synth, it defined the sound of '80s electronic keyboard music.

"Live, Brent used the Kurzweil as the controller, but the first thing I did was try to give him access to *all* of the sounds that he had," Bob says. "The idea was first to put all that stuff in racks and make it road-worthy, and then wire it all so he would have some control over everything—so he could bring up anything off the DX7s. Like, some of that calliope or bell sound on 'Touch of Gray' is from a DX7. Another thing Brent used a lot was the Roland MKS-20 [piano module, introduced in 1986]. I brought that in for the overdubs on the album, and they loved it. It had piano, electric piano, vibes, harpsichord, and that's about it…about eight presets. And you could program it in certain ways to do different things, but it ended up being a good piano sound for Brent."

"[Bralove] has really allowed me to do all sorts of things I've wanted to do musically but didn't know how to do," Brent told me in a *Golden Road* interview in the summer of 1987. "Working with him has freed me up from having to read all these tech pamphlets for synthesizers, all of which are different. That can really take up time—you can spend so much time learning how to work computers it takes away from playing music." Asked about the realistic fiddle sound he started dropping into tunes like "Big River" and "When I Paint My Masterpiece," Brent noted, "I used to get a decent fiddle sound from the Minimoog, just working at home on tapes, but never live before I got the Kurzweil.

"Right now I'm more or less playing acoustic instrument sounds instead of coming up with 'out there' stuff. I'm using sounds that are like real instruments—the violin, the sax, the piano—and those blend real well. So if I want a little more attack or want to be more aggressive on, say, the end of 'Sugar Magnolia,' I might drop in a horn part to help accent the piano part. Or, on a ballad I might try to bring in some strings, but I try to make it so you don't notice it too much. As opposed to just pushing a button and having the instrument there or not there, I'll blend it in with a pedal so I can listen to it, and if it seems to work I'll go with it. If it doesn't, I can back off and go onto something else."

"Brent's aesthetic was so amazing to me," Bralove reflects. "He had such great taste. He would do these subtle things where he would play through a verse and chorus using a sound, and then he'd come back and all he'd do is turn on the 'chorus' feature on the same sound he was using, and then all of a sudden he'd play the second verse and chorus similarly except it had a ghostly quality because [the sound] just shifted a little bit. It's not so much about virtuosity, but about each note having a meaning and the relationship to the overall sound. It could be a very simple thing that he did, but the execution…wow!"

DYLAN & THE DEAD

The summer of 1987 turned out to be one of the great peaks of the Grateful Dead's career. In full "comeback" mode following Garcia's '86 meltdown, the band rode a wave of great press and good reviews when *In the Dark* was released in early July. Aided by a clever video (directed by Gary Gutierrez) in which the band members morphed into life-size performing marionette skeletons, the single "Touch of Gray" became their first Top Ten hit, and the album soared all the way to No. 6. They also played a series of well-received shows with Bob Dylan, at which the Dead played their own sets and then backed the Mysterious One for a 90-minute set.

The Dylan union was actually a by-product of a series of shows the Dead and Dylan—backed by Tom Petty & the Heartbreakers—played in the summer of 1986. At a few stops along the way, Dylan joined the Dead onstage for a couple of numbers, performed in that typically sloppy, off-handed way of his, and apparently that was enough to plant the seed to really play together the following year. In May '87, Dylan came up to the Bay Area for a couple weeks of secret rehearsals at Front Street (even though the tour was two months away), and it is those sessions that are the source of The Story of the Pink Guitar—a famous/infamous Modulus axe owned by Mr. Robert Weir. Take it away, Bob:

"We went into rehearsal with Dylan and he needed a guitar; he hadn't brought one, if you can believe that. 'Okay, what do you want? We'll get it for you.' 'Oh, just get me something simple—get me a Strat.' I was working with Modulus a lot by then; in fact, I'd actually bought into the company—I had some nickels in my jeans, and my investment philosophy was I wanted to invest in companies that were furthering musical-instrument technology. So I thought we could quickly get one of the Modulus Strats for him, but the only

Mega-Dead at Giants Stadium for a Dead-Dylan show, 7/12/87. The PA consists of Meyer MSL-3s.

PHOTO: ROBERT MINKIN

Bob onstage with his famous—or is that infamous?—Pepto Bismol-pink Modulus guitar, Frost Amphitheatre 4/30/88.

one they had right then was this pink one. So we presented him with this variety of Strats, and he plugged them in one at a time and played them a little. I was sitting around killing time at Front Street while all this was happening, and I'd check in with him every once in a while, and at one point he was just sitting there looking at the guitars. He said, 'I like the way this one sounds and I like the way this one plays...but this one is the right color,'" Bob says with a laugh. "'And so he went with that one. Later, after the tour was over, he gave it to me. I started playing it and I loved it."

Geoff Gould, founder of Modulus, offers his own take on the story: "That Pepto-Bismol-pink one was one of my favorites. It had a Strat-style body and was made out of poplar. I put on some EMG Select pickups—EMG's passive pickups, which weren't that great—and it had some kind of bridge; I don't even remember what kind. But I kind of whipped it together, took it up there for rehearsal, and Dylan played it. Garcia had one of our guitars that we'd made him, and he played that for a couple of numbers. So there I was in rehearsal and there are Bob Dylan, Jerry, Bob, and Phil, all playing my guitars. And nobody was there to see it! I talked to Dylan briefly afterward, and he said, 'It sounds kinda rinky-dink'; he wasn't very impressed with it. But Bobby really liked it. Of course, once the tour came around, Dylan didn't even play that type of guitar; he played a Washburn acoustic/electric.

"Apparently a lot of Deadheads hated [the pink guitar], but I thought it had an awesome sound, and Bobby loved it...because they hated it! Actually, he did like it for real. He ended up using it on *Built to Last*, on 'Foolish Heart.'" Bob also played it live on numerous occasions.

Weir's main guitar during this period, though, was a beautiful wood Modulus. "That's the one in the *Touch of Gray* video; it was probably my favorite," Gould offers. "It's a through-body Blacknife. It has a bookmatched cocabola top—a ⅛″ veneer instead of ¼″, over a bird's-eye-maple veneer, and the core of the sandwich was mahogany; then [the top] was replicated on the back. That had Bartolini pickups and a Kahler tremolo—Bob was really into tremolo.

"We had what we called a 'Bob Weir setup,' where we had three Strat pickups, but they were within the space of where two normal pickups would be," Gould adds. "In the traditional Strat pickup configuration, the neck pickup and middle pickup are perpendicular to the strings and the bridge pickup is angled, so we made some guitars where we stuck a pickup between what was the bridge pickup and the middle pickup, and then with the middle one we sort of split the difference on the angle. There was no neck pickup, because Bob never played the neck pickup. That one had Bartolini pickups, as well." Gould says that Weir had two other through-body axes built, including a sand-colored model to match his BMW at that time—ah, such decadence!

Phil also started playing a different Modulus bass during this period, a "headless" model which, according to Phil, improved the instrument's balance. Gould notes, "That was a through-body based on the same neck as the earlier ones, but the body was a sandwich of some really light wood—birch—with a graphite top and back. He played it for a while before it had a finish; then we put a blue finish over it. The checkerboard [pattern] on it is a hand-woven graphite basket weave."

Bob plays some slide on one of his most beautiful through-body Modulus Blacknife axes, sometime in 1986.

Jerry continued playing Tiger, but for the Dylan shows only, he also thrilled the crowd by playing pedal-steel guitar on a song at five of the six concerts, for the first time onstage with the Dead since the early '70s.

DRUMMERS IN ZONE

Like Brent, the drummers also benefited from Bralove's technical expertise. Following his work on *The Twilight Zone* and *In the Dark*, he set about developing a reliable MIDI system they could employ live, especially during the Rhythm Devils solo. "One thing I brought them that became an important part of what they did—particularly Mickey—was a Dynacord [ADD-One], which was an eight-channel system that you could configure in all sorts of very interesting

One month apart in mid-1987, Phil can be seen playing two different Modulus basses. The vertical shot is from Frost Amphitheatre in May, the horizontal one with the headless bass, is from the Greek Theatre in June.

ways," Bralove says. "It was MIDI, but it also had its own custom-designed triggers that were kind of bizarrely shaped rubber mats; at the time, they were very effective. It also had samples—it had onboard sounds, and it also had a floppy disk you could load up. You could configure its eight voices to be triggered by any of the eight inputs, so you could say, 'I'm going to put three voices on this one pad, so all three will combine to create this wonderful sound whenever he hits it.' You could also add delays and repeats in it, so you could have all eight voices trigger off one pad, but they would then loop and create these little *ch-cha-ch-cha-ch-cha* grooves. If you listen to shows from that time, you hear a lot of that. Those sounds were all out of the Dynacord." (Dynacord is a German company that was founded by Werner Pinternagel in 1946, originally as an amplifier manufacturer. Through the years Dynacord expanded its repertoire of products to include echo/reverb units, loudspeaker cabinets, and more.)

Another facet of the Rhythm Devils solos in this era was "these store-bought volume pedals that Tom Paddock, who was another guy who did electronics work for the Dead, rebuilt for low noise so we had dynamic volume," Bralove recalls. "The idea of the pedals was that we could route The Beam, route *anything*, through pedals—we must have had 15 or 20 pedals down there. We could route anything dry or wet [i.e., with or without reverb]; [Mickey] could control all sorts of things. I had marked all the levels and we'd trimmed it out so beautifully. Well, the first show for me [touring with the Dead] was in Ventura [6/12/87]; I had this big Peavey mixer, and we'd been rehearsing with Mickey like crazy. So we get to Ventura and the drum solo starts, and Mickey kicks down every single pedal *full volume*, stomping on everything! It just sounded like pure distortion. I spent the whole drum solo trying to figure out what was distorting and how to turn it down, but of course he

The drummers close out the banner year of 1987 at Oakland Coliseum Dec. 30 and 31: Billy goes nuts on his Roto-toms, while Mickey looks comparatively serene at his set.

loved it!" Welcome to Mickey's World, eh? "Exactly! It was hysterical." Mickey nicknamed his electronics setup Big Hair, because "it makes your big hair stand up," he explained in 1988.

Of course Mickey always had another partner in crime when it came to unleashing wild weirdness—and I don't mean Billy. Basically from the birth of The Beast until the Dead's final show in '95, the Rhythm Devils segment was also a playground for Dan Healy and his racks of processors and synths at front-of-house. "I'd hear tapes of the drum solos, and sometimes it wasn't anything like I remembered it," Bill says, "and that's because Dan was always doing stuff out there. I could almost never hear what was going on out [in the house]. Sometimes we'd hear something bouncing off a back wall, but mostly we were just hearing what we were doing, and that was *loud* onstage."

Healy also brought his twisted audio sensibilities to the "space" segment following the Rhythm Devils. "We sort of play together," Dan told me in 1985. "A lot of the equipment [I have] is home-brew stuff. I have about six different kinds of delay systems that are basically all the popular varieties you find in recording systems. I also have three or four pieces of equipment that we have the only ones of, because John Cutler and I designed them. One thing I have now allows the sound to be controllable by a computer. The sound can move around the room, and as it moves it turns inside-out and upside-down.... I [also] have the equivalent of the elements found in most synthesizers, like a ring modulator, envelope generators, envelope followers, burst generators, sine wave and square wave and triangle wave generators, and all that stuff. But I have it as separate components rather than built into one device, because I completely restructure the uses of these things so radically that it would be impractical to turn it into a synthesizer unit without limiting myself. Then I have a matrix system that enables me to connect them together in every configuration....

"Rhythm Devils and the weirdness after it is an experimental area, so it's legitimate to try out your most outside stuff—things that don't have to make sense, or don't have to ring true. You wouldn't want to mess with something like 'Stella Blue,' but you *do* need a place to try out stuff."

GOODBYE, BRENT; HELLO, VINCE

IN THE DARK was an unprecedented success for the Grateful Dead, selling
more than two million copies. And a long-form video—*So Far*, culled from the
original 1985 Marin Vets sessions, combined with live concert footage and a
few conceptual pieces—was a bestseller and award-winner in 1987, as well.
Len Dell'Amico and Jerry were co-directors on that project; John Cutler was
in charge of creating a seamless 55-minute musical presentation from the
disparate elements. It was a strong piece of work all the way around.

Chapter Fifteen
1987-1991

To no one's surprise, the Grateful Dead's brief incursion into the pop mainstream courtesy of "Touch of Gray" (the single and video) attracted thousands of new fans to an already crowded scene. Tickets were hard to come by, and increasing numbers of people came 'round to the venues where the Dead played just to be part of the hippie bazaar that invariably sprang up outside the large arenas and stadiums the Dead were forced into by their growing success. During the summer months, too, the Dead would often play "sheds"—outdoor amphitheaters that combined conventional seating for several thousand with a large general-admission lawn area in the back. Alpine Valley and Irvine Meadows (south of L.A.) were early sheds; in the late '80s and into the '90s the Dead started playing many more, including Deer Creek Music Center in Indiana, the Bay Area's Shoreline Amphitheatre, Sandstone Amphitheatre near Kansas City, and the World Music Center outside of Chicago.

Jerry looks happy and relaxed as he plays "Tiger" at the Greek Theatre in Berkeley, 7/16/88.

In the second half of 1987 Garcia also found time to re-connect with his folk roots. With two of his picking partners from the early '60s—David Nelson (acoustic guitar) and Sandy Rothman (banjo, dobro, mandolin)—and good ol' John Kahn (upright bass), he formed the Jerry Garcia Acoustic Band, which was devoted to playing old-time country, bluegrass, and folk tunes. Along with the electric Jerry Garcia Band, the JGAB (with JGB drummer David Kemper added to the lineup) played a memorable series of shows in October '87 at the Lunt-Fontanne Theatre on Broadway, and later brought the show to the Bay Area and L.A. For all the JGAB shows, Garcia played a Takamine electric-acoustic guitar, though this was a single-cutaway model, whereas the one he played in 1980 was not.

PHOTO: JAY BLAKESBERG

MIDI GUITARS

In the summer of 1988, Bob Weir joined Brent and the drummers in the MIDI universe when he started playing a Strat-style Casio/Modulus axe with an onboard synthesizer. The Casio PG-380 was a brand-new instrument then; it had just been introduced in Japan in February. The Casio Computer Company dates back to post-war Japan, when Tadao Kashio (hence the name) enlisted the help of his three brothers to create some of the first high-quality electronic calculators. Calculators, cash registers, and various hand-held electronic devices became Casio's bread-and-butter through the years, although the company also got involved with TVs, word processors, and digital cameras. Casio's first electronic musical instrument, the cheesy-sounding Casiotone keyboard, came out in 1980, but its guitar synths were considerably better. They were built by Fuji-Gen-Gakki, the same folks who built MIDI guitars for Ibanez and Roland. The PG-380 was notable because the onboard synth was battery-powered (although this made it rather heavy). It contained 64 preset sounds with internal ROM and also had a slot in the back for a RAM card. Its pitch-to-MIDI system operated through a magnetic "hex" pickup near the bridge. The great jazz guitarist Stanley Jordan was an early endorser of the 380.

Bob with one of his many Casio MIDI guitars (with a Modulus graphite neck), Shoreline Amphitheatre, June 1990.

PHOTO: BOB MINKIN

"I picked the Casio because it was portable," Weir says. "It put out audio; the rest of them just put out MIDI, and I wanted to be wireless because I was done with that ball and chain. And it simplified your choices, too. You could re-program it to some degree and that was fun, but really, for the amount that I used the synth, I wasn't into putting that much time into building sounds. All we were doing was wigging out for ten minutes or so with the MIDI stuff [during "space"], and every now and again I'd pull out some horn stops; it had good horn stops."

Bob Bralove comments, "In those days, processing speed was an issue a lot more than it is now. Pitch-to-MIDI translation can cause delays in terms of the performance—it was especially bad on basses, because the wavelengths are so long. On Bob's guitar we installed a system out of Australia [designed by Steve Chick] that would calculate the wave's trajectory—it could calculate the MIDI note from only the first half of the wave. That made it a little faster. The thing about the Casio guitar, too, is that Bob had a lot of control over it right on the guitar—he had up and down preset switches. Then on top of that he'd add various processing; like, I know he used the [T.C. Electronic] 2290 [Dynamic Digital Delay] quite a bit. Sometimes he'd have me running out and changing delay settings right before the show."

A number of months after Bob, Jerry and Phil entered the MIDI realm. "The thing about Jerry and Jerry's system—and this I learned from listening and focusing on his playing—is that a lot of his expression and the unique-ness of his sound comes from the subtle but *constant* movement in his left hand, fingering the notes," Bralove said in 1992. "A note rarely sits flat; it's always alive, always moving…. But you give him one of the early [synth] systems or one that's not real customized, and you take away that nuance from his playing. So it took a lot of effort to hear, 'Well, he's doing a subtle thing that's going in quarter-tones, and I'm hearing half-steps'…. The first things we tried were slow and not responsive."

The system that eventually passed the acid test, so to speak, was the Roland GR-50. Bralove says, "When I first wired the Roland for a Strat for Jerry to test out, I spent this long, long afternoon trying to make it suitable. He came in for an hour and fooled around with it a lot, and he seemed to be pretty pleased with it. He walked out of the studio and Steve [Parish] turned to me and said [gruffly], 'He'll *never* use it live, man. He'll *never* use that.' It was very Steve," he laughs. "But of course he did use it eventually." Garcia played that black Strat with a Roland MIDI system just a few times during "space" in the spring of 1989. Then Jerry's beloved Wolf became his MIDI guitar, with the Roland MIDI controller externally mounted at first. Then, the San Francisco-based guitar tech Gary Brawer installed the Roland system into Wolf. For a while there, however, Garcia would play Tiger during the show, switch to the MIDI'd Wolf for "space," then return to Tiger. It wasn't long, however, before

Garcia wanted to introduce some of his MIDI effects into the regular sets, so Wolf became his main guitar again for a period.

Check out photos of Phil during "space" from the fall of '88 and you'll see him playing a Modulus bass with a MIDI unit actually attached to the point of one of the cutaways, and what looks like masking tape right where the neck meets the body. "That's a copy of my bass, with a synth pickup taped onto it," says Geoff Gould when shown a photo. "I saw him use it at Laguna Seca [Monterey, California, summer of '88]. The bass is a Quantum 6 through-body with a red narra top. [Native to the Philippines, narra is also known as red sandlewood.] I'm not sure about the pickup he's using; it's probably a Roland."

This was a short-lived MIDI arrangement for Phil, however. The next stage in his MIDI evolution was facilitated by the aforementioned Australian tech wizard (and bassist) named Steve Chick, who tackled head-on the inadequacy of the typical pitch-to-MIDI setup in basses. He devised a system whereby the instrument's frets themselves were wired. As Bob Bralove puts it, "When the player contacted the finger to the string to the fretboard and then plucked, it

Phil had a makeshift MIDI box literally taped to one of his Modulus basses for a brief period. This is from 10/2/88 Shoreline.

PHOTO: JAY BLAKESBERG

would generate the MIDI note from the *contact*, as opposed to the pitch. It was much more immediate and solved the problem of typical MIDI basses' slow response time."

In a 1998 interview with *Bassist* magazine, Chick explained, "I took a regular bass and performed open neck-surgery with various tools and chemicals and eventually built my first wired-fret neck. Building the neck was the easy part. It then took me six months to work out an algorithm that could accurately read the finger position off the neck, but this is what made the MIDI bass system possible.

"The prototype proved rather popular, but because I wasn't in the bass-building business, I designed a retrofit kit that could be installed in virtually any 4- or 5-string bass. We were doing retrofits ourselves in Australia and eventually got Valley Arts Guitars [in Southern California], Wal [in the U.K.], and Maton [in Australia] to install the systems in their basses and do retrofits. We engineered a neat way of installing the wired frets into virtually any bass. It was more complicated than other systems, but the tracking was much faster. On the slowest setting, the delay was still less than 10ms, which was acceptable." (By 1991, Chick had made a licensing deal with Peavey Electronics, which launched its own line of MIDI basses that used his system. However, the Dead's initial work with Chick's electronics, which involved tearing apart a 4-string bolt-on Modulus bass, was through Valley Arts.)

BUILT TO LAST

A fair amount of MIDI experimentation can be heard on the Grateful Dead album that was recorded during the first half of 1989—*Built to Last*, their final completed studio effort. Initially, the Dead thought they would try to record the album using the same methodology as *In the Dark*: recording "live" on the stage of the Marin Vets, and then overdubbing at Club Front and in the band members' personal studios. For whatever reasons, however, that didn't work out, so the action shifted to Skywalker Studios in rural West Marin, on the expansive ranch property that is the headquarters of George Lucas's film and recording empire. Skywalker is probably the most beautiful studio in the Bay Area, and also one of the best-equipped. Built in 1988 and located in the Technology Building, which is tucked amidst rolling vineyards, up the road from the pond and the baseball diamond, the giant $60 \times 80 \times 30$ scoring stage can accommodate a full symphony orchestra or provide a fully adjustable but still live-sounding environment for a rock band like the Dead. The band managed to take a stab at a number of basic tracks at Skywalker, but once again, something wasn't quite right.

"What we started to discover," Garcia told *Relix* magazine in the fall of 1989, "was that our material was saying something else about itself, and that approach was not going to work on this record—and that we're really looking

Crew stalwarts captured at Frost Amphitheatre, 1989: Kidd Candelario (in front of Phil's rack), Steve Parish (behind Jerry's rig) and the late, great Ram Rod.

PHOTOS: JON SIEVERT

for something entirely different. So we screwed around there for about a year, a year-and-a-half, and then right around April ['89] we started to get serious and sort of focus in on the record."

In the end, most of the usable basics were cut at Club Front, but actually, the methodology they ultimately chose meant that over the course of making the album, almost everything was continually being updated and replaced. Or, as Garcia explained in *The Golden Road* in the fall of '89, "We didn't do basics

Mickey got to use The Beam (above) and all sorts of sampled percussion effects during the making of *Built to Last*.

in the normal sense at all. What we did was spend a lot of time trying to figure out what the right tempo for the tune was going to be, and then we took a piece of tape and a dumb-shit drum machine, and set up a basic feeling for the tune on the drum machine—like an enhanced click-track, a track that says a little more about the rhythm than just a square 4/4. It has a little more of the feeling in it, whether it's a little bit of a shuffle feeling or whatever else it has in the groove.

"So we set that up and ran it the length of the tune; then Bob and I and Phil and Brent would work together just with that to get a sense of how the song would hang together. Once we had established the length and tempo, we started working on it individually. So Bob would go home and work on his guitar part until he felt he had one that was really successful, and so on....

"We had plenty of time for trial and error on the individual parts, but not on the mixing, which was sort of one-shot. Really, this music was not heard in its entirety until we mixed it, because it was all out on slave reels. I mean, Mickey usually accumulates no less than 11 or 12 tracks just for his stuff, so that's a whole sub-mix where you have no idea what you're actually dealing with and how it will fit in with the rest of the music until you get to it during the mix." Garcia spent a lot of time up at Mickey's home studio in Petaluma [Sonoma County], working on percussion ideas for the album. Mickey went wild with his samplers this time out: On Weir's ominous "Victim or the Crime," Garcia noted, "There's sort of an anvil sound, and there's also machine-shop sounds in there that are big crushers and stampers and grinders we use in various parts," as well as a generous dose of The Beam. "There's a four-bar rhythm pattern where every other four has a different stamper crunching, and also there's the sound of broken lightbulbs on the *twos* and *fours* that sounds a little like a tambourine.... Using metal-shop sounds—metal on metal—was an early idea of mine that actually ended up working really well."

Garcia and John Cutler once again took the reins on the album, and though the approach was unorthodox—really the antithesis of how the band usually liked to work in the studio—the results were impressive. *Built to Last* is a great-sounding CD where every individual part is distinct, yet it still creates the illusion of being a performance. The team of Brent and John Barlow actually had the most tracks on the album, with four: "Blow Away," "Just a Little Light," "We Can Run," and "I Will Take You Home." Weir had "Victim" and "Picasso Moon," and Hunter-Garcia contributed three outstanding tunes—"Foolish Heart" (the first "single," such as it was; it was not a success), the title track, and "Standing on the Moon."

Although Garcia hadn't been playing his MIDI axe onstage for very long when the *Built to Last* sessions took place, he still managed to incorporate a few interesting parts, including some MIDI "trumpet" on both "Built to Last" and "I Will Take You Home." In general during this period, when Garcia and Weir were feeling out their systems, Garcia tended to employ more literal sounds—flute, trumpet, sax, etc.—than Weir, who went for more abstract and less-defined sounds.

Discussing that aspect of his MIDI vocabulary in 1989, Garcia said, "[Those literal sounds] are the ones that are most playable for me right now. I go on how much my touch can be transferred to the MIDI realm. What's interesting is that if I play harder on the horn thing, I can actually over-blow it, just like you can with a horn. So what I'm looking for is getting some of the expression you get from a horn, except on a guitar. I look for the things that are most interactive that I can affect by my touch. But I'm on the ground floor still."

The system that Bralove developed for Garcia was foot-controlled. "It had 'pages' that could go up or down with a few presets on each page," says Bralove. "Each preset came up with three names, and there were three pedals controlling various configurations of synthesizers—so when he hit the preset and it said, for example, TRUMPETS, TROMBONES, STRINGS, that would be the order of his three pedals—so he could put down the trumpet pedal and play the trumpet, then add strings to it with another pedal. The trick was to imagine it as modular components that would have to be unified in the performance. And we kept it fairly simple, because you didn't want him getting lost in the pedal looking for things."

Garcia told me in '89, "I can do combinations, plus I can do the guitar [sound] in combination with anything else to whatever extent I want. I've started to do some stuff on ballads that's kind of interesting, where I'll add little voicings against the guitar so it's not actually adding to the guitar note, but it's sort of adding a halo around the sound. Some of it is very subtle."

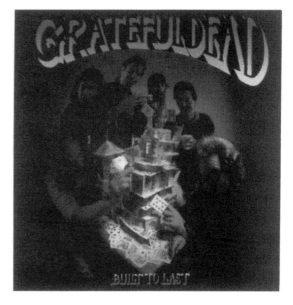

Suggested listening/viewing: The Dead's final studio album, *Built to Last* is a highly underrated disc, superbly recorded and containing several powerful tunes. The expanded/remastered version also contains exciting live versions of "Foolish Heart" and "Victim or the Crime." Two DVDs from this era that are definitely worth ogling are *Downhill From Here* (Alpine Valley, 7/17/89) and *Truckin' Up to Buffalo* (Buffalo, 7/4/89).

Phil with one of his Ken Smith six-string basses, 6/10/90.

ANOTHER NEW BASS

At the tail end of 1989, Phil adopted a new main bass that would carry him through the next couple of years: a Ken Smith BT-G6 6-string model. It was Jerry, indirectly, who led to the switch, as Phil told me in a *Golden Road* interview in April 1990: "When Jerry was so turned on to the Chick Corea Elektric Band and their guitar player, Frank Gambale, he had me check it out, and they had an outstanding bass player as well, John Patitucci. I picked up one of his records and saw him holding the bass, so I looked into it more."

"He called me out of the blue in the late '80s," recalls Ken Smith, whose business at that point was operating out of New York but is now headquartered near Philadelphia. A former session bassist, Smith started his bass company in 1978, delivered his first instrument around 1980, and experienced steady growth for his hand-built instruments throughout the 1980s. "That first bass we built for him was very special and exotic. We mixed up several different woods: It had a beautiful tiger-maple front and maybe ebony for the back, for projection or whatever, and a mahogany core. The neck was most likely maple and morado with an ebony fingerboard. It had only three knobs—bass, treble, and volume, and then a push-pull for active or passive bypass. We have our own pickups, which are these ceramic adjustable-polepiece magnetic pickups we've been using since 1982, and still use."

Phil noted in our *Golden Road* interview that the Smith neck "is wider than what I've been using, and it's actually forced me to re-examine my whole left-hand technique, which was getting really sloppy. The [hand] position the neck requires is the correct position—in other words, the position that allows you to reach as many of the strings as quickly as possible. My other instruments with narrower necks tended to give me more of a guitar positioning, where the hand is dropped from the wrist, rather than the wrist dropping from the fin-

Jerry's beloved "Rosebud" MIDI-ready guitar, designed by Doug Irwin.

gertips, as in bass or violin technique. So the new instrument is a good excuse to put myself in shape, because I won't be able to play well unless I really work at it. It's been fun." Eventually the "too wide" Smith neck would be a factor in Phil's decision to go back to Modulus basses. "I had to play it for a while to understand that [it was a problem]," he says.

In the first months of using the Smith bass, Phil still switched over to a Steve Chick-modded Modulus to play MIDI during "space." "Unfortunately, that system is only good for a 4-string mix," Phil said, "and I hate switching instruments, so hopefully they can build it into the Smith. If they can't build a 6-string system, I could have one where the center four strings are MIDI and the outer two aren't, and then I'll be able to switch back and forth—like Bobby and Jerry can."

Ken Smith: "Then Phil calls up, or maybe it was a manager, and says, 'We want a MIDI bass but we don't want to cut up the one he's playing.' So he asked me for two more so they could convert them to MIDI. These were a little simpler—they weren't the fancy ebony or high-flame maple; we had some quilted maple—but they were still our top-of-the-line basses. They also ordered two other complete sets of the

PHOTO: JOHN SIEVERT

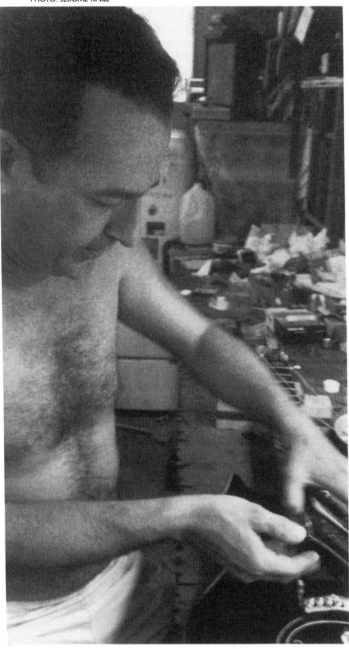

PHOTO: JEROME KNILL

In this 1990 photo, Doug Irwin does some tweaking on "Tiger" in his Sonoma County workshop.

pickups and circuits and hardware—one in gold, the other in black, in case something failed on the road, they said. It was almost the price of a whole other bass. Anyway, we didn't have anything to do with the MIDI work; that was done at Valley Arts. We just supplied the bass and then he did whatever he wanted; he voided the warranty, I'm sure," Smith laughs.

Talking about his own MIDI setup, Bill Kreutzmann told me in a 1989 *Golden Road* interview that he was using mainly a Roland Octapad as a controller. "It's got eight switches under these black pads—four on top, four on the bottom—and you activate it by hitting it with a drumstick.... [Bralove and I] work together getting sounds for the Octapad. I have a long list of sounds on a big sheet of paper near me, and then I have to initiate the number of each sound on a switching box that I can hit with a stick. So No. 1 might be 'high jingly thing,' and then there's a single boom on the No. 4 pad, handclaps on 3, a shaker on 2. It's neat. And sometimes I'll use things during the regular part of the set, too—I'll throw a hand-clap into 'Gimme Some Lovin',' just for fun."

At the first Dead shows of 1990, Garcia debuted a new axe: an $11,000 Irwin guitar that looked virtually identical to Tiger but had a different oval inlay, this one depicting a dancing skeleton holding a rose. Irwin originally referred to this axe as "The Saint" (he described the figure as "a skeleton saint in the act of repelling death"), but when he asked Garcia, Jerry said he had named it "Rosebud," perhaps after the iconic sled in Orson Welles's *Citizen Kane* (as Irwin speculated). Rosebud's pickups were three DiMarzio Super II split-coil humbuckers. The big difference between Tiger and Rosebud—aside from the important fact that the newer guitar weighed two pounds less, thanks to its hollowed-out flame-maple core—is that Gary Brawer had wired Rosebud internally with a Roland GK-2 guitar-synth interface, which hooked into a rackmount GR-50 controller. So, once Garcia got this guitar, it replaced Wolf as his everyday instrument; Wolf became a backup (used for the final time with the Grateful Dead in February 1993, when Rosebud's peghead broke and had to be fixed). The GR-50 was also connected via MIDI-interface cabling to a Korg M1R and a Lake Butler Sound RFC-1 Midigator foot-controller, which gave Garcia convenient access to his library of some 500 sounds and combinations.

"Jerry was always into experimenting with his guitars, particularly trying out different pickups," says Gary Brawer. "He was always changing his pickups because he felt their magnetic field didn't last long at all and that the high end would go quickly. We went through a phase where he wanted to try a lot of different pickups—he played Lindys [Lindy Fralin pickups] at a couple of shows; in fact, I still have Jerry's Lindys at my shop. He also tried some [Seymour] Duncans and a different model of DiMarzio, but he always seemed to go back to the DiMarzio Super IIs."

VINCE AND BRUCE

The next big change in the Grateful Dead's sound came in the summer/fall of 1990. In July, Brent Mydland died of a drug overdose, after more than ten years in the keyboard slot. It was a devastating blow to the band at a time when they were at an undeniable peak. However, after a relatively brief round of auditions for a new keyboardist that summer, Vince Welnick, late of the Tubes and Todd Rundgren's band, was chosen to replace Brent. The effect on the Dead's instrumental blend was immediate and profound.

First of all, the Hammond B-3 organ, which was such a major part of Brent's sound, was completely eliminated. One-time B-3 tech Peter Miller notes, "That was like a personal stab; that hurt. Jerry made the decision not to have a B-3 on the stage." Why? "It was strictly superstition; he didn't want to lose another keyboard player." Really? Any chance he was kidding? "Maybe, but that's what he told me." For the record, I've heard it said that neither Jerry nor Phil was hot to have another B-3 onstage. "Anyway," Miller continues, "as a result of not having the B-3, Bob Bralove and I spent weeks, months—and thousands of dollars—trying different combinations of sound modules and mixing everything we had available to imitate the B-3 sound without having the B-3 console. In the early days [of Vince's tenure] we used the Voce DMI-64, which at that time was the closest thing to it. We had three or four of those units and mixed them together, and then on top of that we had a Groove Tubes Trio preamp that we used as a distortion box, because we couldn't get the right distortion character out of the stock DMI."

When Vince made his debut appearance the first week of September 1990, he had a single MIDI keyboard controller—a Roland RD-300—making for quite a spare-looking stage compared to Brent's beefy setup. Vince had previously used the RD-300 during his time with Todd Rundgren, so he came into the band playing an instrument he was comfortable with.

Though the Roland RD-300 had a better-than-average piano sound, its main function was to be a portal to an extensive world of offstage MIDI sounds that had been assembled by Bob Bralove—and, in fact, the bulk of Vince's piano sounds came from a Kurzweil RMX module and a Roland MKS-20 (same as with Brent). Bralove had an expanded role with Vince: Not only did he help

Vince develop his sonic vocabulary, he actually worked with him during every performance, feeding him timbral possibilities in real time from his position on the side of the stage.

"I have all sorts of sounds—vibes, piano, Clavinet, harpsichord—that I can combine together with the faders in any way I want," Vince told me in February 1991, "but then Bralove also has sounds that he can put together to make the designated song sound." For instance, if there was a notion to put a fiddle sound on, say, "Me and My Uncle," "[Bralove] might look at me and pretend to be playing violin, and I'll nod my head in agreement if I want to do it. On something like 'Wharf Rat' we might use acoustic guitar sounds blended in with vocal sounds, strings, or whatever. Sometimes, on a long song, he turns strings into horns and adds rattling bones as texture…he's the one in control. He might give it to me piecemeal and stack it up, but as I hear it, I just interpret it the way it sounds to me, and it kind of dictates the way I play it …. It's really fun for me. It keeps me on my toes."

Bruce and Vince sometimes struggled to find space in the music for their respective keyboards, but mostly played together very well. This is from 5/12/91.

PHOTO: JAY BLAKESBERG

Just a few shows into Vince's run with the band, he was joined by a powerful second keyboardist—Bruce Hornsby, who had played Grateful Dead music while he was in college, but had long since moved on to a *very* successful career as a solo artist beginning in the mid '80s. His band, Bruce Hornsby & the Range, played on the same bill as the Dead a few times in the late '80s, and he even joined the boys onstage a couple of times. He was a fellow traveler, you might say, so after Brent died Garcia suggested that Bruce might be able to help fill the void, at least on a temporary basis. And so, on September 15, 1990, at Madison Square Garden (nothing like starting *big*), Vince and his rig moved a few feet back on a riser, and in front of him suddenly was a nine-foot

Baldwin grand piano (with Helpinstill pickups), topped by a Korg M1 16-voice polyphonic synthesizer (which Bruce rarely used). Hornsby also played accordion on a few songs, most notably "Uncle John's Band" and "It's All Over Now, Baby Blue."

Asked what kind of accordion he used with the Dead, the always affable keyboardist says, "For about the first year I was playing this complete *bullshit* rig—it was basically this big hulk that was sort of like a regular accordion, but it was [actually] a MIDI controller for a synth. I couldn't even tell you what kind [of controller] it was. But it had this calliope-esque synth sound from an old Roland Juno-16. I had used that when I played accordion in the Range—that group was pretty loud, with two guitars, and a regular miked accordion wasn't cutting through. We tried that setup and it was okay, so that's what I did when I came to the Dead, because they were also fairly loud, you might recall," he says with a laugh. "After a while,

Bruce at the Baldwin grand, 5/12/91.

PHOTO: JAY BLAKESBERG

though, I got burnt with that because there was no dynamic range. So in the latter stages of my time with them I started playing a real accordion, a Hohner, and that sounded much better to me."

Bruce's contribution to the band's sound made for a pretty thick stew sometimes, though he was undeniably a great addition—a virtuoso who fully understood the Dead's music and legacy and was not afraid to push the other members musically. Despite the trauma of Brent's death and the difficult task of quickly bringing Vince up to speed, 1991 ended up being a great year for the band, filled with interesting shows and adventurous playing—much of which was undoubtedly a result of Hornsby's positive influence.

NEW ELECTRIC/ACOUSTICS

Outside the Dead, during this era, both Garcia and Weir were playing a fair amount of acoustic music in their spare time—Weir with bassist Rob Wasserman, Garcia with mandolinist David Grisman and Grisman's rhythm section of

Garcia with one of his Alvarez axes at a benefit concert with Phil, Bob and Vince at Berkeley Community Theatre, 9/24/94.

PHOTO: JAY BLAKESBERG

bassist Jim Kerwin and percussionist/fiddler Joe Craven. (Somehow Garcia also found time to play electric music with the Jerry Garcia Band, which by 1991 had graduated to arenas.) For these two acoustic ventures both Weir and Garcia played custom single-cutaway Alvarez-Yairi guitars, and in fact both became endorsers. Like Ibanez, Alvarez was a Spanish name adopted by a Japanese company. In this case, there is a family of luthiers, of which Kazuo Yairi is the most notable current artisan.

Garcia's guitar, which he actually obtained in the late '80s and nearly used with the Jerry Garcia Acoustic Band, according to David Nelson, had a tree-of-life inlay on a graphite neck. "It's rigged up so it's not only got the [piezo] bridge pickup, but there's a microphone inside it," Jerry told *Guitar Player*'s Jon Sievert in 1993. "I love that guitar. It's not quirky, and mine is set up for performing." Garcia's axe had a Sitka spruce top, rosewood back and sides, and a rosewood fingerboard over the graphite neck. He had three nearly identical guitars.

"The graphite neck seems to help produce a better sound, but to me it's all mojo," he told Sievert in an earlier (1991) interview. "The physics of a guitar are beyond me. I don't know why good ones sound good. You can get two consecutively numbered assembly-line guitars and one will sound fabulous and the other as dead as a doornail. I don't even know why I like one better than another, but this is the one that seems to speak clearest and is most even from string to string. To me, that's what a guitar needs—at least it's a great place to start from. I've got some *f*-hole guitars that I love; I just got a beautiful D'Angelico, and I've got a beautiful classic [Gibson] L-5 that barks like a dog. The Alvarez-Yairis are my favorite so far, though, just because they allow me that pickup. From the onstage point of view, it's the best all around."

As for Weir's Alvarez, Bob told Sievert, "I presided over the design of mine. We took [Jerry's Alvarez] to start with, which is a Dreadnought, and asked, 'Okay, what is it I don't like about this?' Well, okay, there's too much bass. For my purposes of playing with Wasserman, I don't want to get into a pissing match with the bass in that register. I need something a little tighter—not thin by any means, but a balanced guitar with tighter bass. That suggests that we go to a smaller box. And the grand concert size, the triple 'O' box, will give you that. Then we need the cutaway. So that's the major difference. Our guitars are set up basically the same; they both have the piezo bridge pickup and an interior mic, and you can balance those. The piezo sounds like shit all by itself, but it gives you more projection and delivery, as opposed to feedback, in a concert situation." Weir's Alvarez had a cedar top and Indonesian coral rosewood back and sides, and a Modulus graphite neck.

Working closely with Grisman, who is a collector and connoisseur of vintage acoustic instruments, seemed to rub off on Garcia. Over the course of numerous sessions they recorded together at Grisman's Mill Valley home studio, called the Dawg House, Garcia eagerly tried out a number of different axes, including an incredibly rare 1939 natural-finish Gibson Super 400N. "I think there are only seven of them," Grisman told *Acoustic Guitar* in 1993. In the same joint interview, Garcia added, "It sure is a wonderful guitar. I wound up buying it." He played it on several tracks of the children's record the duo made together, *Not for Kids Only*; other axes he used on that disc included a Martin D-18 owned by Grisman's son, Monroe, Garcia's own D-28, and the Alvarez, which, he admitted, "doesn't have the refinement that some of these [vintage] instruments have—the depth, the character."

Depth and character are also qualities that Garcia and Weir (and all their various musical cohorts) seemed to have in abundance, as well.

GOIN' DOWN THE ROAD

IT'S truly difficult to grasp the complexity of what the Grateful Dead's equipment scene had become by the early 1990s. Think back for a moment to the *Live Dead* era: 14 microphones to capture all the instruments for the PA/recording split; no effect pedals for any of the guitarists; a few Fender amps and JBL extensions; a small PA probably consisting of just a few Acoustic and/or Sunn cabinets; a Vox portable organ; two drum kits, a couple of gongs, and some congas; a few stacked MX-10s at the front-of-house...*and* a hot band playing some of the most adventurous rock music ever performed on Planet Earth, mostly in theaters, ballrooms, college gymnasiums, and small civic centers. Fast forward to 1993. Same band, mostly—but things had gotten a little...er...*bigger*. To put it mildly.

Chapter Sixteen
1992-1995

Now, a 20,000-seat basketball arena or comparable outdoor shed was considered "intimate," and every spring and summer brought a gaggle of stadium shows, with venues ranging from 30,000 to 70,000. The Dead/Ultrasound PA system had been based entirely around Meyer loudspeakers for more than a decade. At a series of May 1993 concerts at the Sam Boyd Silver Bowl in Las Vegas (one of the "small" stadiums), for example, the main stacks consisted of 96 modified MSL-3s—48 per side—plus 32 double-18″ subwoofers, 12 UPAs under the stage to aid with the center fill, and delay towers containing a dozen of Meyer's humongous MSL-10 units. Crest 8001 amplifiers powered the system, which had enough sheer wattage to make the old Wall of Sound seem like a megaphone in comparison—okay, that part is writer's hyperbole. But it was a very loud and, fortunately, very clear system.

"There was nowhere to go but to keeping adding stuff," Mickey Hart says good-naturedly. "Even in the old days, that's where it was headed. When Jorma got an amp, Cipollina got an amp, and James Gurley [of Big Brother], and Jerry was right in there, too. There was a volume war between all the guitarists! As the amps went up and you grew in volume, it was also almost like you had to re-learn how to play your instrument. You had to become more facile and learn how to play *with* the volume. You can't play the same with four Twins as you can with two; it's a completely different technique. And it was like that across the board. As drummers, we had to learn to play louder and differently, too. Then you put that together with better and more powerful equipment in bigger places..." he laughs heartily.

There had been a big change in the band's monitoring setup by the spring of '93: The Dead had gone to an in-ear system and removed all amps and loudspeakers from the stage, a major move with profound implications. Though in-ears have become downright common today, in the early and mid '90s relatively few artists used them. The Dead had looked into the burgeoning technology as soon as systems started popping up with this or that band, but it appears the direct impetus to make the switchover came from touring with Steve Miller during the summer of 1992. Always a technical innovator (remember, John Meyer even worked for him back in 1967!), Miller was an early adopter of Future Sonics in-ear systems. The company was founded in 1991 by a one-time live-sound engineer named Marty Garcia, who had spent a decade experimenting with different personal monitoring systems. By the time the Dead and Future Sonics hooked up, the company had its Ear Monitors (a trademarked name which, to Marty Garcia's chagrin, has become genericized through the years) on tours with the likes of Phil Collins, Gloria Estefan, U2, Reba McEntire, and Miller.

"In 1992 things really came together," Marty told *Mix* magazine in 2005. "I got my Ear Monitor trademark. That was the time I started working with the Grateful Dead, who went full-tilt into the Ears. I consulted with them for about a year, starting with Phil Lesh, who helped me talk the band into them. Steve Miller was already using Ear Monitors, and his band and the Dead co-headlined a stadium tour that was not only completely wedgeless, but also had no back-line speakers onstage."

Not surprisingly, multiple members of the Dead's sound crew were also intimately involved in designing the full system for these always-particular musicians. Harry Popick, Dan Healy, Don Pearson, Peter Miller, and others consulted or were involved with designing different components, though at the heart of it was the Future Sonics ear buds themselves, each custom-molded to fit the players' ear cavities.

"We'll never claim to have the highest highs," Marty Garcia said. "However, those [frequencies] are the easiest for the end-user to adjust with a little equalization. The hardest thing to create in an earpiece is low, dynamic frequencies that don't distort, which is what we focused on ... .

"The transducer has to be right, too. It's amazing how little power an earpiece requires to sound good. However, in 1992, the Grateful Dead's Don Pearson

Garcia playing "Rosebud" in Las Vegas, 5/15/93. He has his Ear Monitors in. Note that his effects pedals are now mounted behind him on a flat surface.

PHOTO: JAY BLAKESBERG

proved to me that the bigger and better the Class-A amplifier was, the better the sound. We could take a Crown D-75—a good-sounding amp for the time—and current-limit its 75-watt output down to a couple of watts. We could hear all the transients, and the Ear Monitors had an unbelievable sound." (By '93, the in-ears were powered by Crest amps.)

Musicians have gone to in-ears for a variety of reasons, but certainly paramount is the hearing protection they offer—long an issue with the Dead, where no member was immune to ear damage (Mickey Hart was affected seriously enough that today he wears hearing aids). The removal of amps from the stage immediately cut the decibel level drastically, and the ear pieces themselves were highly controllable in terms of both volume and frequencies, with each being equipped with a built-in limiter. Vocal microphones also became less susceptible to feedback. Each musician got his own personal stereo mix that was completely unaffected by the amps and speakers, which were now miked in enclosed areas offstage, often *under* the stage.

IN-EAR LOVE

To a person, the band members seemed to like the change. It definitely improved the group's harmonies, and in general they seemed to feel that they could be more "inside" the music wearing the in-ears.

"I love it!" Garcia enthused in 1993. "I think it's just amazing. I mean, the amount we've gained on our part singing is just… *boy!* Now we can really hear what we're doing…. You can start to use your voice as an instrument more…. You don't get the kick-in-the-ass physical low, the through-the-roots-of-your-feet low end. But you can hear. And also you can hear the notes that the bass is playing, and you get the drive. Even outdoors you get plenty of low end." It helped, too, that electronics designer Tom Paddock had built special emulators that simulated the sound of a power amp feeding a speaker, and this realistic approximation could be pumped into the Ear Monitors.

From chief monitor mixer Harry Popick's perspective, "[The in-ears] made my life easier. I wasn't struggling and fighting the room every day; it sounded the same wherever we went. Once you got them on and had the reverb dialed up, we had what we called 'Oakland Coliseum' everywhere! I didn't have to deal with so many wires and speaker cabinets, and I had a rack underneath [the Gamble console] that had a really nice T.C. Electronic reverb and the Crest 60- or 70-watt amplifiers for the in-ear monitors." Harry also had a special system, developed primarily by Peter Miller and Don Pearson, that allowed him to monitor how loud each musician had his volume relative to the others.

"The great thing about the in-ears," Harry continues, "is you could essentially give a guy a studio mix in his ears—construct a truly personal mix. You could pan the organ left and right if you wanted, or put more or less of someone

PHOTO SUSANA MILLMAN

Monitor mixer Harry Popick
and Ultrasound co-founder and
all-around audio guru Don
Pearson, early '90s.

in a mix so easily. Phil's mix was completely different from everybody else's. He kept his in-ears quieter than the others' because he wanted to listen to the PA more."

Garcia said in *Guitar Player* in 1993, "I have a mix that's basically like onstage: Vince on the left, Bob on the right, drums across the center, bass in the center, and me in the center. And the vocals with just the tiniest spread.... I like to play it and sing it as though it's the final mix of a record. That's what I want to hear."

In the same joint interview, Weir agreed: "[My mix] features my voice and my guitar a few dB louder than anyone else, to give me the advantage of hearing really clearly what I'm doing. But the rest of it should sound like a record, exactly. And it does pretty much."

Not everyone was delighted by the switch to in-ears. In fact, there was considerable grumbling in the audience about the issue. First of all, the removal of the amps fundamentally changed the experience of being up close in front of the stage; the air that had previously been moved by the backline amps had a real physical quality and immediacy, one that was not comparable to getting a

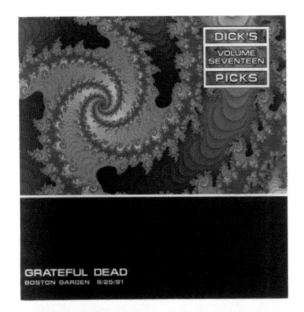

GRATEFUL DEAD
BOSTON GARDEN 9/25/91

CD releases from the '90s have been few and far between, but a couple of good ones are *Dicks Picks Vol. 17, 9/25/91* (from the group's epic run at the Boston Garden) and *Dick's Picks Vol. 27, 12/16/92* Oakland Coliseum. Additionally, live and rehearsal versions of some of the unrecorded songs the band introduced in the early '90s appear on the fine box set *So Many Roads,* released in 1999.

feed off even a well-placed fill-in PA (which usually wasn't loud enough to please the die-hards in front, anyway). There was also the sense that the band was suddenly less connected to the crowd, wrapped up in their own world. Harry notes, "Bob liked to have some of the audience mic pumped into the in-ears so he could still hear the crowd, but the other guys were in their own world entirely." Adding to that feeling of separation from the crowd was the fact that the musicians had a talkback system that allowed them to converse with each other, or a member of the tech crew—even mid-song—without the audience hearing them. (Sort of: In fact, because the talkback went out over a radio frequency, audience members with the right equipment could, and did, pick up the little bursts of conversation.) It was a slightly disconcerting sight to be hearing a song and seeing Jerry or Phil talking inaudibly into a microphone.

Ultrasound's Howard Danchik notes, "I thought going to the in-ears was a great idea until I heard what it did to the band. Nobody was playing to the same band anymore. They'd be playing to some mix of these instruments, and if they were pissed off at someone they could turn off everyone but themselves—which *did* happen. Up until then, the band had played to what they were hearing together, but now everyone was hearing something different, so the dynamic range suffered and caused the advent of compressors on a lot of the instruments, something we had strenuously avoided before. Yes, they could sing a little better and it might have been better for them—for their hearing—but I'm not sure the music was better for it, frankly."

By the band's last couple of years, they were carrying *six* Gamble consoles: two at the front-of-house, three monitor consoles (two at Harry's position, and one back by the drummers for their acoustic percussion, mixed by a tech named Mike Brady), and then one devoted to Bob Bralove's electronic-instrument line inputs, which fed into the monitor and house systems. Ultrasound's Don Pearson was also a key member of the monitoring team.

Say what you will about the evolution of the Dead's music in the early to mid '90s—certainly there was a precipitous decline in the quality of Garcia's performances in 1994 and 1995, related to various health and drug-dependency issues—but the "drums" and "space" portion of nearly every second set unfailingly delivered the goods, show after show. Has there ever been a more exciting MIDI/electronics playground before or since? I think not. It is to the eternal credit of the Grateful Dead's members that in good times and bad, that experimental portion of the show always retained its vitality and invention. They were always willing to push the technological envelope and kept asking that question: "What if we...?"

BRALOVE AND CHAOS

Dan Healy had long been a willing partner in that exploration, and for the last decade-plus, Bob Bralove was an essential part of the equation, too. In fact, during the Dead's last few years he usually had a little segment after Mickey and Billy's workout (for which he provided all manner of processing from his own backstage rack) and before Garcia, Lesh, and Weir

Front-of-house mixer Dan Healy (R) and Ultrasound's Howard Danchik, Las Vegas 2003.

returned for "space," where he had free rein to add his own musical weirdness as a bridge of sorts. In 1994 he told David Gans how that evolved: "I started to generate these textures to contrast what was happening with The Beam. I wanted to take The Beam performance into a new place, so I started working with these drones, overlays of synthesizers that Mickey could play against or into or away from, so that [The Beam] would be by itself. And then there would be these lengths of time when Mickey would leave, and he'd say, 'Let that thing go!' and The Beam would resonate, and he'd say, 'Go ahead and bring up that other stuff you've been doing,' and then he'd be off the stage. So that little section started to open up a little bit, and I was pretty cautious about it—as soon as somebody would step out [onstage] I'd pull out. I think Phil was the first guy who came back, as he was heading toward the stage [for "space"], and said, 'Keep playin', man!' The headphone systems allow me to plug into Jerry's headphone or Phil's headphone while I'm playing to hear how I'm playing with them from their perspective."

And it was partly Bralove's indefatigable, searching nature that helped keep the Rhythm Devils and "space" segments so sonically fresh year after year. "It was my policy to bring something new for everybody every tour—not just the drummers," he says. "They had to have new sounds. I had to feel like we were moving forward. So we might put in some new samples or maybe some new processors, or maybe attach a new controller to something. They would quickly tell me what they liked and didn't like. But we had this constantly growing body of sounds that they liked, and understanding what they liked then informed me about who each of them was in this [electronic] realm. Language is often very difficult for these things; hearing what they wanted to play told me more."

In Mickey's case, he had sampled nearly every exotic instrument in his collection, so he could access them easily through electronic pads. "There was a massive amount of sounds I wanted to use, and I wanted to explore the combination of acoustic sounds and electronics, but I found out early on you couldn't really process the acoustic sounds the way you could the electronics, because of feedback. So we got the pads and started going to town, sampling whips and motorcycles—we had tried real motorcycles in Madison Square Garden and we choked on the fumes," he laughs. "We were miking the pipes in stereo, and there were these huge clouds of exhaust. So it became mo' bettah to use stuff I had already recorded. We'd do our recordings and then put them in early samplers, like the Dynacord. Then, once we had MIDI, we were able to combine them in interesting ways we couldn't previously. The other thing that sampling did is it preserved all those pieces of percussion, because we didn't have to bring them on the road anymore. A lot of people don't understand that all drums decompose in some way after you play them for a while. You play them hard and beat them, and they give their voice in the name of the music. All drums have a certain lifespan, and they also have a peak—which could be many years, of course—but you never know. So I got into the habit of whenever I got a drum, it would come into my bedroom first and I'd get to know it, find out its nuances, before I or any of my associates would go in and sample it. There's still nothing like putting hand or stick to drum, but sampling and MIDI actually give you more control over the sounds. So it was a trade-off."

Vince at his Wersi keyboard, 5/15/93.

PHOTO: JAY BLAKESBERG

Not that he (or Bralove) was always in full control over the electronic percussion: "I remember hitting a pad at a show one time and it was like an atomic bomb went off or something," Mickey says with a chuckle. "And Garcia just kind of looked at me over his glasses. He didn't give me the death-ray, but the eyes said everything: 'You are louder than the whole fucking band!' The problem with sampled sounds is if you didn't soundcheck, and Bralove's been turning knobs all night, God knows what might happen!" Among the processors Bralove had in his rack were T.C. 2290s, Eventide's H3000 Ultra-Harmonizer processor, Lexicon PCM 70 and PCM 90 digital reverbs, the Quantec room simulator/signal processor, and more. And out at front-of-house, Healy had similar tools at his disposal, all under MIDI control through a Macintosh computer and an Opcode Studio 5 MIDI interface. (Healy's partner in crime when it came to custom programming during this period was Uwe Willenbacher.)

Vince's setup still looked spare, with his main controller now a German-made Wersi digital, which Peter Miller says had a Fatar-style keyboard. That was augmented by a Hammond-Suzuki XB-2 keyboard which, at the time, offered the most accurate electronic re-creation of the old B-3 (plus MIDI capability and onboard digital reverb). All of his sounds and processing equipment were stored in racks and synths offstage. Mickey and Billy were both using kits from a combination of manufacturers, including Sonar, Yamaha, and, in Mickey's case, Rogers. And, of course, they still had their tons and tons of Beast-ly drums and MIDI gear.

The guitarists, too, always seemed to have a ball putting their MIDI setups through their paces. Altered pipe-organ sounds might be mixed with clay-pipe flutes and weird percussive clonks and clangs in a delirious cacophony. There were times when Jerry, Phil, and Bob all played "drums" through their setups—and pretty well, too! Ethereal voices might cascade through the sound system in quad, like angels falling through space, or Garcia might play a "bassoon" that was beyond diabolical. Everything was possible, all the time.

LIGHTNING BOLT

During the winter of 1993, Garcia acquired his final Grateful Dead guitar: a custom axe, nicknamed Lightning Bolt (after its dominant wood and mother-of-pearl inlay design), crafted by a heretofore unknown Florida woodworker named Steve Cripe. Garcia debuted the new guitar at Shoreline Amphitheatre in August 1993 and played it regularly until his death in 1995, with the exception of a few shows when the guitar was in the shop.

A Deadhead since the early '70s, Cripe was not a guitar-maker by trade—he was a yacht restorer and woodworking expert who started designing guitars as a hobby. He got it in his head that he wanted to build a guitar for Garcia, so over and over he watched the video *Dead Ahead*—from the 1980 Radio City shows, where Garcia played Tiger—and then copied the Irwin guitar's contours, crafting the body of his version out of cocobolo taken from an old Chinese opium bed, ironically enough. The neck differed considerably from an Irwin's: It was a through-body made of nine-ply strips of alternating maple and cocobolo.

"He went through several different variations of the Lightning Bolt before he ended up with the one that Jerry got," says Adam Palow, head of South Florida's Tungsten Amplification (which makes a renowned line of classic hand-wired tube amps) and a friend of Cripe's who has owned several of his guitars. "I've probably played a dozen of the Cripe guitars [only about 25 were ever made], including a couple of the early Lightning Bolts, and the contours were slightly different." The finished Lightning Bolt was only the seventh guitar Cripe had built.

Actually getting the guitar to Garcia proved to be difficult. After making numerous inquiries and getting nowhere, Cripe ultimately used one of the few contacts he had and sent the guitar to Pam Grisman, David Grisman's wife, who then gave it to Jerry. A few months later, much to his surprise, Cripe learned that Garcia was using Lightning Bolt onstage with the Dead. He was also contacted about building a second guitar for Garcia and sent a check for $6,500 to cover the expense of both that guitar—nicknamed *Top Hat*, after its inlay—*and* the first axe, which had actually been a gift from Cripe. The guitar-maker met

The Final Days: Jerry with his Cripe "Lightning Bolt" guitar, Shoreline 6/4/95.

Garcia only once—in Miami on the spring '94 tour—and, Cripe told the *St. Petersburg Times*, "It took me a while to get anything out of him about how he would change the guitar." However, Cripe noted that Garcia said, "'It's almost like I sent you the specs for what I was really looking for in a guitar.' The whole thing was just great; it was a highlight of my life."

Palow notes that Cripe "wasn't much of an electronics guy. I know he'd seen the *Guitar Player* article [from 1988] that discussed the [Garcia] effect loop, and he'd seen some things about the Irwin guitars. I think for Lightning Bolt he basically set it up with five-way Stratocaster switching with the three humbuckers. But I know that when Jerry got it, the first thing he did was send it over to Gary Brawer to have the electronics re-done the way he preferred," which of course included making it MIDI-compatible.

Luthier Steve Cripe holds two of his creations, shortly before his tragic death in 1996.

"When Jerry first got it, it was completely different from what he was used to," Brawer comments. "It had Schaller humbucking pickups and a few other things Jerry wasn't used to, so Parish came over and said, 'Here, make this a Jerry guitar.' So we changed the pickups [to DiMarzio Super IIs], put in the MIDI, and I had to re-do the frets. In general, Jerry's setups on the guitar were pretty much like nobody else's: The bow in the neck was tremendous, the nut height above the 1st fret was two or three times higher than what it might normally be, and he kept his string height pretty high."

Why opt for a high action? "Jerry told me that he wanted everything he did to be *intentional*," Brawer says. "He didn't want to make it so easy that his fingers started doing things he didn't want them to do. He was very clear about that."

What was so special about Lightning Bolt? Palow believes it was the neck-through: "By using that nine-ply neck-through design, instead of a bolt-on, you've got an incredible amount of sustain. Those [Cripe] guitars just ring on and on and on. The tone is affected, too: If you listen to post-August 1993 Dead and Jerry shows, you can tell the guitar has more upper-midrange presence. A lot of people describe that sound as 'acoustic,' but it was a straight electric tone. It's just the way Cripe guitars sound."

"What's funny about that tone," adds Gary Brawer, "is when he played it, everyone called me and asked what kind of piezo pickup was in the bridge! And of course there wasn't one. I did use a slightly different buffer in that guitar. I have a schematic of the original Cutler buffer, and we made a copy of the original at some point, and we changed a couple of things to make it more electrically correct, though it didn't really affect the sound. What I was told is that at the same time he played the Cripe guitar, he actually had changed the way he was buffering his pedals, and the impedance wasn't exactly right and it filtered out the bass—it was an impedance mismatch. It made everything very clear and bright."

That "acoustic" tone during this period was not universally adored. (Nor was it confined to Lightning Bolt—there are pre-Bolt shows where that sound is evident.) Though it definitely added a nice, almost lacy quality to some of the more folky material—such as the new Hunter-Garcia tunes "So Many Roads" and "Lazy River Road"—that timbre was not as suitable to more rocking numbers, and in general it lacked the *heft* that Rosebud's regular sound, with some light added distortion, had. Some have speculated that the clarity of that "acoustic" guitar sound in his Ear Monitors was also very appealing to Garcia.

Meanwhile, Bob Weir took to playing a couple of different Alvarez-Yairi electric-acoustics—including a rather homely battleship-gray one—for a couple of songs at most shows beginning in the spring of 1994. (He played it at a handful of shows in the fall of '93, as well.) "Once we got the Ear Monitors," he says, "it seemed like you could bring an acoustic guitar onstage and fit it into our sound easier than when we had all those amps out there. We could hear everything more clearly, no doubt about it." This immediately fueled rumors that the Dead might try playing acoustic sets again, but it was not to be, even though in 1993 Garcia told Jon Sievert, "I would love to play acoustic in the context of the band." The Cripe guitar is as close as he got.

Also new to Garcia's setup was a DigiTech Whammy pitch-bend pedal that allowed him to play a note, bend it up a 3rd with his hand and another 3rd with the pedal, making for some rather extreme and eerie slide effects. Occasionally, when he hit it just right, the effect had an ethereal, almost pedal-steel sound—but in my view he never learned to control it very well, and most of his solos using the pitch bend just sounded out of tune and unsettling. (Actually, some

Some of Phil's foot pedals, early '90s.

PHOTO: SUSANA MILLMAN

of his best pitch-bend work came with the Garcia Band on the song "The Maker"—somewhat unusual, as Garcia kept his JGB setup relatively simple and MIDI-free.)

A peek into Garcia's rack in the '90s, as revealed in a photo on dozin.com, shows a relatively straightforward setup, including old favorites like the Mu-Tron III, the MXR Phase 100, a Boss (Roland) OC-2 Octave pedal, Boss OD-2R Turbo OverDrive, Boss GE-7 7-band equalizer, an ADA Multi-Effects Delay, a Groove Tubes Trio preamp, a (B.K. Butler) Real Tube reverb unit, and a Korg DTR-1 digital rack tuner. Other gear included Chandler Digital Stereo Echo, Korg 01R/W synth module, E-mu Proteus/1 sound module (which included many samples from the Emulator III library), an ADA MicroCab guitar speaker-cabinet emulator, and an Alesis MidiVerb signal processor.

As he would through the end of the Dead's reign, Phil was playing a wide-body Modulus Quantum 6 Throughbody TBX. "The top is book-matched quilted maple over maple, with a special black cherry finish," Geoff Gould said in 1993. "It uses EMG pickups, except for the Gotoh 510 piezo at the bridge. That feeds into six EMG modified acoustic guitar preamps that all sum together on the balance knob. The neck has a clear red finish and a cocobolo fingerboard." At the time of that interview, Lesh still used a Ken Smith for the MIDI "space" segment, but shortly after that he had a Quantum 6 outfitted for MIDI, too.

CUTLER TAKES THE REINS

In March 1994, the Dead made a change that virtually no one outside of the six band members had foreseen: They relieved Dan Healy of his duties as front-of-house mixer, after 25-plus years of service to the band. What happened? Well, the details are still shrouded in mystery more than a decade later, in part because the musicians never liked to trash each other or their close work associates in print—an admirable quality, I'm sure we can all agree. Different explanations have filtered out through the years: everything from Healy's supposedly shabby sonic treatment of support acts at early-'90s stadium shows, including Sting and Crosby, Stills & Nash, to what was widely regarded as ongoing disrespect to Bob Weir, who often found himself barely audible in Healy's mixes. Some didn't care for his somewhat extreme stereo mixes. Others thought that he used too much processing and, in effect, junked up the Dead's sound. He could be haughty on occasion, and it didn't help that he, too, had some substance issues. At any rate, it all added up to enough of a problem that the band unanimously decided that the time had come for him to go—always a tough, tough call in the Dead world; none had been harder, I'm sure.

Don Pearson summed up one of his friend and work-mate's best qualities as a mixer in the *Deadhead's Taping Compendium, Vol. II*: "Dan had the innate, uncanny, magical ability to find out early on in the night who was 'on' and who wasn't—to foresee the magic. He was able to find out who was playing with any redeeming value and would build his mix around that person; so regardless of how good or bad the band was playing, there were thrilling moments every night because Dan was able to find that portion of redeeming value. And a lot of other [mixers] never do find that—they just turn it up, and they expect the band to find the handle." And, of course, Healy's impact on the overall development of the group's live-sound setup through the years cannot be overstated, either.

But at Chicago's Rosemont Horizon arena the third week of March 1994, there was a new person manning the Gamble consoles at front-of-house, although it was hardly a new face in the Dead scene: John Cutler had been part of the Dead's world for 25 years, had recorded and co-produced their last two studio albums (and the 1990 double-CD live set *Without a Net*), presided over numerous radio and television broadcasts, and been the front-of-house mixer for the Jerry Garcia Band for the past several years. He was the obvious choice, and the fact that he *was* around to step into the breach no doubt made Healy's departure slightly less traumatic for the Dead, who always *hated* letting anyone go, and were notoriously bad at it.

John Cutler at the Gamble front-of-house console.

PHOTO: SUSANA MILLMAN

"The last couple of years before that," Weir comments, "we had been work-ing a lot more closely with Cutler, and we had more of a *simpatico* going with him. I don't want to talk out of school, but we were all having problems with Dan in the live situation, and at one point enough became enough. No one had issues with Cutler, so we said, 'Let's see what he can do out front.' And that's what happened. I'm sure it wasn't that easy for Cutler—not technically, of course; that was no problem. But just the thing of replacing someone who'd done it for so long."

Though the job might seem to be a plum, Cutler was actually thrust into a rather unenviable position: working with a notoriously difficult-to-please band with one of the most complex gear setups in rock music, and following in the

John Meyer stands below a hanging array of his speakers in Las Vegas, 1992.

footsteps of someone who had become famous in his own right and was beloved by many fans. Healy had always been "the tapers' friend" for allowing the Deadhead recording and tape-trading community to flourish in the late '70s and early '80s, and for instigating the more formal "taping section" (usually behind the sound board) beginning in the late fall of 1984. Mixing for the Jerry Garcia Band was a much different expe-rience: They still had amps and wedges on the stage—old school—and carried so little compared to the Dead. And even working with the Dead so much in the studio couldn't have prepared him fully for the challenge of mixing front-of-house in arenas/sheds/stadiums. It might have been helpful, too, if Don Pearson—who had such great ears and could trouble-shoot a system as well as anyone—had been available to offer his sage wisdom on a regular basis, but he was helping Harry Popick with monitor concerns during this period and wasn't out front as much.

The sound during that first Cutler tour in '94 drew mixed reviews from the fans. It seemed as though he had, in fact, reduced the clutter of signals coursing through the system at any given moment; it sounded cleaner. He

PHOTO: SUSANA MILLMAN

appeared to soften the stereo image somewhat, making it easier to hear all the instruments clearly regardless of where one was sitting in the venue. But there were also complaints that he had reduced the volume in a trade-off for clarity; indeed, there were chants of "Turn it up!" at a number of shows that year and in 1995.

It didn't help that Garcia was not at the top of his game and would actually turn his guitar *down* in the mix from his position onstage. What was going on with him? Well, he was suffering from a recurrence of the diabetes that had nearly killed him 1986, causing him to periodically lose sensation in his fingers, which certainly affected his dexterity. He also had been afflicted for a number of years with carpal tunnel syndrome, a repetitive stress injury brought on by years and years of playing heavy guitars in poor ergonomic positions. He had pain in his back, shoulders, forearms, and wrist and was being treated by a chiropractor and acupuncturist, with varying degrees of success. Add to that his troubling drug dependency, which definitely contributed to his appearing vacant and spaced from time to time, an enlarged heart, and early symptoms of emphysema, and you have a portrait of a man who was not in good shape *at all*. Ironically, Phil, Bob, Bill, and Mickey were in top form during this period of Jerry's slow decline, and they tried admirably to make up for their comrade's failings and lapses.

Some of those lapses were helped by the addition, beginning in December 1994, of lyric TelePrompTers—a move that horrified many Deadheads, who believed that at best it was a sign of laziness, and at worst just a Band-Aid and further proof of Garcia's ongoing malaise, as he was the main (but certainly not the only) culprit. Besides, blowing lyrics was a Grateful Dead tradition, the thinking went. In the end, only the band's new songs—and a couple of recent covers—showed up on the TelePrompTers (sorry, no help for "Eyes of the World" today, Jer!), and they definitely helped considerably on wordy tunes such as the Hunter-Garcia gem "Days Between," and Jerry's spellbinding version of Dylan's "Vision of Johanna."

LAST TOURS

As 1995 began, there were, as usual, many plans afoot.

The band had convened a few times in 1994 and early '95 trying to get going on their first studio album since 1989's *Built to Last*, but the sessions were mostly unfocused and lethargic, mainly due to Garcia's diminished state. Working at a lovely studio in West Marin called The Site, they never really got beyond a few basic tracks; indeed, when John Cutler went through the session tapes after Garcia's death wondering if there was some salvageable material, he came up empty.

Changes continued on the sound front: For the group's late-spring and early-summer tours, they shifted their usual SR setup from a combination of

Meyer MSL-3s and MSL-10s, to eight MSL-10s per side, augmented with 16 650-R2 subwoofers per side. At the Western shows in May, the three delay towers each held two MSL-5s. For the tour's Eastern portion in June and early July, both the mains and the delay towers were MSL-10s.

Bob Weir started playing a new guitar onstage occasionally that spring—a James Trussart "Steelcaster," which was a hollow Telecaster-style instrument fashioned out of sheet-steel, plated with brushed nickel, and coated with polyurethane. Originally from Paris, Trussart had been a guitar luthier since 1980, mostly in the Los Angeles area. "I hadn't really worked with metal much before I started making the guitars," he says, "but I actually got to be pretty good at it. The metal [body] gives them a distinctive sound, but it's not *too*

Bob with his James Trussart Steelcaster guitar, Shoreline 6/4/95.

much." Not like a Dobro, I ask? "No, no, not at all," he laughs. "It's still an electric guitar." Trussart says that Weir's axe (actually, he had two) has a koa and maple neck and a rosewood fingerboard.

The Dead bid adieu to Club Front (and the old clapboard San Rafael house that was their main office) and opened a wonderful, spacious new headquarters in a nondescript warehouse building in the Bel Marin Keys section of Novato. Besides offering luxurious office digs for the Dead staff, it had a sizable, semi-isolated studio control room, an adjacent rehearsal room, a large, climate-controlled tape vault, and plenty of warehouse space for gear and to house the group's very successful merchandising operation. Garcia was excited that there was going to be an entire room devoted just to musical instruments.

Speaking of which, Steve Cripe sent Garcia a second guitar, Top Hat, but Jerry never played it onstage. Cripe was also working on a third axe for Garcia, "which was going to be Steve's masterwork," Adam Palow says. "There are 64 pieces of mother-of-pearl inlay all down the neck and into the headstock, with a palm tree, a dolphin, and a Saturn that had sterling-silver rings—it's gorgeous!" (Alas, the Steve Cripe story has a tragic

PHOTO: JAY BLAKESBERG

ending: A year after Jerry died, Cripe, who was also an expert designer/builder of aerial fireworks displays—hence the exploding firecracker emblem he put on his guitars' headstocks—was killed when some gunpowder in one of his work sheds detonated. Several guitars-in-progress were also lost in the intense explosion.) As fate would have it, however, at what would turn out to be the Dead's final gig, at Soldier Field in Chicago on July 9, 1995, Garcia didn't play Lightning Bolt; it needed some minor work. So he used both Tiger and Rosebud.

Ten days after the tour ended, Garcia went into rehab at the Betty Ford Clinic in Southern California. He left the program early, however, swearing that he'd changed his ways, was feeling good, and would thrive closer to home. When he slipped back into using drugs after returning to the Bay Area, he checked himself into a drug treatment center in Marin called Serenity Knolls. It was there, early in the morning of August 9, that Jerry died, and with him, the Grateful Dead.

What has happened in the decade-plus since Garcia's demise could be a book in itself: All the other members of the Dead have played in a vast assortment of different bands, sometimes together, but mostly apart. And a lot of the music has been *really* good. Musically, they have honored Garcia's questing spirit, taking the Dead's incredible repertoire to previously unexplored realms, and also bringing dozens of new players into this unusual world of melody, rhythm, and space that remains uniquely their own—even through all the changes.

The Great Experiment continues.

BIBLIOGRAPHY

BOOKS

Babiuk, Andy. *Beatles Gear: All the Fab Four's Instruments, From Stage to Studio*. Backbeat, 2001.

Blakesberg, Jay. *Between the Dark and Light: The Grateful Dead Photography of Jay Blakesberg*. Backbeat, 2004.

Brandelius, Jerilyn Lee. *Grateful Dead Family Album*. Warner Books, 1989.

Gans, David. *Conversations with the Dead: The Grateful Dead Interview Book*. Citadel Press, 1991.

Gans, David and Peter Simon (photo editor), *Playing in the Band: An Oral and Visual Portrait of the Grateful Dead*. St. Martin's Press, 1985. Revised/updated edition, 1996.

Gleason, Ralph. *The Jefferson Airplane and the San Francisco Sound*. Ballantine, 1969.

Harrison, Hank. *The Dead, Vol. 1*. The Archives Press, 1973. (Originally published as *The Dead Book*.)

Harrison, Hank. *The Dead, Vol. II*, The Archives Press, 1980.

Hart, Mickey (with Jay Stevens). *Drumming at the Edge of Magic: A Journey Into the Spirit of Percussion*. Harper Collins, 1990.

Lesh, Phil. *Searching for the Sound: My Life with the Grateful Dead*. Little Brown & Co., 2005.

McNally, Dennis. A *Long Strange Trip: The Inside History of the Grateful Dead*. Broadway Books, 2002.

Parish, Steve. *Home Before Daylight: My Life on the Road with the Grateful Dead*. St. Martin's Griffin, 2003.

Peters, Stephen and Chuck Wills, Dennis McNally, and Blair Jackson. *Grateful Dead: The Illustrated Trip*. Dorling Kindersley (DK), 2003.

Reich, Charles and Jann Wenner. *Garcia: Signpost to a New Space*. Straight Arrow, 1972. Out of print.

Scott, John W., Mike Dolgushkin, and Stu Nixon. *DeadBase XI: The Complete Guide to Grateful Dead Songlists*. DeadBase, 1999.

Shenk, David and Steve Silberman. *Skeleton Key: A Dictionary for Deadheads.* Doubleday, 1994.

Trynka, Paul (editor). *The Electric Guitar: An Illustrated History.* Chronicle, 1993.

NEWSPAPER AND MAGAZINE ARTICLES

Abbott, Lee. "Dead Reckoning and Hamburger Metaphysics." *Feature* (March 1979).

Block, Adam. "Garcia on Garcia, 1977." *BAM* (December '77 and January '78).

Brainerd, Jeffrey. "Steve Cripe: Guitarmaker's Idea Was Dead Reckoning." *St. Petersburg Times* (January 18, 1996).

Carlini, John. "Jerry Garcia and David Grisman: The Continuing Process." *Guitar Extra!* (Fall 1991).

Coryat, Karl. "Lesh is More! Portrait of an American Beauty." *Bass Player* (June and July 2000).

"Dead Heads" newsletter, 1972–1975.

Doerschuk, Robert. "Brent Mydland: Taking Over Keyboards for the Grateful Dead." *Keyboard* (September 1982).

Doerschuk, Robert. "Keyboards Down the Years." *Keyboard* (March 1991).

Dwork, John. "DDN Interviews Owsley." *Dupree's Diamond News* (Issue 25, August 1993).

Eisenhart, Mary. "Aging Gratefully: The Dead's Flattering Touch of Grey." (December 18, 1987).

Gans, David. "Alembic: Tools for the Musical Alchemist." *BAM* (October 20, 1978).

Garbarini, Vic. "In Search of the Grateful Dead." *Musician* (September 1981).

The Golden Road. Material was drawn from many of the 27 issues published by Blair Jackson and Regan McMahon from Winter 1984 through the 1993 annual, including interviews with Dan Healy, Jerry Garcia, Bob Weir, Phil Lesh, Mickey Hart, Bill Kreutzmann, and Brent Mydland. Article *not* written by Blair quoted in the book:

- Groenke, Randy and Mike Cramer. "One Afternoon Long Ago.... : A Previously Unpublished 1967 Interview With Jerry Garcia" (Issue 7, Spring 1985).

From *Guitar Player* magazine:

- Stuckey, Fred. "Jerry Garcia: It's All Music" (April 1971).
- Mulhern, Tom and Dominic Milano. "Phil Lesh: A Zone of His Own" (November 1977).
- Sievert, Jon. "Jerry Garcia: Founder of the Grateful Dead" (October 1978).
- Sievert, Jon. "Bob Weir: Rhythm Ace" (August 1981).
- Sievert, Jon. "Jerry Garcia: New Life With the Dead" (July 1988).
- Sievert, Jon. "Garcia & Grisman: Jerry's Acoustic Side" (September 1991).

• Sievert, Jon. "Garcia & Weir: Further." Special Grateful Dead issue (Fall 1993).

• Tywoniak, Ed. "Showtime: A Dedicated Crew of Alchemist Magicians Keeps the Magic Jamming." Special Grateful Dead issue (Fall 1993).

• Obrecht, Jas. "Turn On, Turn Up, Trip Out: The Rise and Fall of San Francisco Psychedelia" (February 1997).

Hopkins, Jerry. "The Beautiful Dead Hit Europe." *Rolling Stone* (June 22, 1972).

Hunt, Ken. "Jerry Garcia: Folk, Bluegrass and Beyond." *Swing 51* (Issue 7).

Jackson, Blair. "In the Dark With the Grateful Dead." *Mix* (July 1987).

Jackson, Blair. "Classic Tracks: the Grateful Dead's 'Truckin.'" *Mix* (May 1996).

Lawson, Steve. "MIDI Bass." *Bassist* (October 1998).

Perry, Charles. "Alembic: Sound Wizards to the Grateful Dead." *Rolling Stone* (September 27, 1973).

Petersen, George. "All You Need Is In-Ears: Marty Garcia and the Evolution of Personal Monitoring." *Mix* (July 2005).

Peterson, Jonathon. "Rick Turner Interview." *American Lutherie* (Winter 2000).

Rodgers, Jeffrey Pepper. "In the Dawg House: Jerry Garcia and David Grisman's Acoustic Reunion." *Acoustic Guitar* (January 1994).

Relix magazine (in chronological order):

• Hall, John. "Jerry Garcia: True Confessions in Hartford, Parts 1 and 2" (November 1977, January 1978).

• Brown, Toni. "So Far: A Transcript of a Grateful Dead Press Conference" (February 1988).

• Peters, Steve. "Built to Last: An Exclusive Interview With Jerry Garcia" (December 1989).

Selvin, Joel. "Strings of Gold: There Was Something Special About Doug Irwin's Guitars…." *SF Chronicle* (November 6, 2001).

Simons, David. "The Grateful Dead: Built to Last." *Acoustic Guitar* (March 2002).

Spiegel, Joseph. "Industry Weighs Potential Demise of Grateful Dead." *Pro Sound News* (November 1996).

Trubitt, Rudy. "Live Sounds: The Grateful Dead." *Mix* (September 1993).

Watrous, Peter. "Touch of Grey Matter: The Grateful Dead Are Different From You and Me." *Musician* (December 1989).

Wickersham, Susan. "Alembic's History: 1968–81." (original source unknown).

Wendling, Diana. "Dan Healy on Recording the Dead 'Live.'" *BAM* (May 8, 1981).

INTERNET WEBSITES

This is the first book I've written where the Internet was an important tool in my research (my last book was written in 1998). I fully understand that there is plenty of unreliable information on the 'Net, but there is also a plethora of pure gold if you know how to look for it. I must have visited over a thousand websites in my search for information about matters large and small. (If I'd been smart, five years ago I would've bought Google stock!) Here are some of the ones that were particularly useful to me. I'd like to single out dozin.com, which is an entire website dedicated to the Dead's equipment, with reprinted interviews (band members, Doug Irwin, et al.) and tech specs galore. Also, Yahoo's Gearheads conference (http://launch.groups.yahoo.com/groups/gearheads) had many interesting conversations germane to the book.

Vintageguitar.com; Edromanguitars.com; Everythingsg.com; Precambrianmusic.com; Dangpow.com; Bassplayer.com; Studioelectronics.biz; Homestudio.thing.net; Roger-russell .com; Ominous-valve.com; Adirondackguitar.com; Audioworld.com; Audioheritage.org; Sweetwater.com; Gibson.com; Fender.com; Infomaniac.net; Wikipedia.com; History.acusd .edu; Alteclansing.com; Stratcollector.com; Leee-virtual-museum.org; Combo-organ.com; Theatreorgans.com; Ampwares.com; Voxshowroom.com; Vkmag.alphabeck.co.uk; Alphaentek.com; Provide.net; Meyersound.com; Guitarhq.com; Dvanet.net/timesteel.html; Ovationguitars.com; guitargearheads.com; kensmithbasses.com; Exboard.com (the dudepit forum); Keyboardmuseum.org; Harmony-central.com; Livesoundint.com; Autohobbydigest.com; Cathedralstone.net; Sonicstate.com; Worldmusicsupply.com; Ibanezcollectors.com; Modulusguitars.com; Stevelawson.net; Ampexdata.com; Barncard.com

OTHER MISCELLANEOUS SOURCES

David Gans interviews for KPFA with Dan Healy (5/19/93), Bob Bralove (1/5/94), and Don Pearson (5/19/93).

The Key-Z Productions DVD *The Acid Test*.

Jeremy Marre's 1997 documentary *Anthem to Beauty*.

Grateful Dead DVDs: *The Grateful Dead Movie* (1974 show); *Closing of Winterland* (1978); *Dead Ahead* (1980); *View from the Vault IV* (1987); *Truckin' Up to Buffalo* (1990).

Interviews by the author cited in the Acknowledgments.

Interviews by the author originally conducted for *Garcia: An American Life* (1999, Viking Books), including some material which originally appeared on blairjackson.com.

INDEX